British National Cinema

Second edition

Sarah Street

Routledge
Taylor & Francis Group

LONDON AND NEW YORK

10065319

First edition published 1997   791. 430941
by Routledge
2 Park Square, Milton Park, Abingdon, Oxon OX14 4RN

Simultaneously published in the USA and Canada
by Routledge
270 Madison Ave, New York, NY 10016

Reprinted 2001, 2002, 2004

This edition published 2009

Routledge is an imprint of the Taylor & Francis Group, an informa business

© 1997, 2009 Sarah Street

Typeset in Times by
Book Now Ltd, London
Printed and bound in Great Britain by
CPI Antony Rowe, Chippenham, Wiltshire

British Library Cataloguing in Publication Data
A catalogue record for this book is available from the British Library

Library of Congress Cataloging in Publication Data
Street, Sarah.
   British national cinema/Sarah Street. – 2nd ed.
     p. cm. – (National cinemas)
   Includes bibliographical references and index.
   1. Motion pictures–Great Britain–History. 2. Motion picture
industry–Great Britain–History. I. Title.

PN1993.5.G7S75 2008
791.43'0941–dc22   2008010267

ISBN10: 0–415–38421–4 (hbk)
ISBN10: 0–415–38422–2 (pbk)

ISBN13: 978–0–415–38421–6 (hbk)
ISBN13: 978–0–415–38422–3 (pbk)

British

With films a
Draughtsma
Atonement,
identity and
to the British

Describin
orothers' firs
and the sev
Palace Pictu
Council, Sara
society. Usin
strates how E
to the prevai
revised secor
well as select

British Na
context with
questions wh
subject to go
and Hollywo
and what was
ated with Bri
hybrid forms
British film, s
lenges the traditional concept of cinema and operates outside mainstream structures in order to deconstruct and replace classical styles and conventions.

Illustrated with over thirty stills from classic British films, *British National Cinema* provides an accessible and comprehensive exploration of the fascinating development of British cinema.

Sarah Street is Professor of Film at the University of Bristol. She is the joint author of *Cinema and State* (with Margaret Dickinson, 1985) and *Film Architecture and the Transnational Imagination: Set Design in 1930s European Cinema* (with Tim Bergfelder and Sue Harris, 2007), author of *British Cinema in Documents* (2000), *Costume and Cinema* (2001), *Transatlantic Crossings: British Feature Films in the USA* (2002) and *Black Narcissus* (2005). She is co-editor of *Moving Performance: British Stage and Screen* (with Linda Fitzsimmons, 2001), *European Cinema* (with Jill Forbes, 2001), *The Titanic in Myth and Memory* (with Tim Bergfelder, 2004) and *The Queer Screen Reader* (with Jackie Stacey, 2007).

National Cinemas
Series editor: Susan Hayward

For Sue (again)

Contents

List of plates

Acknowledgements

I would like to thank Rebecca Barden for inviting me to produce a second, expanded edition of *British National Cinema*. Throughout the process of revision I have been struck by how so much has happened in the decade since its first publication, in terms of both film scholarship and Britsh cinema. As for the former, there has been a burgeoning of academic interest in the subject, producing many books and commentaries that have influenced the growth and direction of this fertile sub-field of Film Studies. I have drawn upon these in the revision where appropriate. Also, the films continue to provide fascinating insights into realms of experience that reach beyond questions of national identity and frequently challenge and test the limits of academic analysis. This time I would like to acknowledge the support from many of my friends and colleagues in the field including Tim Bergfelder, Pam Cook, Richard Dyer, Christine Geraghty, Mark Glancy, Sue Harper, Sue Harris and Andrew Higson. As last time I dedicate this book to Sue Simkin.

The film stills featured in this book were reproduced by the British Film Institute's Stills, Posters and Designs Department, with the exception of *Trainspotting*, *Vera Drake*, *Atonement*, *28 Days Later*, *Last Resort*, *Bullet Boy* and *Young Adam* which are reproduced courtesy of The Kobal Collection.

Introduction: British national cinema

> It is quite possible to conceive of a national cinema, in the sense of one which works with or addresses nationally specific materials, which is none the less critical of inherited notions of national identity, which does not assume the existence of a unique or unchanging 'national culture', and which is quite capable of dealing with social divisions and differences.
>
> (Hill, 1992: 17)

As the above quotation indicates, the question of national cinema is complex and contentious. On the one hand, there is a British film industry with relatively clearly defined economic boundaries and methods of classification, producing films which may not necessarily involve British themes or preoccupations, often including financial and labour participation from other countries. On the other hand, there is the cultural conception of what we mean by British films: the extent to which they participate in establishing nationhood as a distinct, familiar sense of belonging which is shared by people from different social and regional backgrounds. We have inherited a dominant conception of what it is to be British, a collective consciousness about nationhood which has, in part, been constructed by cultural referents, including cinema.

Nationhood as the expression of a collective consciousness, rather than the sole product of militaristic conquest, is an idea derived from Benedict Anderson (1983) who argues that mass communication assists in the complex process of creating an 'imagined community' which differentiates itself from others. As Andrew Higson has pointed out, the achievement of this is often at the expense of representing the diversity of British society: 'This imaginative process must be able to resolve the actual history of conflict and negotiation in the experience of community. It must be able to hold in place – or specifically to exclude – any number of other experiences of belonging' (1995: 6). Until relatively recently the diversity of Britishness referred to by Hill and Higson has not been fully represented on screen. With some notable exceptions, until the 1960s the dominant construction involved films which reflected a limited, often privileged experience of the class system, starring actors and actresses with BBC English accents and set in metropolitan locations. While audiences may well have read against the grain, the ideological construction of most pre-1960 British films encouraged acceptance of the *status quo*.

Yet despite the ascendancy of particular recurring filmic representations of British people and aspects of their lives, for example in films which employed the documentary realist tradition, the term 'British national cinema' is clearly not homogenous. A person's experience of being British will depend on a variety of factors which influence their production and consumption of films: place of birth; gender and sexuality; race; class, education and occupation. National cinema is inflected with a multitude of different connotations, often implying a jingoistic, nationalist imperative, while at other times challenging that view by giving a voice to those who have had very different experiences of living in Britain. British film styles and themes have not been totally uniform and in their different ways have contributed to the cultural construction of Britishness. Some films are concerned with questions of national identity at a more obvious level than others, so it is essential to examine production as a whole, a wide-ranging spectrum of representation which might at different times support, contest or ignore the dominant articulation of the imagined British community. As the concept of 'national cinema' has been much debated in film studies, the changing nature of community, representation and the existence of transnational identities are indeed reflected in cinema (Vitali and Willemen, 2006). The production of films in Wales and Scotland, especially since the mid-1990s and the election of the Scottish Parliament and Welsh Assembly, further challenges conventional notions of British cinema. The films of 'New Scottish Cinema', for example, 'can be regarded as part of a larger British national cinema' (Petrie in Hjort and Mackenzie, 2000: 153). Alternatively, they can be regarded as national cinemas of their own which draw on traditions, sensibilities and experiences that do not necessarily relate to those which can be identified as being connected to British cinema. Films such as *Hedd Wynn* (Paul Turner, 1991), which was nominated for an Academy Award for best foreign-language film, turned attention to Wales as a film-producing nation whose films frequently challenge dominant stereotypes about Wales and Welshness (Stanton, 2002). In sum, ideas about national cinemas have developed to such an extent that for many critics we are now living in a 'post-national' period which acknowledges the need to examine cinema from perspectives that celebrate pluralities and the blurring of boundaries instead of seeking to locate an essentialised notion of national identity.

I do not intend however to completely dispense with the concept of national cinema for the second edition of this book, particularly since the first edition placed the existence of divergent representations within a history of film genres at its heart and recognised the pluralities that are blatantly there. Indeed, the existence of a variety of film-making themes and practices was revealed to provide a central dynamic. As Thomas Elsaesser has argued, British cinema 'always functions around another polarization – what one might call an "official" cinema and an "unofficial" cinema, a respectable cinema and a disreputable one' (1993: 64). This book demonstrates how British cinema has been both respectable and disreputable, according to the prevailing notions of what constituted a 'good' British film. Despite the chronic instability of the industry's economic infrastructure, the range and diversity of British films suggests dynamism, not stasis. For the sake of definition, my focus is on production: films registered as British, not always dealing with British subject-matter at an overt level, often seeking to differentiate themselves from films made in Hollywood, while at other times attempting to beat Hollywood at its own game. Different styles, different themes, but nevertheless British films. Writing for the second edition of this book I find that institutional categorization is still a real fact of life that needs to be negotiated by filmmakers, even when operating in a context of co-production or trans-national financial co-operation. As such, a British film may not look or feel particularly 'British', yet this tag will be visible in award ceremonies, box-office listings, reviews and media commentary; applications for tax breaks or in tables of production activity. The production still on the cover of this book demonstrates the eclecticism of much contemporary cinema at the level of production. *Elizabeth: The Golden Age* (2007) is an Anglo-French production by Working Title and Studio Canal, distributed by Universal Pictures. It is directed by Shekhar Kapur, born in India (now Pakistan), scripted by British writers and based on British history. The lead actors include Australians Cate Blanchett and Geoffrey Rush as well as British actors, including Samantha Morton and Clive Owen. It was filmed at Shepperton Studios as well as in a variety of other UK locations. The cover image on the first edition of this book was of Anna Neagle in *Victoria the Great* (1937), produced by Herbert Wilcox in an irrefutably patriotic representation of nation and collective identity. *Elizabeth: The Golden Age* is also a patriotic account of history with an emphasis on romance and adventure, demonstrating continuities within the genre of the historical film that have been incorporated in this instance into the big budget, trans-national context of contemporary film-making. In generic terms it is representative of the 'post-heritage' film which above all celebrates the spectacle of cinema rather than deliver an accurate history lesson.

Continuities clearly also persist in regard to the financial make-up of international media institutions. Hollywood's ascendancy has been, and continues to be, particularly significant in the British context. As this book demonstrates on many occasions, American domination has had a profound impact on the British film industry, from production to exhibition. Producers have been caught in a perpetual bind: should they make films for the

British market or for international export? Is it possible to aim for both, at the risk of satisfying neither? Market decisions like this have a considerable influence on a film's style, subject matter and perception of itself as a national product. It is always important to acknowledge the extent to which Hollywood influenced British audiences through its domination of Britain's cinema screens. Hollywood's successful international standards and democratic values exercised an enormous influence on British film culture. In one way or another, the Hollywood factor is acknowledged throughout this book. Anglo-American film relations are explored in an economic and political context, as well as Hollywood's influence on British genre cinema and the character of the British star system. The sections on avant-garde, art and independent cinema chart how British film-makers operating outside mainstream traditions and structures were determined to deconstruct and replace classical Hollywood styles and conventions. On the other hand, British cinema as a key component of European cinema must be emphasised, particularly since in terms of personnel, recurrent thematic preoccupations and style, British films can be seen to belong to international traditions which reside in Europe as well as in Hollywood.

The chapters outline the main chronological developments in each chosen theme. A book of this nature, covering just over an entire century, cannot be completely comprehensive, but where necessary the reader will be directed to relevant further reading. Chapter 1 on 'The Fiscal Politics of Film' establishes the difficult economic context within which British producers and directors have worked, focusing on the role played by the state in regulating the film industry's affairs. From the 1927 Cinematograph Films Act to the formation of the UK Film Council, the state has played a significant role in guiding the affairs of the film industry, albeit from a limited perspective. At the same time fundamental economic structures have influenced the ways in which the industry is able to manoeuvre itself within a context of intense international competition. The following four chapters cover the main contours of generic production, decade by decade, concentrating on British films which were most popular at the box office; how generic production has evolved over the years and the ideological imperatives which have preoccupied British film-makers. Chapter 6 on the nature and functioning of British stardom explores the extent to which stars have represented images of the nation at particular historical junctures, including a case study of Anna Neagle. Frequently functioning in opposition to Hollywood's stars, it is possible to locate a sense of national specificity in connection with the roles and marketing of British stars. While the majority of British film production has been genre-related, operating in the mainstream market, there is an 'unofficial' tradition of film-making, surveyed in the last two chapters. These make clear the range of possibilities for British cinema suggested by John Hill in the opening quotation. The increasing blurring of boundaries between art or oppositional cinema and the mainstream has created opportunities for 'other cinemas' which challenge traditional conceptions of British cinema. It is, however, crucial that these are supported, not overwhelmed by the fast-developing global, televisual and digital networks which have, in turn, shattered long-held notions of what is cinema, let alone what is British national cinema.

Chapter 1

The fiscal politics of film

THE EVOLUTION OF AN INDUSTRY

Cinema was born in the 1890s, the 'last machine' of Victorian invention.[1] British inventors had been involved in experiments with photography and Thomas Edison's 'peep show' kinetoscope was developed in America with the assistance of Englishman W. K. Dickson. The first public cinema exhibition in Britain is recorded as being organised by a representative of the French producers, the Lumière brothers, at Marlborough Hall in Regent Street, London, on 21 February 1896. British manufacturer Robert Paul invented the first film projector to be placed on the open market, also in 1896. It was not yet clear that America would dominate the world's cinema screens and for a time British manufacturers of projectors and cameras were able to hold their own against foreign competition. Concentrating on supplying its vast home market, the American film industry had not yet begun its aggressive export drive. It was not until the early 1900s that American manufacturers began to take the entrepreneurial initiative, in close competition with the French companies Gaumont and Pathé. In many ways, however, the history of early film was about international experiment, with similar techniques and developments towards the institutional mode of representation occurring in many different countries at different times.[2] The popular themes used in magic lantern exhibitions featured in early films and there was a great deal of thematic and stylistic repetition, particularly in early French, American and British productions.

Music halls were the first real home of the commercial cinema and during the years 1896–1906 many thousands of short films were produced in Britain, including innovative work by Cecil Hepworth, William Haggar, G. A. Smith, James Williamson, R. W. Paul and the Sheffield Photo Company. Most film-makers sold their films outright to travelling showmen and music-hall exhibitors. 'Moving pictures' were so popular that new premises had to be built: 1907–8 saw the erection of the first theatres entirely devoted to showing films. In 1908 there were only three exhibition companies registered, but by the end of 1914 there were 1,833 (PEP, 1952: 26).

The number of cinemas also rose dramatically from 1,600 in 1910 to 3,500 by 1915 (Perelli, 1983: 375). The industry was evolving from a proliferation of small companies into a more or less tripartite structure, determined by the functions of production, distribution and exhibition which became increasingly distinct by 1914. It was not until around 1910 that exclusive (as opposed to open market) rental contracts came into being, escalating film prices and increasing competition.[3] Exhibitors had to bid for the most popular films but once booked they were entitled to exclusive exhibition rights in their local area: the films could not be shown concurrently at other cinemas. Distribution became the most crucial element in film supply. Films were hired on increasingly competitive terms which encouraged product differentiation: for example, if a film was unusually long or if it required a limited run it was offered for a high price. This chain of relations gave distributors enormous power, as Michael Chanan (1990: 187) has explained: 'A process began to unfold which step by step propelled them towards better control over the terms and conditions of supply and demand than either producers or exhibitors'. Once this trend was entrenched British producers were unable to keep pace with Hollywood's quick turnover of cheap, popular films which distributors clamoured to hire.

Despite the innovative work of British producers and the increasing capitalisation of the exhibition sector, in 1910 only 15 per cent of films released in Britain were of British origin. Box office profits were used to hire American films rather than finance British production. During the years 1906–11 the pioneer producing companies did not consolidate or make advances on their early promising start. From 1911–14 there was a brief revival of the British industry, fuelled by a spate of longer films, mostly adaptations of plays and novels, but on the whole the most startling development was the success of America's film export strategies. Kristin Thompson (1985) has shown how from 1909 American producers concentrated on distributing their films abroad. Britain was an especially important market because of London's position as the centre for international trade and the world's clearing house for films. The expansion of exhibition was also an incentive, together with the popularity of American films in Britain. By contrast, British producers had little success with their films in America and could not afford to compete with Hollywood's high production values or turnover. This difficult situation was exacerbated by accusations that British films were primitive compared with Hollywood and the elaboration of myths about British cinema being uncinematic, tedious and too reliant on the theatre. This is not the place to examine these criticisms in detail, but it is clear that early British cinema needs to be examined *on its own terms* and in a European context rather than solely in relation to Hollywood. But from an economic standpoint, it is incontestable that American films enjoyed a highly advantageous position in the British market from an early stage. This had an impact on British producers in terms of creating an example of the

stylistics of popular cinema and on audiences in terms of inculcating codes
of generic expectation and viewing habits.

HOLLYWOOD'S EXPANSION AND QUOTA PROTECTIONISM

America was a leading force in the British market before 1914 and the First
World War merely consolidated that hegemonic position. In 1914, 25 per
cent of films shown in British cinemas were British, but by 1923 this figure
had fallen to 10 per cent. In 1924 the total number of British films shown
was 56 and in 1926 there were only 37 (Low, 1971: 156). America dominated
its home market and the major film companies had amalgamated to become
vertically integrated, uniting production, distribution and exhibition interests, with box-office profits providing their studios with production finance
and cinemas guaranteeing automatic outlets for their films. Most of the
majors had distribution subsidiaries abroad. In 1920 amongst the 14 leading
distributors in Britain were Famous-Lasky (Paramount), Jury's Imperial
(MGM), Fox (Twentieth-Century Fox), Vitagraph (Warner Brothers) and
Goldwyn (MGM). Between them these companies offered 310 American
and British films but only 15 of these were British (PEP, 1952: 40). Films
were particularly suited for world-wide distribution since almost the entire
cost was incurred in making the first copy – by comparison marketing costs
were very low. Hollywood could therefore supply its vast home market and
the rest of the world's cinema screens: there were 22,000 cinemas in the
USA in the mid-1920s and 4,000 in Britain (Dickinson and Street, 1985: 10).
This unbalanced relationship did not facilitate an exchange. The vertically
integrated structure of the American industry made the American market
a virtually closed one to foreign films, as an American study explained in
1926:

> This market can now be profitably reached only through one or more of
> a group of not more than ten American distributors of pictures each of
> which is busily engaged in marketing its own brand of pictures through
> the theatres owned, controlled or operated by one or more of this group.
>
> (Seabury, 1926: 195)

American producers also had the advantage of an effective trade organisation, the Motion Picture Producers and Distributors of America (MPPDA),
which devoted considerable energy to researching the export of motion
pictures.

Vertical integration, the foundation of American domination at home
and abroad, did not develop in the British industry until the late 1920s and
early 1930s. The outstanding development in the British industry in the
1920s was the growth of cinema circuits which formed the basis of the major

combines of the 1930s, the Associated British Picture Corporation (ABPC) and the Gaumont-British Picture Corporation (GBPC). In the 1920s, exhibition was the most profitable element of the British industry: attendances were rising, American films were cheap and in plentiful supply, and in the ultimate distribution of box-office receipts exhibitors retained by far the lion's share, while producers received a very small percentage. In 1925 economist Simon Rowson calculated that out of £35 million invested in the British film industry, producers only received £500,000 (Rowson, 1925: 41). When British exhibition interests linked up with production units in the 1930s there was always a tension between the need to produce more British films and the temptation to rely on American. Hollywood further consolidated its hold over exhibition by means of booking practices known as blind and block booking. Renters would agree to hire out a popular film only if the exhibitor agreed to take with it a series of unseen, often as yet unmade films which tied the exhibitor to one or more renters for a long period, leaving scant screen space for British films.

The Cinematograph Films Act, 1927, aimed to foster production by encouraging the exhibition of British films. The Act imposed a statutory obligation on renters and exhibitors to acquire and show a quota of British films. In the first year the renters' quota was 7.5 per cent and the exhibitors' was 5 per cent (the renters' was higher so that exhibitors would be able to exercise an element of choice). Both were to increase by stages to 20 per cent by 1936, and to remain at that level until 1938 when the Act expired. A British film was defined as one made by a British subject or company, but the definition did not specify that control had to be in British hands, only that the majority of the company directors should be British. All studio scenes had to be shot within the Empire, and not less than 75 per cent of the labour costs incurred in a film's production, excluding payments for copyright and to one foreign actor, actress or director, had to be paid to British subjects, or to persons domiciled in the Empire. The scenario had to be written by a British author, and the Act attempted to abolish blind and block booking. The Board of Trade was to register British films and to consult with a trade-dominated Advisory Committee.

The Act was the result of some fascinating debates on the role of film as an industrial commodity and as propaganda. The first active steps were taken by the government in 1925 in response to agitation from producers. A Joint Trade Committee was established to report to the Board of Trade on possible remedies for the decline in production. It was known that some members of the Conservative Party, back in office after the fall of the Labour Government in 1924, were sympathetic towards protection for industry, even though at the time Britain pursued a policy of free trade. Even though the Conservatives had lost the 1906 and 1923 elections over tariff reform, and Baldwin had pledged not to introduce a general tariff in his 1924 election address, many hoped that a measure of protection for the film industry might be secured. There was no question of a subsidy for producers or an import duty on American films: a quota, however, was considered to be an appropriate option. The debate on the protection of the film industry was therefore caught up in wider debates about the protection of British industry against foreign competition, and the propaganda elements of film were uppermost in official concern to counter the Hollywood invasion. Viscount Sandon, a Conservative MP, was hostile towards Hollywood films and on 25th January 1927 wrote an impassioned letter to *The Times*:

> Children and young men and women, who pour nightly into the cinemas in the UK, see perpetually stories of divorce, of running away with other men's wives, distorted home life, burglaries, murders, revolvers, produced as a matter of course by all and sundry . . . evidence of police, judges, school teachers, all accumulates to prove the disastrous effect of this on the rising generation.

Comments like this were common as increasing cultural and ideological alarm was expressed about American films. Another argument frequently put forward was that trade 'followed the film': Britain and the Empire were in danger of over-exposure to screen advertisement of American goods and lifestyles. Concern over the propaganda value of film and anti-Americanism therefore played a large part in securing the passage of the Cinematograph Films Act, 1927.

THE 1930s: CONSOLIDATION AND EXPANSION

The Act's provisions afforded some protection for producers but did not seriously threaten box-office takings for popular American films. According however to Political and Economic Planning, the years 1927–30 were 'the most momentous in the history of the British film industry' (PEP, 1952: 45) because of state protection, the coming of sound and the formation of vertically integrated combines. State protection encouraged optimism about British production and as a consequence a plethora of companies were formed immediately after the Films Bill became law. The increased capital available to film producers enabled many to buy equipment for the conversion to sound, a process which, while not without its problems, was achieved with relative success by 1933 (see Murphy, 1984). The most far-reaching development was the formation of GBPC 1927 and ABPC 1928, highly capitalised, vertically integrated companies whose films were guaranteed an exhibition outlet. Financed by the Ostrer brothers, GBPC was an amalgamation of the interests of Gaumont, Ideal Films, the W. & F. Film Service and some cinema circuits. ABPC was the creation of Scottish solicitor John Maxwell, an amalgamation of British International Pictures, Wardour

Films, First-National Pathé and several important cinema circuits including Provincial Cinematograph Theatres, the largest circuit in the 1920s. The Films Act's promise of increased production further encouraged the growth of exhibition: between 1927 and 1932 715 new cinemas were built (Dickinson and Street, 1985: 35). The late silent period and the early years of sound films also fostered international co-operation between European cinemas, culminating in the 'Film Europe' movement which was formed to combat Hollywood's domination and for a few years at least provided some evidence of pan-European cinema activity at the level of trade congress discussions and co-productions (Higson and Maltby, 1999). Relations between the film industries of Britain and Germany were particularly fruitful, as well as co-operation that was encouraged by the Multi-Language-Version (MLVs) industry when versions of the same film were made in several different languages.

The Films Act required American renters to handle British films. Many did this by sponsoring quota quickies, cheap films made purely to satisfy the letter of the law without providing serious competition for American films. Much maligned, quota quickies nevertheless provided work for British technicians and valuable experience for directors, and there is evidence that some were popular with regional audiences (ibid.: 45–46 and Chibnall, 2007). In 1931 the seven major American distributors had their 44 quota films supplied by 36 different British producers. Exhibitors exceeded their quota requirements, indicating that British films did fair business: in 1934 Simon Rowson discovered that in the year ending September 1934 exhibitors showed 26.4 per cent British films, when their statutory liability was only 15 per cent (Rowson, 1936: 118). The recovery and expansion of British production in the early 1930s has also been documented by Sedgwick (1994 and 2000) and success with exporting British films in the 1930s by Street (2002).

THE QUOTA, FILM FINANCE AND HOLLYWOOD

In 1938 a second Cinematograph Films Act was passed, modifying the basic framework of its predecessor and making some important changes. The legislation had been preceded by a report of a Committee chaired by Lord Moyne (Cmd. 5320, 1936), which drew attention to the shortcomings of the 1927 Act, including quota quickies, the need for a shorts quota and the persistence of booking offences. The 1938 Act continued protectionism via quotas for a further ten years and introduced a quota for short and documentary films. To encourage quality, a cost test was instituted whereby long films had to have cost a minimum of £1 a foot with a minimum total of £7,500 a film. A controversial system of double and treble quotas was available to facilitate American production of expensive feature films in Britain. The motives involved in the Cinematograph Films Act 1938 were in many respects similar to those of a decade earlier: an economic and ideological imperative to foster an alternative to Hollywood. But there were also two crucial developments in the 1930s resulting in a government policy which encouraged a new alignment with the American film industry: film finance and the international situation. These factors became essential determinants of the film industry's future during the rest of the century.

Production expanded well into the 1930s. New companies were formed, 640 between 1935 and 1937 (Dickinson and Street, 1985: 76). The boom was encouraged by the international success of Alexander Korda's *The Private Life of Henry VIII*, a film which made £500,000 on its first world run and was still earning £10,000 a year ten years later (Kulik, 1975: 89). The American success of *Henry VIII* can be largely explained by the link between Korda's company, London Film Productions, and United Artists. Most other British companies did not have access to American cinemas via an astute distributor and, in retrospect, *Henry VIII* might be seen as an isolated case of a British film conquering international markets. On the other hand, some films during the 1930s managed to gain distribution outlets in America including *The Ghost Goes West* (1935), musicals starring Jessie Matthews and films with imperial themes such as *The Drum* (1938) whose paths were eased via agreements between the larger British companies such as Gaumont-British and Hollywood studios (Street, 2002: 43–90). But as far as the domestic industry was concerned, by 1937 the boom was over and the industry was in dire financial straits. Short-term, unstable methods of film finance had facilitated the mid-1930s boom but, when many of the films lost money, financiers withdrew their support and company after company went into liquidation. Film business had always been risky business and the crisis confirmed the City's formerly cautious attitude. The Prudential Assurance Company had backed Korda, only to regret its investment when the company lurched from crisis to crisis throughout the 1930s (see Street, 1986). When the Films Act was being debated in Parliament the industry's financial plight was therefore a major concern.

The severity of the 1937 crash, and the government's unwillingness to encourage proposals for a Film Bank (ibid.: 81–88), prompted the Board of Trade to look to Hollywood to finance British films, initiating a policy which had a profound impact on the industry's subsequent history. Hollywood was highly capitalised and deals with American companies brought with them the promise of access to the closed American market. The Moyne Committee had expressed concern about control passing abroad, but as yet there was little evidence of American companies with sinister motives towards the British industry. In 1935 United Artists purchased a 50 per cent interest in Odeon Cinemas, the third largest circuit, but Odeon's owner, Oscar Deutsch, retained the casting vote and control. J. Arthur Rank hoped that a deal between the General Cinema Finance Corporation (GCFC) and Universal in 1936 would facilitate access to American cinema screens and be of considerable benefit to the British industry. The group's distribution company, General Film Distributors (GFD) also handled Universal's product in Britain. Dismissing the conspiracy theory of an American take-over, the Board of Trade's main concern therefore was to revive production: the multiple quota clauses of the Films Act 1938 were designed to foster Anglo-American productions.

Outside the film world, collaboration was also desirable on the diplomatic front. As the international situation worsened, the British government was keen to court American support against Fascism. A prelude to this rapprochement was the negotiation of an Anglo-American Trade Agreement which coincided with the debate on the renewal of the Films Act. From this perspective, a major confrontation with Hollywood producers, who formed a powerful lobby in the US Congress, was out of the question. During the 1930s the American film industry became increasingly concerned about protectionist measures for European film industries and did its best to make the 1938 Films Act as acceptable to Hollywood as possible (see Street, 1985). The American Ambassador, Joseph Kennedy, negotiated with Oliver Stanley, the President of the Board of Trade, for a settlement which was more favourable to the Americans than the original Films Bill of 1937.

The Second World War inaugurated yet another stage in Anglo-American film relations, but the 1938 Films Act was crucial in extending quotas and drawing further attention to the difficulties of financing British production. At the end of the 1930s, therefore, the British industry had been through a major stage of development and consolidation and was optimistic about winning international success. British production was served by two major studios, Denham and Pinewood, and despite the repercussions of the 1937 crash was assured a future because of the continuing structural integration of the major companies. American renters handled over 50 per cent of long films and exhibition had expanded with three main circuits (GBPC, ABPC and Odeon), each owning about 300 cinemas.

THE SECOND WORLD WAR

The Second World War had profound effects on production, distribution and exhibition. There were fears that, as in the First World War, production would collapse altogether. Indeed, the early years of the war were characterised by disruption, requisitioning of studios and uncertainty over state protection and production finance. Studio space was severely restricted: over half was required for war purposes and for the production of Ministry of Information-sponsored propaganda films. Even so, studios managed to produce an average of 60 feature films a year (PEP, 1952: 83), a third of the average annual output in the 1930s, but of a high standard. Companies which expanded most noticeably were Ealing, British National and Rank.

The Ministry of Information's Films Division sponsored documentaries and feature films, indicating an unprecedented degree of state involvement in film production. The average cost of feature films rose, as did their overall quality, which can be explained by the convergence of notions of wartime consensus, a heightened sense of national identity and the propagandist imperative which brought about, as Murphy has noted, 'a genuine rapport between British film-makers and their audiences' (Murphy, 1984: 17).

During the years 1939–42 the government was preoccupied with the question of adapting its film policy to wartime conditions. Plans for a state Films Bank were discussed and rejected, but were influential in post-war schemes to assist producers (see Dickinson and Street, 1985: 129–39). A major concern was to limit the large amount of dollars remitted by American companies to the US on account of their films screened in Britain. Estimates of the annual amount reaching America in payment for films exploited in Britain varied between £6–10 million. The need to conserve dollar reserves demanded another set of negotiations with the American industry, resulting in the first Anglo-American Film Agreement in November 1939, which set a limit on remittable income at $17.5 million but also required American companies to maintain their customary level of film exports to Britain. Since British production was curtailed by wartime conditions, it was considered essential that cinemas were well stocked with a plentiful supply of films.

The policy of encouraging American finance for British production continued with the easing of quota obligations and the establishment of the 'monetary quota', reducing quota obligations for American companies that used blocked earnings to make films in Britain. A second Film Agreement in 1940 was more lenient, permitting American companies to release $12 million in 'blocked dollars', that is, monies which were earned by American companies in Britain and, because of exchange control restrictions, could not be transferred back to America. The Treasury had backed down on its original hardline approach because of American pressure and fears about prejudicing wider Anglo-American relations. These considerations were all the more important after America's entry into the war in December 1941, and in October 1942 all blocked funds were released. The quota was further revised to encourage the purchase of foreign rights of British films. The need to win American support against Hitler, and secure and maintain the financial security of Lend-Lease,[4] outweighed arguments about the need to discriminate against American films.

British cinemas needed to maintain a healthy film supply which depended in large part on popular American films. This was not too much of a problem because they were supplemented with British films and reissues. Cinemas did very well during the war: average weekly attendances increased from 19 million in 1939 to over 30 million in 1945 (PEP, 1952: 83). Exhibitors' profits were reduced by Entertainments Tax[5] and Excess Profits

Tax, but very few cinemas were closed during the war and the total number slightly increased: in 1940 there were 4,671 cinemas in Britain and 4,703 in 1945 (Perelli, 1983: 375). Screen entertainment played a crucial role in maintaining morale on the home front and cinema-going trends which had been established in the 1930s were consolidated and extended. *The Cinema Audience*, a survey undertaken in 1943 by the Ministry of Information, discovered that the most frequent cinema-goers were young town-dwellers from lower-income groups who lived in the North, North-West, the Midlands and Scotland (see Aldgate and Richards, 1986: 3–4).

A major development was the progress of integration in the industry into a duopoly: ABPC and the Rank Organisation. J. Arthur Rank, a Methodist flour miller who was first interested in films as religious propaganda, had acquired an interest in 1935 in GFD and Pinewood Studios. In 1936 he formed GCFC as a holding company for subsequent deals. By 1941 GCFC had absorbed GFD, Denham and Pinewood, purchased an interest in Odeon and gained eventual control of GBPC. The industry was therefore divided between two major combines, a situation which caused concern among independents, particularly Michael Balcon, about 'tendencies to monopoly' in the film industry.[6] A committee chaired by Albert Palache was appointed by Hugh Dalton, President of the Board of Trade, to investigate in 1944.

The report considered it particularly dangerous for two companies to dominate exhibition (Rank and ABPC between them owned a quarter of all cinemas and a third of cinema seats) and drew attention to their links with American companies, reviving the Moyne Committee's concern about control passing abroad. The amalgamation of interests which formed the Rank Organisation in 1941 absorbed ties with Universal, United Artists and Twentieth-Century Fox and ABPC was linked with Warner. The combines owned 70 per cent of studio space, a situation which forced independent producers to enter into agreements which were not always to their advantage. The Report's most important recommendations were the imposition of restrictions on further circuit expansion; the prevention of booking practices which discriminated against independents and the establishment of a Films Bank. A degree of progress was made towards rectifying some of the problems identified in the report: the combines agreed not to increase the strength of their circuits and the film trade pledged to sort out internal disputes. In a longer-term trajectory, however, many of the issues raised in the report anticipated the fundamental concerns of post-war film policy: the structure of the industry, relations with America and film finance.

THE LABOUR GOVERNMENT AND FILM

The question of monopoly and the film industry remained on the agenda of unfinished business after 1945, but little was done to address the imbalance of power between the combines and independents. This was because government officials and the film trade were unconvinced that Rank's position was harmful: a strong British company was needed to counter Hollywood and secure the distribution of British films abroad but, on the other hand, the work of independent producers was a crucial component of national output, particularly in terms of their preference for films aimed primarily at the domestic market. Surely there was room for both? As the PEP report put it:

> Catastrophe to Mr. Rank would mean catastrophe to British film production, for while the financiers were prepared to back a solidly based combine there was no evidence that they had forgotten the affairs of ten years earlier and were willing to renew their support of small independent, or more correctly, free-lance, producers.
>
> (PEP, 1952: 96)

A 'wait and see' policy continued while Rank entered into distribution contracts with many independent producers including Michael Balcon, arch-champion of the independents, who secured a financial and distribution deal for Ealing in 1944. Monopoly continued to be a live issue for the next twenty years, but the government was not willing to follow the American industry's example of divorcement decrees[7] whereby the majors were forced to sell cinemas in order to create more competitive market conditions.

BOGART OR BACON?

It soon became clear that the whole question of the structure of the industry was influenced by relations with America. The government was reluctant to interfere with companies like Rank who offered some hope of penetrating the American market. After 1945 Hollywood was keener than ever to export films to Europe and, as Ian Jarvie (1990) has shown, was determined to dismantle trade barriers and protective quotas for indigenous film industries. In the context of Europe's need for American economic assistance after 1945, debates on the international film trade once again became inextricably linked with wider issues. A major one was the shortage of dollars which handicapped the British economy. Film imports were expensive and concern was expressed about high sums remitted to the US which exacerbated Britain's acute balance of payments problem: in 1947 American film earnings were calculated at $70 million (PEP, 1952: 98). The debate centred on the dilemma of 'bacon or Bogart?'.[8] Despite the popularity of Bogart, bacon won out and in August 1947 a 75 per cent *ad valorem* duty, the Dalton duty,[9] was imposed on American films, a move of unprecedented severity against Hollywood. This was very surprising in view of the Board of Trade's previous leniency towards American producers who vociferously opposed the duty, but the public debate's polarisation between 'food or flicks' demanded a tough approach during the severe winter of 1946–47 and a fuel crisis. Three schemes competed for official favour between 1944 and 1947, and the 75 per cent duty won out as the best way to reduce the cost of film entertainment (see Dickinson and Street, 1985: 184).

The Board of Trade and Treasury miscalculated when they ignored warnings that Hollywood might boycott the British market as a retaliatory measure: one Treasury official reported to the Chancellor in April 1947 that 'the Board of Trade are inclined to think that rather than [boycott our important market] . . . the companies would still carry on and make the best of a bad job' (Public Record Office, BT 64 2283). The boycott was instituted by the Motion Picture Association of America (MPAA) almost immediately after the duty was announced. British producers finally got their chance to dominate the home market, although many were totally unprepared for the crisis and lacked the financial backing and resources for a production drive. Rank feared that the duty would jeopardise the distribution of British films in America and sabotage his well-publicised deals with American companies.[10] Exhibitors protested against the inevitable reduction in film supply, and Rank desperately attempted to fill the gap with some success, as Geoffrey Macnab (1993: 183) has argued: 'The overall quality of his output may have been variable, but several excellent films were made at Rank's studios in the wake of the Dalton duty', including *The Red Shoes* (1948) and *Oliver Twist* (1948). At the same time, negotiations were under way to end the boycott and reach agreement with the Americans. Pressure to reach a settlement was particularly acute because of the need to secure American financial aid via the Marshall Plan.[11] Also, British producers were still keen to get their films shown abroad. *The Red Shoes* was successful in America, as were other British films during the 1940s that benefited from links between British and American companies (Street, 2002: 91–118). The solution came in March 1948 when the duty was removed in exchange for a blocking arrangement whereby American companies could remit no more than $17 million a year, plus a sum equal to the earnings of British films abroad. As with the blocking arrangement of the early war years, it was intended that the money would be used to finance production in Britain.

FILM FINANCE

After the Anglo-American Film Agreement in 1948 the emphasis of government policy shifted from dollar-saving back to protection for the film industry. As soon as American films re-entered the market, British producers were faced with severe competition, and American companies, including Warner, MGM and Twentieth-Century Fox, started to initiate projects in Britain, although fears that they would invade British studios on a major scale proved to be unfounded. In anticipation of this scenario the Bank of England had been granted powers in October 1947 to keep a close watch on American activities in Britain and, in any case, the American film unions were opposed to large production programmes in Britain when there was unemployment in Hollywood. Nevertheless, between 1948 and 1950 the five Hollywood majors spent nearly £6 million of frozen sterling on production activities (PEP, 1952: 160). American investment in Britain increased, however, to unprecedented levels later on in the 1950s and 1960s as the trend of runaway production in Europe became an essential part of Hollywood's overseas operations. The post-war years were therefore crucial in continuing the Board of Trade's 1938 policy of looking to America to solve the British industry's chronic financial problems.

The renters' quota had been abolished in 1947 as a result of American pressure during the General Agreement on Trade and Tariffs (GATT) negotiations. The Cinematograph Films Act of 1948 imposed a 45 per cent exhibitors' quota, which exhibitors succeeded in reducing to 30 per cent in 1950 where it remained until its abolition in 1983. Two important new schemes were adopted by the Labour Government to assist producers: the National Film Finance Corporation (1949) and the Eady Levy (1950). Independent companies, particularly Korda's British Lion and Filippo del Guidice's Two Cities, were in dire financial straits and Harold Wilson, the President of the Board of Trade, examined plans to assist independent producers as a means of encouraging competition with the combines.[12] He favoured a non-confrontational approach of curbing, but not dismantling, the power of the combines by creating a third force of independents. The Board of Trade was drawn into devising the National Film Finance Corporation (NFFC) when the Finance Corporation for Industry and the Industrial and Commercial Finance Corporation (organisations funded by the Bank of England and major banks to provide loans for the postwar rehabilitation of industry) refused to assist British Lion when it applied for help in 1948. The birth of the NFFC was very much conceived as a short-term plan to rescue British Lion, but it ended up being an essential, if limited, element of government policy.

The NFFC did not award money to producers directly but contributed 'end money' via distribution companies. The initial revolving fund was £5 million, which was increased to £6 million in 1950. British Lion was the first distribution company to receive money, and in the initial years much was lost through mismanagement. But many important films were made with assistance from the NFFC, including *The Third Man* (1949), *The Small Black Room* (1949), *The Wooden Horse* (1950) and *The Happiest Days of Your Life* (1950). It also sponsored three special groups of film-makers: two were associated with the combines and a third consisted of new directors and makers of short films (see Dickinson and Street, 1985: 218–19).

Unfortunately, these groups had collapsed by 1955 and over the years the NFFC's finances were whittled down: in 1970 it was allocated only £1 million. Nevertheless it assisted over 750 films and functioned as an important resource for many independent producers until its cessation in 1985.

The Eady Levy, named after the Treasury official who was involved in devising the scheme, was a further attempt to assist producers. The idea was to create a production fund from a levy on cinema tickets which would be distributed to British producers on the basis of box-office takings. The most successful British films would, therefore, be the major beneficiaries. Exhibitors agreed to participate in the scheme in exchange for a reduction in Entertainments Tax and an increase in seat prices. Like the NFFC, the scheme was introduced as a temporary measure, but it became statutory in 1957. Along with the NFFC the Eady Levy was abolished in 1985, after a controversial history during which it was widely known that Americans producing in Britain had taken the lion's share.

By 1950, therefore, the major components of state policy had been established: quotas, the NFFC and the Eady Levy. The commitment to assist the film industry had been beset with problems involving the accommodation of major conflicting interests: the film trade which was consistently divided over how best to assist producers, and the Americans who could not be dealt with purely in terms of film issues. International economic and political affairs provided an ever-present backdrop to bargaining over celluloid diplomacy. At best, the structures which were established provided some access to the market and an element of support for producers, and maintained a consistent Parliamentary rhetorical position on the importance of a British film industry 'in the national interest'. At worst, they did little to assist independent producers or facilitate an environment in which films intended primarily for the domestic market might flourish, nor did they insist on effective foreign distribution of British films in America and they did little to foster independence from Hollywood in economic or aesthetic terms. The history of the film industry after 1950 reflected these fundamental contradictions from the perspective of changing conditions of exhibition, the structure of the industry, relations with America and the perennial problem of raising production finance. In 1952 Political and Economic Planning published the first in-depth, book-length study of the film industry. Its introduction stated:

> The crisis in British film-making – where lies the main problem of the industry – started long ago, and only at rare intervals during the past forty years have there been short periods of prosperity to lighten an otherwise depressing canvas. Of a stable production industry there has been no sign.
>
> (PEP, 1952: 11).

EXHIBITION AND THE SHRINKING AUDIENCE

The most striking factor affecting cinema exhibition since 1950 was the decline in admissions from 1,635 million in 1946 to 54 million in 1984 (*BFI Handbook*, 1996: 62). During the peak years in the 1940s, the most regular cinema-goers were young, urban and working class, but this audience was lost by stages, particularly during 1955–59. It is only in recent years, with the building of large multiplex cinemas, that the youth audience has been to some extent recaptured. Docherty, Morrison and Tracey (1987: 5) argue that the causes of this decline were a combination of 'Elvis Presley, espresso coffee, the Town and Country Planning Act of 1947 and the sclerosis of the British exhibition industry'. Rather than place the blame squarely on competition from television, it is clear that social factors – including the rise of consumer culture, the nuclear family and the stagnation and demise of the inner cities – dictated new leisure patterns which were not effectively exploited by cinema entrepreneurs (ibid.: 25).

The domination of the market by the duopoly of Rank and ABPC continued until 1969 when ABPC was absorbed by EMI, which later became Thorn-EMI Screen Entertainment. In 1972 the circuits controlled 32 per cent of cinemas, which generated 52 per cent of total takings (Economic Intelligence Unit, *Retail Business*, 177, 1972). Further ownership changes occurred when Thorn-EMI Screen Entertainment, with its large cinema circuit, was taken over by the multinational company Cannon in 1986 (see Stanbrook, 1986). Despite successive official reports warning of the dangers of monopoly, the power of the two dominant companies remained unchecked, although only one remained British. In 1990 there were 1,561 screens in Britain: Cannon operated 381 of them on 138 sites and Rank's Odeon chain ran 256 screens on 75 sites (*BFI Handbook*, 1991: 36, 41). Each combine engaged in barring restrictions in their first-run cinemas which gave preferential treatment to films produced by their American affiliates, Columbia and Warner (Cannon) and Disney, Twentieth-Century Fox, United Artists and Universal (Rank). Stephen Woolley of Palace Pictures expressed the acute concern felt by independent producers and exhibitors:

> We have survived by ducking and weaving between the majors, releasing when we know they are not. It is getting more difficult to get theatres, they have just got too many films lined up and we have to fight tooth and nail to keep our cinemas.
>
> (Quoted in Hacker and Price, 1991: 15)

In the late 1980s, exhibition practices and patterns of ownership were profoundly affected by the spread of multiplexes. Cinema screens and seating capacity increased, and the youth audience (aged 15–24) was lured back to cinema-going with some success: in 1989 admissions totalled 94.5 million, a figure which rose to 114.3 million in 1993 and again to 123.5 in

1994 (*BFI Handbook* 1996: 62). Allen Eyles explained the attractions offered by the multiplex: 'With as many as 14 screens, they give cinema-goers a wide choice of films at one location. . . . They also offer clean pleasant surroundings, convenient parking, and are often part of larger developments which include other attractions such as eating-places and shops' (*BFI Handbook* 1991: 37). From a financial point of view, the arrival of the multiplex inaugurated a further wave of Hollywood intervention in the exhibition industry. Rank and Cannon were joined by powerful interests who dominated the multiplex scene very quickly: United Cinemas International (UK), owned by Paramount Communications, MCA, National Amusements (Showcase) and Warner Brothers. Cannon over-extended itself in the late 1980s and its cinemas were absorbed by MGM Pathé, making them the largest operator in the UK, owning 406 screens out of a total of 1,558 in 1990 (*BFI Handbook*, 1992: 41).

The trend towards greater concentration and intensification of American interests continued unabated with 697 new screens being added in 1993, 37 per cent of the total number of 1,890 (*BFI Handbook*, 1995: 32). The majority of the multiplexes were owned by MGM, Odeon and US-owned UCI, Warner Brothers and Showcase, giving the majors a much greater degree of control over exhibition than they were permitted by law in the US. The BFI Film and Television Handbook expressed anxiety about this situation:

> The Americans, of course, have been very welcome in the UK, since it is they who have invested most heavily in new multiplexes. But there is a growing awareness that the hegemony of Hollywood in both exhibition and distribution – films distributed by the major studios accounted for 80.5 per cent of all tickets sold in Britain in 1993 – makes it even more difficult . . . for independent British films to gain effective access to the market.
>
> (1995: 35)

The Monopolies and Mergers Commission's Report of 1995 discovered that 'all the leading exhibitors except Odeon have some ownership link, direct or indirect, with a Hollywood studio' (*Report on the Supply of Films for Exhibition in Cinemas in the UK*: Summary 1.3.) In keeping, however, with previous investigations into monopoly in the film industry the report concluded that, although there was cause for anxiety, 'the scale monopoly situation does not in itself raise concerns for the public interest' (ibid.: 112), and recommended that two obstructive booking practices should be abolished and restricted.[13] It is ironic that the duopoly of Rank and EMI, whose existence had been tolerated by the government as a bolster against American domination, was finally broken by American companies – United Cinemas International, MGM Cinemas, Warner Theatres and National

Amusements. Along with Rank, by 1992 they controlled 77 per cent of the market (*BFI Handbook*, 1994: 29). This situation was somewhat checked by the acquisition of MGM, the largest circuit in the UK, by the Virgin Group in 1995 which was in turn sold for £215 million in 1999 to the French company UGC. In 2003 two major chains, Odeon and Warner Villages were sold, respectively, to a consortium of German/British investors and to the British independent exhibitor SBC International Cinemas which operate the cinemas through the Vue company (*BFI Handbook*, 2004: 39–40). Cinema admissions continued to increase in the first years of the twenty-first century, reaching 176 million in 2002, with a slight decrease in the following year to 167.3 million. This is an interesting situation, especially considering that new cinemas continued to be built, bringing the total number of multiplex screens in 2003 to 2,362, and admissions prices increased (*BFI Handbook*, 2004: 39–40). Films funded, or part-funded, by American companies continue to dominate the box-office. The UK Film Council's plans to extend the range of films screened in British cinemas via the Digital Screen Network promises to reduce costs for exhibitors by supplementing expensive 35mm exhibition with the use of digital copies of 'specialised' films (foreign language, subtitled films; documentaries; archive/classic films; non-mainstream films with complex and challenging subject matter; films that are innovative in terms of storytelling devices and aesthetics) that might not otherwise be screened (Hanson, 2007: 370–83). In addition to cinemas, British films are also screened on television, particularly with the availability of Film 4 on Freeview digital set-top boxes, and on DVD. Home screens are getting bigger and the sales push for high-definition emphasises the similarities between what home technologies can deliver and the cinema experience.

DISTRIBUTION AND FILM FINANCE

Distribution also continued to be dominated by American interests. In 1993 five American-affiliated companies led the field: Buena Vista, Columbia, Fox, UIP and Warner Distributors. The most important independent distributors were Entertainment, First Independent, Guild and Rank Film Distributors who handled British films. Historically, the monopolistic nature of distribution and exhibition has prevented films from being widely available on an even geographic basis, as Julian Petley has explained:

> It delivers a large amount of mainstream Hollywood product fairly effectively to audiences in large metropolitan areas but gives those audiences little opportunity to widen their tastes. Meanwhile, certain audiences (particularly those looking for non-Hollywood, even British, films) and, increasingly, certain geographical areas, remain virtually uncatered for.
>
> (*BFI Handbook*, 1992: 26)

American companies spent huge sums on marketing their films, and links with the combines and multiplexes left little screen space for independents. Even so, astute advertising campaigns by independents were occasionally successful, as demonstrated by Palace's marketing of *Company of Wolves* in 1984 (Petrie, 1991: 132–33). One venture which attempted to redress the imbalance was devised in 1988 by the Commission of the European Communities: MEDIA 92's EFDO scheme. This provided interest-free loans to assist with the pre-distribution costs of low-budget films. In 1990, it was announced that over the next five years £100 million would be available towards distribution costs of MEDIA 92 projects. British films to benefit from this assistance have included *Distant Voices, Still Lives* (1988), *Drowning By Numbers* (1988) and *Orlando* (1992).

As well as difficulties arising from the external domination of exhibition and distribution, British producers continued to struggle to finance their films. In the 1950s Rank went through a period of retrenchment after attempts to penetrate the American market had failed (see Murphy, 1983). Although the Anglo-American Film Agreements of the early 1950s were designed to attract dollars to Britain, American finance for British production was not available on a major scale until the 1960s. American companies were however responsible for producing over 100 films in Britain between 1950 and 1957. A combination of factors explained American interest during that period and into the 1960s. Anti-trust legislation which had forced the majors to relinquish their cinemas placed greater stress on foreign markets and the attractive possibilities of 'runaway production' (US-financed or part-financed productions abroad). The Eady Levy was also an incentive as a production subsidy for films registered as British, regardless of their source of finance. The quality and availability of British studios, relatively cheap labour and the popularity of British films in the 1960s also account for the proliferation of American finance which reached a peak of £31.3 million imported by the American majors in 1968 for production by their British subsidiaries (Dickinson and Street, 1985: 240). The success of the New Wave, the Beatles, James Bond films and the prospect of making big-budget films in Britain attracted dollars: 90 per cent of production finance was American in 1967 (Murphy, 1992: 258). The key American companies operating production programmes in Britain in the 1960s were United Artists, Paramount, Warner Brothers, MGM, Twentieth-Century Fox, Columbia, Universal and Disney.

This trend did not, however, continue and by 1974 the sum imported by US companies had fallen to £2.9 million (Dickinson and Street, 1985: 240). The majors showed catastrophic losses on big-budget extravaganzas and problems at home dictated a drastic decline in foreign investment. After a period of economic growth and artistic exuberance in the 1960s, British producers were left without reliable sources of finance in the 1970s as the NFFC's resources dwindled: during the years 1973–81 it contributed only

£4 million towards 31 features and six shorts (Dickinson and Street, 1985: 241). In yet another bid to find success in America, the British majors (EMI, Lord Grade's Associated Communications Corporation and Rank), embarked on a series of disastrous blockbusters, the most spectacular being *Raise the Titanic* (1980), a box-office flop which cost $35 million. The total number of British films registered fell from 98 in 1971 to 70 in 1976 and then to 36 in 1981 (Wood, 1983: 143). The Conservative government realigned the NFFC in 1972 with a consortium of private interests, and in 1981 it was completely restructured: the government contributed £1 million as a small incentive to encourage up to £5 million from the private sector. It was also entitled to receive money from the proceeds of the Eady Levy – £1.5 million or 20 per cent of the Levy's gross receipts. The Levy also contributed funds to the National Film and Television School and the BFI Production Board.[14]

In the 1980s British production revived, particularly during the years 1983–85, followed by yet another slump in 1988–91. Throughout the decade an average of 46 feature films per year was produced and, for a brief period, financial backing for British films from the private sector was healthier than it had been for a long time. Independent production companies enjoyed a brief, but significant phase of activity, the most important companies being Goldcrest, Handmade Films, Palace Pictures, Virgin and Working Title.[15] Goldcrest alone invested £63 million, mostly during 1983–85, and Britain was once again an attractive location for the American majors. The boom can be explained by a variety of factors: 'The existence of 100 per cent first-year capital allowances, combined with a strong dollar and the growing worldwide demand for movies renewed Britain's popularity as a base for production' (*BFI Handbook*, 1993: 18). Under this impetus it appeared that a renaissance in British film-making was under way with films like *Chariots of Fire* (1981), *Gandhi* (1982), *Local Hero* (1983), *A Passage to India* (1985) and *A Room With a View* (1986).

Capital allowances were a major incentive for producers, providing a tax-shelter device from 1979 until they were phased out by the Chancellor of the Exchequer in 1984–86. Alan Stanbrook explained how they worked:

> For tax and depreciation purposes, films have been treated in just the same way as a piece of plant and machinery. Companies have been allowed to write off their entire investment in a particular picture in the very first year. This meant in practice that profits from one picture could escape tax to the extent that they were matched by capital expenditure on another. In short, so long as the company continued to make successful films, it could enjoy a tax holiday.
>
> (1984: 172)

As a consequence of the Chancellor's decision to phase out capital allowances, the abolition of the Eady Levy and the decline of the dollar, investment in British films decreased after 1985. Goldcrest survived near-bankruptcy in 1987, Handmade was forced to retrench and was purchased by a Canadian, Virgin quit film production in 1986 and Palace went into liquidation in 1992. Thorn EMI Screen Entertainment's importance as a production company ceased when it was taken over by Cannon in 1986, a company which concentrated on cinema exhibition rather than production. American investment in British production declined from £142 million in 1984 to £67.8 million in 1993 (*BFI Handbook*, 1994: 25). American companies continued to prefer to make big-budget American films in Britain than to finance British companies.

In the 1990s the major sources of funding available to producers were British Screen, the European Co-production Fund, the BFI Production Board, Channel 4, ITV and the BBC. British Screen replaced the NFFC in 1986 as a private company consisting of initially three major shareholders: Rank, EMI, Channel 4; in 1987 Granada joined the grouping. Additional monies were inherited from the NFFC and in all the Department of Trade contributed £10 million over five years. By the early 1990s however private investment in British Screen declined but from 1994 funding became available from the Pay-TV channel BSkyB.[16] Essentially a 'quango' (quasi-autonomous non-governmental organisation), a type of financial grouping favoured by the Tories, British Screen's first chief executive was Simon Relph, son of the respected British producer Michael Relph. The organisation's brief was to develop treatments, drafts of scripts and preparation to

> encourage the making of British films on a commercially successful basis. There should therefore be a considered relationship between the cost of the film and its income potential sufficient to demonstrate the potential profitability of the project. Sadly, most films must therefore have commercial appeal outside the United Kingdom.
>
> (British Screen, 1987: 3)

Nevertheless, some experimental small films were assisted, for example, Jarman's *The Last of England* (1987) and *Edward II* (1991), and there was considerable variation in the budgets of films supported by British Screen. Films made possible with British Screen input included *Belly of an Architect* (1987), *Prick Up Your Ears* (1987) and *The Kitchen Toto* (1987). British Screen often co-financed films along with the European Co-production Fund (which was established in 1990) and with Channel 4. Simon Perry took over from Relph as British Screen's chief executive in 1991 and was responsible for the deal with BSkyB. Some significant films were funded including *The Crying Game* (1992), *Naked* (1993), *One Day In September* (1999), *Butterfly Kiss* (1994) and *Land and Freedom* (1995). Under Perry's direction British Screen increased the trend towards European co-production and collaboration which 'laid the foundation of the production boom of the mid-1990s' (Macnab, 2000). The Greenlight Fund, also under Perry's control, in collaboration with the Arts Council, was established in 1996 to entice filmmakers associated with bigger budget commercial production to work in the UK rather than migrate to Hollywood. Lottery funds, which had first been available for films in 1995 via the Arts Council, then became an important source of funding.

In 1997 the Labour Government appointed a minister, Chris Smith, with special responsibility for the film industry who established a Film Policy Review Group whose report, *A Bigger Picture* (1998), emphasised the importance of effective distribution ('we need to encourage the emergence of a distribution-led industrial process: better capitalised companies which can integrate production with distribution') and marketing. It aimed to address the six aims declared by Smith as fundamental objectives for the British film industry: a doubling of the domestic market share of British films; a larger and more diverse audience for film in general and cinema in particular; training provision that fully meets the industry needs; a financial framework that facilitates and encourages sustained investment in the British film industry and continued success in attracting inward investment. Tax relief mechanisms were also instituted in 1997 to assist small independent filmmakers. In 2000 three major sources of funding – British Screen, the National Lottery and British Film Institute Production – were merged as the UK Film Council, a government-funded body which represented a renewed state commitment to supporting the British film industry. UK films continued to be eligible for receipt of Lottery funds, now dispensed totally via the Film Council. Scottish Screen, Sgrîn of Wales and the Northern Ireland Film Commission made funding awards for a wide range of film-related activity including exhibition, audience development and short films. Early recipients of Lottery funding (back in 1997 via the Arts Council) were three consortia of producers: DNA Films, Pathé Productions and the Film Consortium. The UK Film Council continued with this stream of funding but on the expiry of the agreements in 2004 the only one that continued was with DNA Films which was renewed until 2008. An influential and controversial factor in this decision was DNA's merger with Fox Searchlight, the US distribution chain which contributed production finance as well as guaranteed release for the films in the USA. In addition the Film Council established funds to award money to projects ranging from 'prestige', higher-budget films via the Premiere Fund, to lower-end, experimental work via the New Cinema Fund. In 2004 tax relief for filmmakers was threatened when the Government sought to crack down on the exploitation of tax avoidance partnership schemes, which had an immediate impact on productions already planned for filming in the UK. After much protest filmmakers welcomed the announcement later that year of a new tax credit to support new UK films up to a budget of £15 million. The 2006 Finance Act introduced an enhanced tax relief with maximum deductions for films costing £20 million or less. The impact of the latter encouraged 'inward investment' activity in British studios, since to qualify for UK tax credit a film must be certified as British either because it is an official co-production or because it satisfies the controversial 'cultural test'. The latter involves a company satisfying particular conditions which involve a point-scoring exercise whereby key factors are registered including 'cultural content' (a film set in the UK; lead characters British citizens or residents; a film based on British subject matter or underlying material; original dialogue recorded mainly in the English language); 'cultural contribution' (film represents/reflects a diverse British culture, heritage or creativity); use of 'cultural hubs' (studio and/or location shooting/visual effects/special effects; music recording/audio post production/picture post production); use of 'cultural practitioners' (director, scriptwriter, producer, composer, lead actors, majority of cast, key staff, crew). The heaviest weighting is given to the first two categories, cultural content and cultural contribution. Tax credit can be claimed if a film incurs at least 25 per cent of its total production expenditure on film-making activities in the UK. This explains the relatively high number of productions filmed in Britain by US studios in 2007 with films such as Walt Disney's *The Chronicles of Narnia: Prince Caspian* and Dreamworks' *Sweeney Todd: The Demon Barber of Fleet Street* being shot in the UK. This has also led to an increased interest in heritage subjects for British films, including a film adaptation of *Brideshead Revisited* (2008) which is part-funded by Screen Yorkshire, a regional funding agency which represents an important aspect of current policy that seeks to take advantage of European Regional Development Fund sources. Other regional screen agencies which encourage production in British localities include North West Vision, Screen West Midlands and South West Screen. Scottish Screen continues to administer a production fund, as does the Wales Screen Commission.

The strengths and weaknesses of the Film Council's work continues to be much debated, for example its declaration that in 2005 British films accounted for 33 per cent of UK box-office revenues, a figure that masks the extent to which the films are largely US-financed, although many contain indigenous cultural content, albeit of a particular brand including films such as *Harry Potter and the Prisoner of Azkaban* (2004), *Bridget Jones: The Edge of Reason* (2004) and the re-make of *Alfie* (2004), starring Jude Law and set in Manhattan rather than the London setting of the original film made in 1966. The turn towards greater internationalisation of film finance does indeed put a strain on definitions of 'British' film that seek to demarcate national identity in terms of labour, finance and subject-matter. Critics of the Film Council's work point to its 'reliance upon trade interests, some of which are heavily reliant on the American film industry ... on balance, the policy options that have been adopted ... have been too limited in their range and effects' (Dickinson and Harvey, 2005: 425). On the other hand, the Council has been involved in funding films in which 'the cultural and financial impetus is from the UK and where the majority of the personnel are British' (*BFI Handbook*, 2005: 28), including *Vera Drake*, *Bullet Boy*, *Enduring Love* and *My Summer of Love* (all produced in 2003) as well as co-productions with non-US partners. As noted in Chapter 5, these produce films which often contain fascinating observations about contemporary life in the UK. However, in terms of box office these films generally do not yield nearly as much as those with US involvement, demonstrating yet again the continuing power of the American film industry. As Alex Cox, a fervent critic of the Film Council, argues:

> Labour's attitude to film-making is all over the place. On the one hand, individual ministers claim to be passionate about film and concerned about the survival of the British industry. On the other, New Labour sits in the pocket of the Americans, whether the policy is culture or war.
>
> (2007: 28).

The combination of screen agency activity with the aim of encouraging non-UK producers to make films in Britain has led other commentators to discern a trend that might appear to be contradictory. Nick Redfern argues that as a result of this policy the British film industry is 'a hybrid space of interactions between a trans-national film industry which crosses national boundaries, and a highly territorialized national film industry which is increasingly organized at the regional level' (Redfern, 2007: 150). In this scenario the films that dominate the scene are those which can be said to demonstrate 'British cultural impetus' by having British writers (films such as *Notting Hill* would fit into this category) but are highly exportable, and Hollywood productions filmed on location in the UK and which use British actors, technicians and studios.

TELEVISION, VIDEO AND DVD

The contribution of funding from television is vital although increasingly sparse. Channel 4's commitment to innovative programming since its inception in 1982 encompassed feature films, investing a total of £98 million in 273 films during the years 1982–93. In 2002, however, film funding was scaled-down considerably by two-thirds to £9 million and Film 4, the bastion of the channel's relationship with independent production companies, became more of a cable-TV channel (Roddick, 2007: 23). The BBC has invested in films since the 1970s, although on a much smaller scale than Channel 4, whose Film 4 channel was made available on digital Freeview in 2006, and screened a season of British films. In the 1990s the BBC's Films Unit had an annual budget of £5 million to co-finance five films intended for theatrical release. It also purchased the television rights of five independently produced films which it then broadcast. In the early years of the twenty-first century the BBC's annual budget for film-making increased to £9 million which was intended to fund films with budgets of up to £10 million. Working in partnership with companies, the BBC has funded some significant films including *Sweet Sixteen* (2002), *Bullet Boy* (2004) and *A Cock and Bull Story* (2005). In an increasingly competitive broadcast market, for several years the ITV companies ceased participating in film finance until July 1996 when plans were announced for ITV investment of £100 million in British films (*Screen International*, 19–25 July 1996: 1). The expansion of cable and satellite TV has made more films available on the small screen, but movie channels are in fierce competition with sports and other popular channels. Video and DVD increased demand for film entertainment. In 1991, revenue from UK retail and sell-through reached a peak of £1.18 billion (*BFI Handbook*, 1995: 46). People were watching more films than ever, but on the small screen and increasingly via the sell-through market. The concentration of ownership was similar to the film industry: the main video distributors were American and in 1993 the video rental top twenty consisted entirely of American films. The booming video retail market in 1994 was dominated by Warner Home Video, Columbia TriStar and CIC and, apart from *Four Weddings and a Funeral* (1994), the top ten titles were American (*BFI Handbook*, 1996: 48). As technology changed, DVD took over from video as the cornerstone of the home entertainment market and purchase rather than rental the preferred option, facilitated by the ease of internet shopping.

At the time of writing the first edition of *British National Cinema*, the film industry's future seemed as uncertain as ever: the average budget of a British film fell from £2 million in 1992 to £1.8 million in 1993, with some improvement in 1994, and European co-productions did not seem to have been particularly successful. The prevailing ethos was to produce international films intended for a restricted market before 'crossing over' into wider theatrical distribution. But films aiming for world markets immediately became caught up in complex negotiations for pre-sales and video rights. Although BSkyB supported many films, it would not advance more than £350,000 to a British film, making it more than likely that much of its film budget was spent on assisting American productions in Britain (*BFI Handbook*, 1996: 29). Producers sought finance for one-off projects and with the collapse of vertical integration were totally at the mercy of American distributors. It appeared to be the case that a hundred years after the birth of cinema the production sector had practically returned to its original cottage-industry structure. It is arguable that with the inauguration of the UK Film Council, and an increasing emphasis on the trans-national make-up of British cinema in terms of finance and cultural content, the picture is not quite so bleak at the beginning of the twenty-first century. Hollywood still calls the shots, but perhaps the greater diversity of viewing outlets, the potential of the Digital Screen Network and the quality of many of the films themselves (see Chapter 5) gives grounds for a greater degree of optimism than was possible in the mid-1990s.

CONCLUSION: FROM *HENRY VIII* TO *FOUR WEDDINGS* AND BEYOND

Four Weddings and a Funeral (1994) broke box-office records at home and in America and since its release there have been further international successes in the *Four Weddings* mould with *Sliding Doors* (1997), *Notting Hill* (1999) and *Bridget Jones' Diary* (2001). But are these films indicators of stable and sustained investment, or are they simply examples of the proliferation of the heritage genre in the international market as British films which export well but fail to encourage increased diversification of British film-making? The above survey of the British film industry's political economy describes fundamental problems which make the latter more likely, although since the first edition of *British National Cinema* was published in 1997 there have been key examples of the co-existence of many varieties of British cinema. Indeed, as Chapters 4 and 5 demonstrate, there have been many interesting representations that challenge the notion that the only films that do well at the box-office or which can be exported reflect very restricted and class-bound notions of 'Britishness'. As ever, film history is instructive in explaining the origins of the industry's vulnerability to market forces and tendency towards cycles of boom followed by slump. Success or failure all too often seems to be contingent on external economic factors including balance of payments, tax incentives and the overall perception of screen entertainment as a viable financial prospect with demonstrable returns. This of course influences the sort of films that dominate the market and, in turn, notions of what constitutes the contestable contours of British cinema's many identities.

The film industry has always been subject to the ebb and flow of financial stringency. The box-office success of *Howards End* (1992) and *Shallow Grave* (1993) are evidence of particular niche British films with international and domestic appeal. So-called 'cross-over' films like *The Crying Game* (1992), which began its theatrical life as an art-house film but went on to win success in the mainstream cinema, and 'post-heritage' films such as *Elizabeth* (1998) or the box-office and film festival success of Mike Leigh's *Vera Drake* (2004) have also been encouraging. But as ever, it is difficult to see how an upturn can be sustained on a long-term basis, given the limited market opportunities and reliance on a few funding bodies which are vulnerable to the punishing fluctuations of the market economy. Far from being greeted as a godsend, there was considerable anxiety about how National Lottery money would be allocated to film-makers (*BFI Handbook*, 1996: 33). Indeed, as soon as the first slate of Lottery-funded films appeared there was much criticism of their quality, as well as reports of how many of the films were never actually distributed. Since its inception, the UK Film Council has been controversial, with filmmakers either welcoming its support or being suspicious of its desire to place British films in international markets. The debates that circulate around the future of the film industry continue to be based on recurrent themes, the most dominant being economic structures and relations with Hollywood. As argued by Alex Cox and representatives from the Independent Film Parliament, a public forum established in 2003 including educationalists, academics and independent film makers, there are nevertheless grounds for concern that these initiatives fail to foster a greater diversity of product.

From an early stage the British industry had to grapple with its home market being dominated by Hollywood. Doubts about the encroachment of American business interests in the British film industry were countered by arguments which emphasised the need for strong British companies with access to the lucrative American market: the only way to achieve this was to do deals with Hollywood. Where there was some commitment to domestic production, as with Rank's production activities and contracts with independent producers, there was always a conflict between supplying cinemas with popular American films and at the same time maintaining an active production programme. In the past Britain's attitude towards Hollywood could not be isolated from America's increasing role in European economies, particularly after the Second World War. The fiasco of the 'Dalton duty' showed that a tough stance could be counter-productive in the wrong circumstances. The aim of encouraging American production in Britain was achieved in waves after 1950, but it is significant that the decision to operate in Britain was dictated by problems in Hollywood and the strength of the dollar rather than by government policy. The largest influx of dollars was in the 1960s, when the existence of Eady money was one among many incentives. Any production activity is important, and the use made by foreign companies of British studios since the 1970s has enhanced the reputation of British technicians and improved technical facilities. But the level of American involvement fluctuates and depends on a variety of factors. To bolster the British film industry's now fragile infrastructure, American investment and collaboration with Europe must play a part in its operation. On the other hand, the level of American interest in distribution and exhibition makes it extremely difficult for British films to get financed and shown. The nightmare scenario of the Hollywood invasion has taken place unwittingly, over many years. The planners of the 1940s did not anticipate the decline of cinema as a mass entertainment, and by allowing box-office takings and the exhibition sector to dominate trade discussions over film, producers lost out.

When Korda, Rank, Lord Grade and Goldcrest attempted to break into the American market, they were, with some important exceptions and trends, often able only to secure one-off successes and not secure sustained profits because of needing to raise generally bigger budgets for films destined for international markets. Hollywood's high production values and budgets dictated a style which British producers were often not resourced to emulate. As long as distribution and exhibition were dominated by American interests it was equally difficult for lower budget, domestically oriented films to get shown, although it is important to note that some British films which were not imitative of Hollywood in style, theme or budget were, and continue to be, successful in UK cinemas and abroad. In spite of the difficulties, there were considerable achievements in production values as well as in returns to the domestic and international box-office. In fact, films marked by their difference could acquire an 'exotic' tag when shown abroad since they became invested with a desirable sense of otherness that could, in certain niche markets, receive enthusiastic reviews and popular followings (Street, 2002).

The conflict with Hollywood was nevertheless reflected in the government's attitude towards the film industry. The state never intended to intervene in the industry's affairs to a great extent: the legislation did not live up to the ideals expressed by forceful Parliamentary rhetoric in support of a British film industry. The quota system avoided questions of film finance, and when the NFFC was established it was always intended that state subsidy should be minimal – the NFFC's primary function being to attract private commercial support. Criticisms about the industry's monopolistic structure conflicted with the need to protect the strongest companies, the Rank/ABPC duopoly. While independent producers were considered to be vital for a healthy film industry it was not recommended that Rank and ABPC should be forced to sell cinemas whose profits were a major source of production finance. If divorcement legislation had been passed (see note 7), the danger was that Hollywood would gain an even greater stranglehold on the British market, which is exactly what happened when the duopoly finally collapsed. But, by that time, Rank was spending minimal sums on production and never evolved into a major in the Hollywood sense.

On the other hand, several schemes which might have helped reduce the three-way conflict between the duopoly, independents and Hollywood were not adopted: for example, plans in the late 1940s for a state-owned Fourth Circuit[17] and successive recommendations for an independent Film Authority to regulate trade affairs. Nationalisation of the film industry had been advocated by the Association of Ciné Technicians for years but when it was most likely, in the late 1940s when the NFFC, the Group Three production scheme and the Eady Levy were being planned, the Board of Trade was cautious. Board of Trade files reveal an interesting exchange of memoranda in the autumn of 1949 between Harold Wilson and R. G. Somervell, a Board of Trade official who specialised in film matters. Wilson was clearly worried about the power of the circuits and contemplated a more interventionist policy in the long term:

> The decision on a film's prospect of circuit release is taken in effect by two men – the appropriate authorities for the Gaumont-Odeon circuits and the ABC circuits respectively. However much work the NFFC may do on the financial standing or even the quality and prospects of scripts etc., in the last resort their action is largely conditioned by the decision of one or both of these two gentlemen. . . . One possibility and radical solution would be to bust up the circuits. This may come in the fullness of time; I hope it will, but I do not consider it a likely development in the immediate future and although I think we should keep it in our minds as a long-term objective I am not sure that we ought to pursue it as national policy in the months that lie immediately ahead. Apart from anything else some proportion of the losses on production are still being made up by circuit profits and to bust up the circuits or to divorce them from production (as in America) might lead to a drying up of such sources of finance as are at present available.
>
> (Public Record Office: BT 64/4519, 25 September 1949)

The memorandum went on to suggest that 'some authority in whom the public, and, so far as possible, individual producers themselves, can have confidence' should be established as a means of monitoring the power of the circuits and making sure that quota films were assisted by the NFFC. Somervell's reply was far more conservative regarding the question of more extensive state intervention. He disagreed with Wilson about the power of the circuits: 'Michael Balcon has told me that he does not think there is any likelihood in practice that a desirable film project for which outside finance was available might be frustrated by the personal prejudice of an individual in a circuit organisation' (Public Record Office, BT 64/4519: 4 October 1949). Somervell advised against a regulatory film authority, recommending instead that the trade should be left to sort itself out: 'The government can only sit on one side and watch for opportunities to remove friction or to exercise discreet pressure on the obstinate' (ibid.).

Had the initiative towards a more enlightened government policy been lost? The complexities of the industry's affairs confounded successive governments and Board of Trade officials, and it is not surprising that radical action was never taken against the duopoly. Whatever long-term strategy Wilson might have been developing, Labour were not back in power until 1964 when the film industry's affairs were very different and the duopoly was even more firmly entrenched. As we have seen, after 1950 policy did not change very much and it contracted in its vision: finance available to the NFFC was reduced and its powers were not extended. Wilson established a Working Party in August 1975 which repeated his 1949 recommendation for a British Film Authority, but yet again the idea was shelved. However, the work of the NFFC's successor, British Screen, provided some grounds for optimism, even though it was a much more commercially dominated body. Petrie (1991: 86–90) has argued that British Screen operated on more realistic, commercial lines than the NFFC which only supplied risky 'end money'. Instead, British Screen backed films costing under £3 million which already had most of their budget. The UK Film Council, with its various funds designed to support films from the 'prestige' end to experimental, continues this trend towards diversification of product. It also shows that a Labour government continues the approach preferred by the Conservatives in its relations with the film industry. While the existence of the Film Council and its 'cultural test' demonstrates a shift in thinking against an entirely commercial conception of British film, it remains to be seen whether in the long-term it will be able to sustain the positive developments noted in Chapter 5, or create the stable structures which are necessary to support a viable production industry for the twenty-first century. While there is a degree of optimism around the inauguration of the Digital Screen Network, whether it will result in a sustained growth of non-mainstream film is not clear, especially since, as critics of the UKFC point out, unless it is accompanied by initiatives that seek to promote 'specialised' film so that audience demand for them is increased, it may well result in simply a re-alignment of screening technologies with commercial gains for the major chains. In many respects, the film policy of New Labour then demonstrates continuities with film history rather than representing a break with the past.

Chapter 2

Studios, directors and genres

> British genres are more than an abstract system of formulas, conventions, and codes that are universally applicable. National identity, social history, and ideology play a central role in their formation.
>
> (Landy, 1991: 11)

British cinema has been characterised as a curious mix of studios, directors and genres, emphasis being frequently placed on key directors who are held responsible for 'great British films' and 'high spots in film history', including *Brief Encounter* (David Lean, 1945), *Henry V* (Laurence Olivier, 1945), *The Third Man* (Carol Reed, 1949) and *Room at the Top* (Jack Clayton, 1959). Their efforts have been praised in auteurist discourse for operating not only against the constraints of studio film-making but also because of the overall economic and cultural oppression by Hollywood. Although directors are important, it is essential however to see their work as part of the larger operation of studios and genres. As the above quotation from Landy shows, British cinema has a strong generic base which has been influenced by a combination of creative abilities, film industry economics and British society.

Until relatively recently, attention has not focused on British cinema in terms of genres, and literature on studios has tended to concentrate on the historical development of Denham, Pinewood, Elstree and Shepperton without placing studio structures within a wider context of creative enterprise. The study of Hollywood cinema has suggested further areas of investigation concerning generic analysis, studio models of film-making and the role of directors (and other creative personnel) within those structures. These themes suggest useful comparative models for analysing British cinema, for example by introducing notions of standardisation, 'repetition' and 'difference' in genre studies; the importance of 'intertextual relay' in promoting generic readings of films and the idea of the 'hybrid' film.[1] They also raise questions about the economic, stylistic and ideological impact of competitive film-making. While detailed research of this nature remains to be done, I want to suggest how these questions are relevant for the study of

British cinema. To what extent can British film-making be described as a variation on the studio system with its own genres, or in stylistic terms as deviating from classical models? I will return to questions of genre/style later, but first will consider British studios.

A BRITISH STUDIO SYSTEM?

The term studio system refers to Hollywood film-making, particularly during the period 1914–60, when production, distribution and exhibition were dominated by an oligopoly of a few very powerful companies, the majors, which derived most of their power from owning cinemas so that production could be financed out of box-office profits. The major companies competed at the production level, but there was little or no competition regarding distribution or exhibition because they had carved up areas of geographic concentration, producing an overall system which thrived on innovation tempered by standardisation, a great degree of stylistic symmetry, mass production and consumption (see Bordwell, Staiger and Thompson, 1985; Gomery, 1986).

A studio system in the Hollywood sense meant a high degree of geographic and economic concentration which to some extent occurred in Britain. British studios were situated in and around London: a survey of British studios lists 86 which have existed, some for a very short time, throughout the twentieth century (Warren, 1995). Of these, 68 were located in and around London, and the 10 which are still operating – Beaconsfield (established in 1921), Bray (1949), Ealing (1902), Elstree (1925), Greenford (1985), Pinewood (1936), Rotherhithe (1975), Shepperton (1931), Southwark (1984) and Twickenham (1913) – are all in the south, which has implications for the technical labour force, actors and actresses and the generally southern bias of British film-making. But, also like Hollywood, this insularity has been offset to some extent by the contribution of many European technicians and directors, particularly in the 1930s and 1960s, who worked in British studios. In addition, some American companies owned, or acquired studio interests: Warner ran Teddington in the 1930s; Fox bought Wembley in 1936 and made films there until well into the 1950s; Amalgamated Studios at Elstree were purchased by MGM in 1948 and remained active until 1970, and Pinewood still functions as a centre for international production.

Most British film studios started out as locations for their owner's film productions and they were also rented or leased to other producers. Some were absorbed by the combines, Rank and ABPC, in the process of vertical integration.[2] The high degree of vertical integration in Hollywood caused problems for independent producers, particularly in the 1930s and 1940s. In Britain the situation was similarly difficult, but competition between producers was less fierce on account of a weak production base and the need to combat Hollywood. Since British producers did not dominate their home market, the production sector was fragmented as British companies came and went in the intermittent cycles of boom and slump.

The Rank Organisation was the closest Britain came to possessing a major, and in the 1940s and 1950s attempted to live up to that image by planning ambitious production programmes, publicising its actors and actresses as stars, and developing new technology: Pinewood remains the British film industry's major asset. But the operating basis for most British studios was different. Since Rank and APBC did not dominate production entirely, there was a small space for independent producers, a space that was encouraged by the NFFC and studios outside the duopoly's control. Rank also fostered several independent companies to assist its own production drive: the Archers, Cineguild, Wessex, Individual and Two Cities. From that point of view, the number of studios available to independents was varied, making for a less closed system than in Hollywood, where it was particularly difficult for independent companies to release their films except through the majors.

Apart from Pinewood and Elstree, several other studios had a good record of catering for independents. Twickenham, Shepperton and Beaconsfield in particular had no connection with the combines and offered good terms. After near collapse in the 1930s Twickenham's fortunes revived in the post-war period, particularly in the 1960s when its stages produced *Saturday Night and Sunday Morning* (Karel Reisz, 1960) and *A Hard Day's Night* (Richard Lester, 1964). Sound City, Shepperton, was developed as a studio in 1932 by Norman Loudon, a Scottish businessman (see Threadgall, 1994). It was purchased in 1946 by Alexander Korda and became the British Lion Studio company, a powerful third force in competition with Rank and ABPC. Herbert Wilcox made his popular Anna Neagle–Michael Wilding 'London series' films there at the end of the 1940s, and Carol Reed's NFFC-backed *The Third Man* (1949) was another triumph of independent production. Many of the British New Wave films were made at Shepperton, including *Room at the Top* (1959), *A Kind of Loving* (John Schlesinger, 1962) and *Billy Liar* (John Schlesinger, 1963). Beaconsfield was also linked with British Lion via Korda and was the studio where the NFFC subsidiary, Group 3, made their films.

Combine-owned or independent, studios which were run with both creative imagination *and* managerial efficiency were able to sustain popular generic cycles most effectively. Korda's historical films were made at Denham in the 1930s, Ealing comedies are synonymous with that studio under Michael Balcon's control in the 1940s, Hammer horrors were made at Bray Studios and James Bond action films at Pinewood. There is no doubt that successful and sustained genre production was partly the result of particular studio policies which were similar to Hollywood's central-producer system: Balcon's celebrated paternal control at Ealing; Ted Black,

Maurice Ostrer and R. J. Minney's economical production schedules at Gainsborough, and cost-efficient management strategies at Hammer.[3] But, as in Hollywood, companies which were identified with particular genres, for example Warner and musicals, often produced a much wider range of films, although Gainsborough (founded in 1924 by Michael Balcon), best known for its costume melodramas, throughout its history produced films across genres, operating mainly in two different studios, Islington and Shepherd's Bush. With a few important exceptions, one should not therefore assume a direct correlation between a studio and a particular genre.

It would appear that British studios operated in similar ways to American, but could hardly be described as a fully integrated and powerful system. The advantages to independent producers of a less rigid regime could be considerable but, in many cases, these were offset by the difficulties of raising film finance. Nevertheless, within this precarious structure a great variety of genres came, went, revived and transformed themselves throughout the century. From time to time there is talk of a revival of classic studio regimes, such as at Ealing or Hammer, but these aspirations always have to be considered in a context of the difficulties of distributing British films, as outlined in Chapter 1. The BBC bought Ealing in 1959 and they spent the next twenty years creating television productions such as *Colditz*, *The Singing Detective* and *Fortunes of War*. The Studios were acquired in mid-2000 by Uri Fruchtmann, Barnaby Thompson, Harry Handelsman and John Kao with the aim of reviving the studio's reputation as a producer of quality films. Even so, a studio system cannot be said to exist today since production is so fractured. While there are studios such as Pinewood that continue to attract a large number of productions, there is little sense of Pinewood as producing a consistent type of product, other than one that is identified with larger budgets and special effects, fuelled by financial incentives for inward investment.

BRITISH DIRECTORS

This somewhat haphazard system nevertheless produced some notable directors, producer-directors and creative teams, including Powell and Pressburger, the Boulting brothers and Launder and Gilliat.[4] British directors have been subject to critical re-evaluation in recent years, with studies of directors who have not received the attention devoted to the likes of Michael Powell or Alfred Hitchcock emerging from the shadows. These include Hammer's Terence Fischer, Joseph Losey, Roy Ward Baker, the Boulting brothers and so on (Shail, 2007). While it is possible to stake a claim for British *auteurs* with distinctive styles and thematic preoccupations which developed across films and genres, the main focus of this book is on generic production and on those who worked broadly within the 'art cinema' tradition. British directors have been influenced by a variety of factors throughout the century. A healthy production environment is important for creating market opportunities and spaces, facilitated by an astute producer in a context where creativity is fostered. As John Caughie has pointed out, the primacy of the producer and producer-director has been particularly significant in the British context:

> In a cinema which lacks stable systems of support, the producer has to create structures in which expression can happen, continually reinventing the wheel, and it may be those structures, rather than the individual artist, which give the cinema its shape.
>
> (Caughie in Vincendeau, 1995: 188)

In one sense, structures can be taken to mean the production companies run by Alexander Korda, Michael Balcon and J. Arthur Rank, which provided commercial environments for the creative work of film-makers like Carol Reed, Alexander Mackendrick and Powell and Pressburger. The term can also be applied to broader funding structures like the National Film Finance Corporation and its inheritor, British Screen, Channel 4 or the British Film Institute Production Board which supported, to a greater or lesser degree, directors including Joseph Losey, Derek Jarman, Stephen Frears and Bill Douglas. While funding bodies do not necessarily impose a house style, they allow directors to develop their work and at the same time teach them the often painful lessons of working within a framework which involves compromise and disappointment.

As far as artistic structures are concerned, it is clear that British directors were influenced by international styles ranging from Hollywood to German and Soviet cinema. The latter's tradition of montage was significant in the development of the Documentary style, while Hollywood contributed continuity principles and tightly organised narrative frameworks. The extent of these influences could in part be determined by the film's intended market, as Andrew Higson's comparative study of *Sing As We Go* (Basil Dean, 1934) and *Evergreen* (Victor Saville, 1934) has shown. While both films can be classed as musicals, *Sing As We Go* was primarily for the domestic market and depended on a fractured narrative structure and a series of spectacles organised around the regional appeal of Gracie Fields. On the other hand, *Evergreen* was aimed at the British and American markets and bears far more resemblance to a classical Hollywood backstage musical (see Higson, 1995: 98–175). *Evergreen* was directed by Victor Saville and produced by Gaumont-British, a major British combine in the 1930s which specialised in British films with international appeal. By contrast, *Sing As We Go* emanated from a smaller company, Associated Talking Pictures, run by Basil Dean who recognised the difficulties of distributing and marketing British films in America, instead favouring a future 'built entirely upon British lines' – by which he meant drawing on Britain's theatrical and music-hall heritage (ibid.: 116). The number of international personnel working in British cinema in the late 1920s and 1930s in particular also had a demonstrable impact in creating films that were designed for export and which in many ways defy narrow conceptions of British cinema as hermetically sealed from other influences in terms of style, content and personnel.

A director's background is also significant. Several dominant career patterns emerge which have had stylistic consequences. Many British directors have come from theatrical backgrounds, from Bryan Forbes to Kenneth Branagh. Films written and/or directed by Forbes utilised a subtle combination of social observation, literate dialogue and awareness of the needs of actors. Branagh's theatrical background is always in evidence in his films, consciously operating in the footsteps of Laurence Olivier and drawing on literary classics for source material. Training in television was the path to film directing for Michael Apted, Ken Loach, Stephen Frears and Mike Leigh, to name a few. Frears and Leigh in particular incorporate the dialogue-based intimacy of television drama in films like *Prick Up Your Ears* (1987) and *Life Is Sweet* (1990).

One prevailing factor for British directors has been perpetual insecurity, a consequence of the industry's weak financial base. As a result, a consistent transition has been made from Britain to Hollywood. Alfred Hitchcock was the first director of major stature to do this in 1940 when he embarked on his American career to direct *Rebecca* (1940). In terms of style, many critics agree that Hitchcock's British films of the 1920s and 1930s bear both thematic and stylistic resemblance to his work in Hollywood, indicating that a contrasting production environment played a small part in the director's overall artistic development which had been heavily influenced by European film-making. By contrast, the films of Ronald Neame, a director who worked in Britain and then intermittently in Hollywood from 1957 onwards, lacked generic or thematic continuity. Neame, a cameraman on Hitchcock's *Blackmail* (1929), collaborated (as cinematographer) with Noël Coward on *In Which We Serve* (1942) and with David Lean (co-scriptwriter and cinematographer) on *This Happy Breed* (1944). Neame's film career was promising, but uneven, and he worked in a variety of genres, ranging from comedy to disaster movies. In 1948 Neame produced *Oliver Twist* (David Lean, 1948) and *The Magic Box* (John Boulting, 1951), and directed a number of thrillers and quality-realist British films, including *Take My Life* (1947) and *The Card* (1952). Once in Hollywood, Neame's films were even more varied, ranging from *The Prime of Miss Jean Brodie* (an adaptation of Muriel Spark's novel about a Scottish schoolmistress, 1969) to *The Poseidon Adventure* (a disaster movie, 1972); in between he returned to Britain in 1970 to direct a musical, *Scrooge*. While this sort of career pattern might appear to be inconsistent, he was known for his professionalism and ability to work very well with actors (Shail, 2007: 154)

Two key British directors of the 1960s, John Schlesinger and Tony

Richardson, left to direct bigger budget films in Hollywood, as did a number of later British directors including Bill Forsyth, Ridley Scott, Alan Parker and Stephen Frears. Some have never come back, with one notable exception. Producer-director David Puttnam, perhaps most famous for producing *Chariots of Fire* (1981), was hired in 1986 to manage Columbia Pictures, a difficult job which lasted only 13 months before he returned to Britain in 1988, disillusioned with the lack of creative opportunities in Hollywood. Danny Boyle's US co-production, *The Beach* (2000) did not result in sustained collaboration with Hollywood. The increasing trends for international co-production mean that directors are less likely to seek a direct move to Hollywood, since many of their films can retain US links without a director having to re-locate on a permanent basis.

A final factor which is important when considering the director's role is the extent to which he or she will be influenced by social and political concerns. Films are not produced in a vacuum and the patterns of repetition and difference (see note 1) which are inherent in genre production are, to some extent, socially and ideologically determined. The relationship is, however, a complex one, and I would not argue for a rigid equation between film and society. Instead, the following survey of British genres will indicate the range and diversity of positions which competed for attention in each particular decade.

BRITISH GENRES: SILENT CINEMA

In the early years, a great number and variety of films were produced which capitalised on the novelty of film spectacle, the 'cinema of attractions' which introduced moving images designed to explore and suggest a thrilling and developing visual potential (see Gunning, 1990). Although many early films have not survived, catalogues give some indication of subject matter. An analysis of Denis Gifford's *British Film Catalogue* shows that throughout the pre-1914 period comedy films were by far the most prolific, followed by crime, trick, drama and chase (Gifford, 1986). Comedy, a staple British genre, soon dominated the scene, numbering as high as 402 films in 1914 out of a total output of 811 films (crime films came second at 143 followed by 75 dramas, 67 war films, 41 trick films, 23 romances, 16 adventure films, 10 fantasy films, 7 chase, 7 pathos, 6 animal, 6 sport, 4 history, 2 westerns, 1 filmed stage performance, 1 horror). According to Gifford's genre definitions, comic elements were also present in films he labels 'trick' and 'chase', so we can be sure that early films were primarily comedy based. As Sargeant's survey (2005: 16) of British cinema at the turn of the century and into the first years of the twentieth century has demonstrated, many early films 'drew their material from older narrative and pictorial subjects which audiences could readily recognise', including the presentation of stock figures for comedic effect, as well as physical comedy. Some of the earliest films were single-shots or reels, featuring natural scenes of breaking waves or various 'rough seas', as well as travelogues of informational interest.

Silent film is an effective form for physical and mime-oriented comedy and many variety acts were filmed, presumably because of the added spectacle of reproducing celebrity, but also because comic situations were suited to short, often disconnected scenes until narratives became longer and more firmly based on continuity principles. Many films containing comic elements showed people as indestructible, using effects like superimposition and stop-motion. In *Extraordinary Cab Accident* (Walter R. Booth, 1903) a man is knocked over by a horse and cab, a policeman pursues the runaway cab and apprehends the driver. On their return they are amazed to see the injured man resurrect himself and run away in triumph with his companion. *The ? Motorist* (Walter R. Booth, 1906) shows a car run over a policeman, who gets up immediately and tries to chase the car as it embarks on a Méliès-style fantastic journey over rooftops and into the sky.[5] Other popular themes for early films were Fire Brigade rescue narratives and policeman chasing various burglars.

These films explored mortality, film space and the spectacle of special effects. A particularly interesting example of this approach is *Mary Jane's Mishap, or Don't Fool With Paraffin* (G. A. Smith, 1903), the story of a housemaid (played by Mrs Smith, an ex-variety artiste) who is blown up while trying to light a kitchen stove with paraffin. The witty and amusing film is a series of linked gags: Mary Jane's comic, irreverent personality is indicated at the beginning when we see her polish a pair of boots and inadvertently wipe her nose with the brush, which gives her a comic moustache. She admires herself in the mirror and then tries to light the stove with bellows. The film uses close shots at key points, for example, when we see Mary Jane slosh paraffin over the stove, winking at the camera with glee before she strikes a match and disappears into the stove as it explodes. A roof-top shot shows her shooting from the chimney in a cloud of smoke, layers of clothing falling from the sky once she has disappeared from the frame, suggesting off-screen space. Ten years before their more common usage, Smith used vertical wipes in the next scene where Mary Jane's gravestone (inscribed 'Here lies Mary Jane who lighted the fire with paraffin. Rest in pieces') serves as a warning to other housemaids who have been brought to visit the grave by their mistress. They are amazed when Mary Jane's ghost emerges triumphant, conjures up a paraffin container and disappears back into the grave.

Films like *Mary Jane's Mishap* imply an awareness of the audience (her cheeky looks at the camera; the performative nature of her various comic acts) which is a key element of the cinema of attractions. *The Countryman and the Cinematograph* (R. W. Paul, 1901) shows a countryman on the left-hand side of the frame as he watches three projected scenes: a dancer, a train and a courting couple. The film is an early demonstration of the spectator's range of responses to cinematic images: he dances along with the dancer (empathy); laughs and then runs away from the oncoming train (excitement and fear/suspense); he points in recognition at the couple (identification: the man looks exactly like the countryman).

The equation of cinema with novelty and even danger is also illustrated by the trick film *How It Feels To Be Run Over* (Cecil Hepworth, 1900) when we see a horse and carriage move towards the camera on the right-hand side of the frame and then disappear out of sight in the same direction, implying a logical sense of movement into off-screen space. By contrast, we then see a motor car head directly at the camera until it fills the frame entirely, cut to black illustrated by stars, flashes and exclamation marks and the title: 'Oh, mother *will* be pleased!'. The spectator is presented with two completely different experiences: the familiar and the unfamiliar, the latter representing something of the first film spectators' conflicting sensations of fascination, fear, excitement and compulsion.

Two films made in 1905 illustrate the range of styles and representations in early British chase films. The genre was very popular at this time and was partly responsible for making films longer. *Rescued By Rover* (Lewin Fitzhamon, Cecil Hepworth, 1905) is famous for its demonstration of fluid continuity principles: a child is stolen by a gypsy and the family dog leads the distraught father to her hiding place where he successfully completes the rescue operation. Shots of the dog running down a road, first on its own and then followed by the anxious father, are matched for continuity, as is the scene when Rover leads the father across a river. In terms of representation, *Rescued By Rover* is a Victorian moral tale of a well-to-do family (indicated by their dress and the fact that they have a maid) whose world is shattered when their baby is stolen by a poor gypsy woman (who is dressed in ragged clothes, and shown swigging drink in her attic and stealing the baby's clothes). The narrative pattern of equilibrium–disruption–restoration of equilibrium is framed decisively at the beginning and end of the film with its emblematic shots of the united family. The audience is not encouraged to sympathise with the gypsy, who is characterised as mercenary, threatening and dirty. Hepworth's celebrated use of the arc light for her attic is an early use of harsh lighting contrasts to indicate a dangerous subcultural world.

On the other hand, *The Life of Charles Peace* (William Haggar, 1905) presents the viewer with a far more contradictory representation of authority/ the status quo. It is based on the celebrated tale of Charles Peace who was executed in 1879 after committing robbery and murder. The story is depicted in a series of tableaux – a common theatrically based form of early film narration – in chronological order telling the story of the criminal's abilities at outwitting the police; his eventual capture; his sensational leap from a train (and instant recovery!); his capture and eventual execution. Unlike *Rover*, intertitles break up the scenes and the audience is encouraged to admire Charles Peace's daring bravado and ability to outwit the bumbling police on several occasions. Even though the film ends with Peace's execution, it is perhaps an early example of the tacked-on ending which fails to match the excitement and humour of watching the criminal get away with so much, including poking fun at authority figures. After the 'Burglary at Black Heath' when Peace gets away with the loot, the incident 'Peace, the parson and the police' shows Peace masquerade as a parson, redirect the police on a false trail and cock a snook at them once they have run on. Haggar and the Sheffield Photo Company both made versions of the story but the Sheffield Photo Company did not show the execution because it was considered to be 'too ghastly and repulsive' (Sheffield Photo Company catalogue, 1906 quoted in Low and Manvell, 1948: 107).

The increasing length of films and shift away from the cinema of attractions towards more narrative-based material had implications for British genres. While some films made before 1913 were based on literature, after that date the trend became more pronounced and, as Sargeant has pointed out (2005: 29), British literary source material was also increasingly utilised by American cinema in this period. Indeed, during the years 1911–18 many films were adaptations of Shakespeare, Victorian novels and stage melodramas. The problems of adapting long classics for the silent screen cannot be underestimated and some critics argue that the challenge prevented concentration on pure cinema, which might, perhaps, have been a more logical development following the cinema of attractions. But the source material contained many familiar characters and references, which perhaps facilitated the daunting task of adapting long plays and novels for the screen. The drive towards narrative and increasing length was encouraged by foreign examples, but an important factor was the new medium's imperative to forge greater links with the stage, its reputation and place in popular cultural experience and its convenient supply of acting talent. Adaptation continued well into the 1920s, and has been a dominant characteristic of British cinema ever since (see McFarlane, 1986). It should also be acknowledged that adaptation in itself was not necessarily a barrier to creativity with the film medium, encouraging as it did some ingenious devices of narrative compression, hastening developments in intertitling, influencing set design and representing a complex, intermedial contract with audiences who may have been familiar with the source texts upon which the films were based.

Will Barker, who built the first Ealing studio in 1910, headed the first spate of ambitious adaptations with his film *Henry VIII* (1911). Before 1910 most British films lasted less than ten minutes, but *Henry VIII* ran for over half an hour. His film version of *East Lynne* (1913) was an important early melodrama, an adaptation of Mrs Henry Wood's popular novel which was staged and filmed many times (see Kaplan, 1992: 76–106). Barker's films were famous for their focus on London life and featured good location work, for example *London By Night* (Alexander Butler, 1913), which portrayed the city as full of danger, fallen women and temptation for a young man who has come down from Oxford to study law. Cecil Hepworth was another important producer in the pre-First World War years who adapted, with the valuable input of character actor Thomas Bentley, three of Dickens' novels between 1912 and 1914, the longest being *David Copperfield* (Thomas Bentley, 1913) which was 7,500 feet, over double the normal length for the period. As Sargeant has detailed (2005: 41–48) serials and series were also popular just before the First World War, some of which drew on music-hall performance styles or presented adaptations of literature in several parts.

The First World War saw some more key developments in film drama relating to structure and content. The trend for literary adaptation continued, utilising bestselling novels which focused on middle-class subjects by Charles Garvice, Robert Hitchens, A. M. Hutchinson, Lucas Malet and Allen Raine, as well as the works of writers including Thomas Hardy, Arthur Conan Doyle, Charles Dickens, Alexandre Dumas, Sir T. H. Hall Caine and Henry Fielding. From about 1915, melodramas began to display greater emotional complexity: Hepworth's *The Confession* (Frank Wilson, 1915) for example, is more accurately described as a psychological drama than a melodrama. As Rachael Low has observed, such films moved 'towards an integrated plot whose situations, often fewer and less sensational, derive from each other through the characters' (Low, 1950: 202). Other popular genres were spy/espionage films; crime melodramas, including George Pearson's popular adventurer 'Ultus, the Man from the Dead'; sporting films mostly adapted from novels about boxing and horse-racing, and war dramas which were particularly popular during the first years of the war. In terms of thematics, there were several recurrent topics which have been neatly summarised by Rachael Low:

> Inheritance and fallen women; the underworld of London with its night clubs and gambling halls; the superiority of honest poverty, with class acting as a one-way barrier to marriage; the regenerating effects of war, the worthlessness of shirkers, and the savage and drunken stupidity of the 'Hun', and death-defying feats by which people won their spurs.
>
> (Low, 1950: 201)

From this list it can be seen that film drama drew heavily on the obsessions of late Victorian dominant ideology: virtue, thrift, temperance, class society, nationalism, xenophobia, heroism. Many of these attitudes were also evident in British comedy.

During the years 1906–18, film comedy was still a dominant genre which underwent some slow but important changes. Instead of deriving from a single comic incident and its repetition (people slipping on banana skins or getting glued to chairs which had been 'treated' by naughty schoolboys), comedy gradually became more subtle, integrated with a narrative structure that was integral to the success of the humour. Although the most popular comedies tended to be American there was some development in the British arena of romance-comedy, and the music-hall artiste 'Pimple' introduced parody with his famous skits on serious films from 1913. It was far more common for the focus of the comedy to be lower-middle-class life than upper-class antics and there was a reactionary bias in many films, the joke frequently being on people who were obese, ugly, spinsters, suffragettes or hen-pecked husbands (see Low, 1949: 168–83). Some popular music-hall artistes adapted their sketches for the screen, most notably Billy Merson, George Robey and Lupino Lane. The stage also supplied personalities like Charles Hawtrey who were already familiar to audiences, although very few came close to competing with Charlie Chaplin who dominated the international scene.

Comedy continued to be an important popular genre in the 1920s and became more sophisticated in terms of narrative construction, characterisation and representation of class relations. George Pearson produced and directed some of the most successful with his 'Squibs' series of four films about a Cockney flower-girl played by Betty Balfour. The second, *Squibs Wins the Calcutta Sweep* (1922), shows the impact of Squibs' win in a sweepstake on every facet of her life: her relationship with her father, her policeman boyfriend, his parents, her position in the local community and her ability to help her sister who has fled to Paris with her husband who is on the run from the police for murder. Pearson intercuts the sister's story as a parallel narrative which adds pathos and suspense to the comic story of Squibs' win. In this instance, a mix of genres works very well as many of the comic scenes are followed by short scenes of Squibs' sister in despair in Paris. The film is mostly studio-based but there are some interesting location shots of Piccadilly Circus and Paris. When news spreads of Squibs' win there is a high-angle shot of Piccadilly Circus which was taken by a cameraman from the top of a restaurant. Pearson wanted the crowd scenes to appear unstaged: low-angle shots of London streets were taken by a cameraman who was hidden from view in a van (Pearson, 1957: 106).

Much of the film is preoccupied with how far Squibs might be changed by her wealth, a question which haunts her boyfriend and his parents (who had previously thought she was not suitable for their son because she was a flower-girl!). In a sequence where Squibs visits her potential in-laws, she arrives in a car all dressed up and pretends to have developed upper-class airs and graces. They are shocked and hurt and Squibs has to change into her flower-girl clothes to reassure them that it was just an act, an incident which nevertheless highlights the film's focus on working-class life and social commentary.

As well as Pearson's film there were other important examples of popular British films which alluded to social issues including *The Rat* (1925), starring Ivor Novello, and Maurice Elvey's adaptation of *Hindle Wakes* (1927).

Plate 2.1 Squibs (Betty Balfour) and her father (Hugh E. Wright) dressed in upper-class attire after Squibs' win on the sweepstake in *Squibs Wins the Calcutta Sweep* (1922).

Indeed, the 1920s has been reclaimed by recent scholarship as a crucial period for British cinema, during which key developments occurred and significant films were produced (Gledhill, 2003 and Sargeant, 2005: 83–110). While British films of this period are often seen as lacking the highly developed continuity principles of Hollywood, or stylistic experiments evident in the rest of Europe, some of the trends evident in British films, most notably pictorialism and the vitality of European co-productions, render this conclusion problematic. *The Life Story of David Lloyd George* (Maurice Elvey, 1918) was produced by Ideal Films and was the longest and in many ways a remarkable film from this period. It was the first film to be based on the life of a living Prime Minister who had agreed to its production and was heralded in the trade press as the most ambitious British film to date. Completed in the last months of the First World War, *The Life Story of David Lloyd George* was suddenly and mysteriously withdrawn before its first trade screening; solicitors, presumably acting for the government or for the Liberal party, paid £20,000 to remove the film from the offices of Ideal, the film's production company. It was long thought that both copies had been lost or destroyed, and then in 1994 the complete negative was found amongst material supplied by Viscount Tenby (Lloyd George's grandson) for examination by the Wales Film and Television Archive (Berry and Horrocks, 1998). This strange tale and the discovery of the film so many years later attracted attention to British cinema of this period, encouraging many to re-evaluate its legacy and resist the grand narrative of Hollywood's dominance of world markets in economic and aesthetic terms. While it is the case that Hollywood norms were fast gaining ground, Europe was nevertheless a key centre of film-making activity to which British cinema was certainly making a notable contribution.

Examples of key films from the 1920s include the experimental films referred to in Chapter 6 as well as Hitchcock's silent British films, discussed in detail by Barr (1999). The first two were shot in Germany, *The Pleasure Garden* (1925) and *The Mountain Eagle* (1926). Germanic influences can also be detected in *The Lodger* (1926) and *Blackmail* (1929), the latter famously demonstrated Hitchcock's desire to experiment with the new technology of sound film. The pictorial strategies developed by Hepworth continued into the mid-1920s with *Comin' Thro' the Rye* (1923), a film which demonstrates an alternative formal approach to that which was developing in Hollywood and which later fell out of favour with critics. Maurice Elvey's style of 'pictorial narration', for example, demonstrates how pictorial film-making could also serve the demands of complex narrative development producing, as in *Mademoiselle d'Armentières* (1926), 'collaged' images to progress narrative that can be compared to 'flicker book' techniques. During this period British cinema needs to be understood as part of a larger culture of 'realisation, recycling, adaptation, deploying existing artefacts and cultural practices as material for new configurations' (Gledhill, 2003: 181). Far from appearing as a backward example of cinema that failed to keep pace with developments elsewhere, British cinema of the 1920s was extremely rich and varied.

GENRE AND 'THE TALKIES'

The 1930s was a decade when many genres underwent a process of develop-ment and consolidation, encouraged by the arrival of sound. The industry's growing concentration and the impact of quota legislation provided a more stable economic backdrop for the increasing visibility of popular British genres. In terms of Britishness, sound films were immediate signifiers of national identity through speech and recurring representations which reflected many of the decade's ideological concerns. Dominant genres were historical/costume; empire; comedy; musicals (musical comedies); melo-dramas. While many of these are part of longer generic trajectories, their deployment nevertheless reveals national and social concerns which are particular to the 1930s. Generally summarised, the most striking of these were the broadening of the middle class and its values; the decline of empire; the extension of the franchise and consensus politics; adjustments after the First World War relating to gender and the workforce; the decline of staple industries, the rise of new ones, unemployment and geographical relocation (see Stevenson, 1990).

A key feature of the 1930s was the gradual ascendancy of the middle class and its values. The landed aristocracy and traditional elites, however, still were powerful and 'on the eve of the Second World War there had been only a minor redistribution of wealth' (Stevenson, 1990: 464). Many films touched on questions of class but few offered a more complex analysis than the all-embracing ethos of consensus, an ethos which concealed the cracks – cracks which on closer analysis were not, as we shall see, entirely absent from many films.[6] By looking at dominant genres it is possible to judge how far a wide range of British films participated in the hegemonic process and the spread of middle-class values. As such, the films comment on social forces and suggest how dominant representations can nevertheless reveal a certain fragility, and be expressive of fears and expectations at the same time as presenting impressions of an apparently non-negotiable 'now'. It is also important to note that audiences only watched British films for some of the time; throughout the decade and as noted in Chapter 1, Hollywood films dominated the market. The all-pervasive habit of cinema-going, became the dominant leisure activity which, as oral history studies have demonstrated, was a key component of the fabric of social life (Kuhn, 2002).

Sue Harper and Marcia Landy have analysed the 1930s historical/ costume film in detail, both adopting broad definitions of historical to include biopics of famous monarchs and fictional stories with historical settings/ period costumes (Landy, 1991; Harper, 1994). The films are important as examples of generic repetition and difference but they are also useful sources of cultural, social and ideological history. Landy argues that the films 'generate a knowledge of the past that is intimately tied to the ideology of the given moment in which they are produced, an ideology that is an amalgam of meanings related to issues of power, community, and continuity' (Landy, 1991: 54). A study of the wide range of films produced in the 1930s illustrates how at any given moment a variety of discourses co-exist, each being representative of particular contemporary fears and anxieties which can be seen to operate on textual and subtextual levels. At the same time, generic analyses acknowledge the crucial importance of reception, the connection between a film's popularity and its ideological significance. A film's discourses will compete for the viewer's attention, often producing a 'preferred' reading which stifles a 'resistant' one which can be derived from notions of 'textual excess'.[7]

The major producers of the 1930s – Alexander Korda, Michael Balcon and Herbert Wilcox – produced historical films which addressed questions of class and gender from different stylistic and ideological perspectives.

Films which drew on episodes in the British past often articulated contemporary concerns. Korda's films were preoccupied with the desirability of 'proletarian–aristocratic alliances' by deploying 'the resonances of the aristocratic ethic while at the same time celebrating popular taste' (Harper, 1994: 38). This allowed audiences of *The Private Life of Henry VIII* (1933) to sympathise with the king via keyhole access to his private boudoir world. *Henry VIII* encourages a class levelling process whereby the monarch is shown to have similar passions and desires as everybody else, particularly his vulnerability to female control of the domestic sphere. Korda articulates this ideological standpoint on class and gender in several important ways: his casting of Charles Laughton as Henry who is played with childlike sympathy and humour, the major focus being on his overeating; Henry being cajoled into successive marriages by his advisers, seemingly not responsible for his wives' executions; his comic exchanges with Anne of Cleves (Elsa Lanchester, Laughton's wife), particularly their card-game pact to get a quick divorce; Henry's hen-pecked old age with Catherine Parr; the inclusion of proletarian servants who gossip about Henry's love-life as if they were his friends; splendid costumes and set pieces of royal pageantry. Henry's statist and religious machinations are entirely absent, as is the violence of the Tudor period. This film was successfully exhibited in the US, demonstrating a cross-cultural address which can be seen to not only relate to British history but also to the contemporary context of the New Deal in the USA. Unusually for a British film, it gained a following in the US outside of the metropolitan centres where foreign films were usually screened (Street, 2002: 51).

Korda's other significant and successful historical film in the 1930s was *The Scarlet Pimpernel* (Harold Young, 1935) (he produced several but these two did best at the box office), in which Leslie Howard plays Sir Percy Blakeney who rescues French aristocrats from revolutionaries. Sue Harper gives three major reasons for the film's popularity: the Regency theme which is sympathetic towards the aristocracy; the popularity of the source novel; and Leslie Howard's role which appealed to female audiences for its combination of 'feminine sensitivity with masculine vigour' (ibid.: 27). Once again, there appears to be an aristocratic–proletarian trajectory at work in Korda's films in which the aristocracy 'functions not solely as itself but as a symbol of repressed desires or inexpressible social fears' (ibid.: 26) with which the audience, particularly female and working class, could identify. As the sections of the population with the least economic, social and political power, women and the working class recognised their unfulfilled desires in historical films which often privileged female sensibilities and suggested that the working class enjoyed a special bond with the upper social echelons.

Unlike Korda's attractive aristocrats, exoticism and appeal to female audiences, Michael Balcon's historical films produced at Gaumont-British extolled middle-class values, aimed for realistic depictions of the past and were addressed mainly to male audiences. *Tudor Rose* (Robert Stevenson, 1936), the story of Lady Jane Grey's claim to the throne after the death of Henry VIII, is a very different portrayal of Tudor England than that of *Henry VIII*. Duty, realism and restraint replace excess, historical inaccuracy and flamboyance. Aristocratic (as opposed to royal) ambition is condemned in an unflattering portrait of the Earl of Warwick's ruthless pursuit of power and exploitation of Jane who, by contrast, demonstrates the virtues of duty, tolerance and, ultimately, sacrifice, as she is executed as a warning against the violation of royal wishes. From this standpoint, *Tudor Rose* expresses Balcon's fears about threats to middle-class values in the 1930s (ibid.: 30).

The third major producer of historical films was Herbert Wilcox, whose *Victoria the Great* (1937) and *Sixty Glorious Years* (1938) represent a reverent depiction of monarchy, a celebration of consensus politics and a nationalistic notion of Britishness which is articulated by reference to Victorianism and the Empire. *Victoria the Great* was a box-office success, which can be partly explained by its appearance just after the Abdication Crisis when confidence in the monarchy needed to be restored.[8] Anna Neagle's depiction of Queen Victoria is completely different from Laughton's humanising approach in *Henry VIII*. She is invested with a sort of regal presence and distance from the audience which encourages worship and deference, not familiarity and laughter. The films can be read differently from Balcon's historical films: although values of hard work and restraint are presented as worthy, they are submerged in the overall call to patriotism and collective consciousness about being British. Individualism only has its place in service to the nation, an idea about Britain as a collective community which was to receive its fullest articulation in World War Two. The last reel of *Victoria the Great* was shot in Technicolor, a colour process that had only recently been introduced to Britain. Its use further demonstrated Wilcox's reverence for his subject since its placement in the narrative was to highlight Victoria's assumption of the title of Empress of India. Colour was used frequently for films with empire themes to emphasise the exoticism of imperial fictions and locations.

Similar in ideological bias is the genre of empire films which were at their most popular in the 1930s, a decade when the empire was, in fact, on the eve of post-colonialism. Marcia Landy has usefully compared empire films to American westerns in their stories of conquest ('civilisation vs wilderness'), nationalism and frontier spirit: 'the empire film translated expansionism, colonisation, and commerce into a spectacle of benevolence of high-minded heroes acting in the name of royal prerogatives, culture against anarchy, and the white man's burden' (Landy, 1991: 97). In general terms, the films focused on the male experience of empire, usually from an upper-class imperialist perspective. The 'white man's burden' was to maintain order and inculcate native obedience in the colonies. As well as articulating this ideological imperative, the empire genre colonised British and American

Plate 2.2 The regal Neagle. Anna Neagle as Queen Victoria in *Victoria the Great* (1937). (Courtesy of Lumière Pictures Limited)

audiences by exploiting elements of spectacular epic cinema: lavish colour, exotic landscapes, large casts, horses, regalia, military trappings, native dances and costumes. Most were produced by Alexander Korda and directed by his brother, Zoltan (particularly *Elephant Boy*, 1937, *The Drum*, 1938 and *The Four Feathers*, 1939), although Michael Balcon produced two notable empire films, *Rhodes of Africa* (B. Viertel, G. Blake, 1936) and *King Solomon's Mines* (R. Stevenson, 1937).

Although the films glorify the imperial mission, the contradictions of imperialism (which were beginning to surface in the 1930s) can be detected in some empire films at a subtextual level. *The Drum* is an interesting case in point where the drum motif, speech and sound in general, are important signifiers of imperial conflict. The story is of Azim, a young pro-British Indian prince (played by Sabu), whose father is murdered by his uncle, Prince Ghul (played by Canadian Raymond Massey!). Ghul then replaces Azim's father as ruler of an independent north-western frontier state. Azim's father had agreed that the state should be protected from invasion by a treaty with the British, a treaty which Ghul pretends to welcome. Azim escapes from his uncle to Pershawa where he befriends the British Governor, his daughter and son-in-law, Captain Carruthers, already acquainted with Azim when his father was ruler. Carruthers is the officer charged with the responsibility of negotiating with Ghul and he accompanies his Scottish regiment to set up residency in the state capital, Tokot. At the same time, Ghul encourages Moslem support against British rule and, in defiance of the Raj, plans to massacre the British troops at a feast. Azim's unquestioning admiration for the British is symbolised by a pact he makes with a young British drummer-boy, Bill Holder, to warn each other of danger by beating a special drum signal which Bill has taught Azim. Azim learns of Ghul's plans in Tokot and alerts Carruthers by using the drum signal. In the following battle Ghul is killed and Azim is proclaimed the new pro-British ruler. Order is re-established and the threat of Ghul and his anti-British attitudes (at one point he comments: 'The empire is ready to be carved to pieces') banished, albeit temporarily because of the film's underlying suggestion of the Raj's instability.

The film begins with a shot of a rotating globe which is stopped to focus on India and the north-west frontier in particular. Some spectacular panning shots of mountainous scenery are followed by a cut to a signpost indicating 'tribal territory' and we hear the thud of tribal drums. The drum-beat then changes to military beats and we see soldiers ascending a mountain path, followed by the sharp sounds of machine-gun fire, a British soldier commenting with surprise that the Indians have such weapons. Ghul's men later use machine-guns against the British at the Tokot massacre. The sounds are being used to signify the conflicting narrative themes which are to follow: native culture vs. British identity; Indian use of western military technology vs. British policing the Raj. The climax of the film is the feast, when the audience knows of Ghul's plans to massacre the British. A long display of Indian dancing is followed by the Scottish regiment's attempt to show 'these people something that'll astonish them': highland sword-dancing accompanied by bagpipes, a jingoistic response to what they clearly find strange. We then hear the drum-beats of Azim's danger signal, the massacre begins and Carruthers' wife, who has previously been depicted as representing a placid corner of England and English womanhood in India, comments 'I never want to hear another drum again'. For most of the film Mrs Carruthers is a plucky Englishwoman until her final intolerant outburst reveals her alienation.

The Drum is riddled with more contradictory themes, sounds and images which emphasise the sense of imperial insecurity which pervaded the 1930s. The British are established as protectors against warring native factions, with Carruthers as the benign English gentleman who teaches Azim clemency when they first meet. Representations such as this suggest the myth that imperialism involved 'good colonisers' with a 'mission' to introduce western notions of 'civilisation' to barbaric territories. Consequently, Carruthers rides into Tokot to negotiate with Azim's father and, as a reprise of the film's opening, is greeted by the sound of native drums which are sharply interrupted by gunshot. It turns out that the shots were instigated by Azim as a test to see 'if the English are easily frightened'. Azim plans to shoot the guilty marksmen while Carruthers recommends whipping as a more suitable punishment, the gentlemanly, more humane alternative to Azim's barbaric tendencies. Carruthers' wife, as the stoical imperial handmaiden, supports this delineation of Britishness. Set against this representation of the British in India is the jingoism of the soldiers and the tension at the feast. The bagpipes are used many times in the film to signify a strident nationalism which qualifies the image of peaceful native and British co-existence. Interestingly, the Scottish regiment is depicted as working class, in opposition to figures like upper-class Captain Carruthers whose view, it is suggested, of the empire is more civilised: conquest with decorum, not violence.

Despite an overtly harmonious representation, the relationship between Azim and Bill the drummer-boy is leaden with class and racial overtones. When Azim asks Bill if he can try on his uniform Bill is hesitant, speaking of 'regulations' and how Azim is a 'toff'. When Ghul has usurped Azim's claim to succeed his father, Azim asks Bill if he can become a drummer in the British army. Bill looks startled at the request, declaring it a 'non-starter' because Azim is not a competent drummer and is a prince. On the contrary, we have already seen him learn the drum signal with no trouble, leading to the unspoken conclusion that the idea of Azim joining the British ranks is unthinkable on racial grounds, although it is possible to argue that this exchange is about class barriers with Bill insisting that 'a toff cannot be a mere drummer'. So, on the one hand we are presented with a picture of tolerance and benign British interest in India, while on the other unspoken prejudices and racial tensions are clearly evident. *The Drum* is therefore an excellent example of how a popular genre film raises questions about the empire, external trappings of Britishness, race and class in the 1930s. These issues are also pertinent in the context of the Depression which affected

Plate 2.3 Bill teaches Azim the danger signal. Imperial co-operation in
The Drum (1938).

Britain in the 1930s, as well as the rise of fascism in Italy and Germany –
countries which appeared to be dealing with the Depression comparatively
well at the same time as expanding into other territories. The British empire
therefore appeared to be under threat from its own internal problems and
also from fascist countries intent on securing their own empires.

Comedy was the most popular and prolific genre in the 1930s. Its success
depended on the long-standing tradition in film comedy of featuring music-
hall/variety performers and well-known West End stage personalities. The
arrival of sound encouraged exploitation of the comic opportunities
presented by verbal repartee, singing and regional accents, as an addition to
the slapstick and situational nature of silent comedy. The most important
star performers were Gracie Fields, Jessie Matthews, Jack Hulbert, Will Hay
and George Formby. According to Raymond Durgnat, Fields and Formby
shared an essential 'dignified cheerfulness' (Durgnat, 1970: 172). George
Formby's star persona was inextricably tied up with his Lancashire accent
and singing voice, accompanied by his banjolele and conscious use of music-
hall tradition. Although frequently imbued with the ideology of inter-war

consensus, the comedies nevertheless often featured working-class characters and issues. This was somewhat ironic because the ideology of consensus played down their particular needs, social, economic and political disadvantages in favour of dominant representations which suggested class unity.

The image of Gracie Fields will be discussed in Chapter 6 which deals with stardom, but it is important to note here that the generic mix of musical-comedy allowed her to inflect her star persona with a utopian sensibility which spoke to working-class audiences of community, solidarity and longing. As well as her singing voice, Fields' northern accent was her most distinctive characteristic, representing a region *and* a class on screen. As Andrew Higson has noted, *Sing As We Go* (Basil Dean, 1934) 'is one of many British films of the period which work self-consciously with cultural traditions, reference-points, and performers which are nationally specific, and in many cases regionally specific' (Higson, 1995: 163). Fields' performance relies primarily on spectacle, a stylistic mode which bears resemblance to the cinema of attractions, displaying tensions between 'narration and description, narrative and spectacle, movement and stasis, voyeurism and exhibitionism' (ibid.: 143).

Another comic personality, Will Hay, typically played a crafty, roguish public-schoolmaster with his mortar board and gold-rimmed glasses askew, in films like *Boys Will Be Boys* (William Beaudine, 1935) and *Good Morning, Boys* (Marcel Varnel, 1937). These films contain potentially anarchic elements in that their 'presentation of community is not idyllic, not a portrait of consensus, but rather a darker picture of a divided society held together by the efforts, often inept, of a few individuals who uncover the disrupting forces' (Landy, 1991: 351). The targeting of British institutions (schools, prisons) as a source of humour and social commentary prefigured the comic style of *St Trinians* and elements of the *Carry On* series.

A popular stage revue star who appeared in musical-comedy films in the 1930s was Jessie Matthews, who also had a considerable following in America. Jessie Matthews' musical-comedies were concerned with issues of gender and sexuality to an extent unusual for British films of the 1930s. They are particularly interesting in terms of the decade's shifting models of masculinity and femininity (see Light, 1991b: 8). The experience of the first total war had profound implications for ideas about conquest, the nature of the home front and male identity in general. At a political level, the extension of the franchise to women in 1918 and 1928 represented a gain, the cumulative result of pressure which had been escalating in the Edwardian period and as a reward for services rendered in the First World War.[9] Women's employment increased, although it was usually unskilled and low paid, and women's lives were becoming more modern in the sense that they participated in the inter-war expansion of leisure. While some of these changes offered ways forward for women, it can be argued that the hegemonic process, which involved the dominance of patriarchal values, operated in such a way as to erode any radical potential or greater political, social and economic equality.

First a Girl (Victor Saville, 1935) is a particularly interesting film regarding the above developments.[10] Matthews' films were designed to appeal to the international market, a strategy which was successful to a degree (see analysis of *Evergreen*, 1934, in Higson, 1995: 131–42 and Street, 2002: 78–83). They were slickly produced, containing Busby Berkeley-style numbers, lavish Art Deco settings, stylish costumes and exotic locations, particularly *First a Girl*, which features the Riviera. In this film Matthews plays Elizabeth, a girl who works for a fashion house but longs to be a show-girl. Her chance comes in an unexpected way when she meets Victor, an aspiring Shakespearian actor who earns his bread and butter by performing a drag act. When Elizabeth is sheltering from a rainstorm in Victor's room he discovers that he has lost his voice and will not be able to perform his drag act that evening. He persuades her to stand in for him by impersonating a young man, singing and dancing on stage as a woman, and pulling off

Plate 2.4 Man to man but 'First a Girl'. Griffith Jones and Jessie Matthews in *First a Girl* (1935). (Courtesy of Rank Film Distributors)

a blonde wig at the end to reveal short-cropped dark hair to the audience as evidence of male gender. The act ends up more slapstick than planned but is nevertheless a great success, so much so that Victor and Elizabeth (as 'Victor') are hired to perform a high-class version of the act all over Europe. They are very popular and Elizabeth's masquerade is not discovered. Comic tension is, however, created when they link up with a couple, Robert (played by Griffith Jones) and a glamorous princess, who gradually begins to suspect that 'Victor' is female.

The sexual innuendo and skits on gender abound when Robert mistakes 'Victor' for a homosexual but decides to put his prejudice aside when 'Victor' out-drinks and out-smokes him, leaving the audience unsure as to whether he prefers 'real men' (but would not admit to homosexual tendencies), or whether evidence of manly activities discounts the assumption that as a female impersonator 'Victor' must be gay. When Robert discovers the truth, Elizabeth entertains the idea that he preferred her as a man, providing further grounds for speculation about his sexuality. There is a similar playfulness around Victor's sexuality. His declaration of love for the princess is never followed through, and his final performance of his original drag act is such a success that he is hired to perform it again, admitting that he would rather do that than *Hamlet*, his original theatrical aspiration. There is an interesting moment during Victor's authentic drag performance when the police, having been tipped off that 'Victor' is female, try to arrest him, a moment which brings to mind the criminalisation of homosexuality. Similar to representations in other female-to-male cross-dressing films, when Elizabeth is in drag she never loses her female identity to us, the audience, and there is no attempt to imply that she prefers dressing as a man. Once it has been discovered that Elizabeth has been masquerading as a man, to be replaced by the real Victor, we assume that she will not return to her cross-dressing activities as a career, instead ending up with Robert, confirming her gender as 'always a girl' with all the concomitant insecurities of employment. Nevertheless, the film's exuberance, spectacle and innuendo play a part in treating gender and sexuality as problematic discourses during a decade when what it meant to be masculine or feminine was being re-evaluated. As observed by Bergfelder (1997: 42), there is a resemblance between the brand of modern femininity represented by Matthews in *First a Girl* and that of female stars in German cinema in the early 1930s. As such it can be seen as representative of the internationalism of British cinema in the 1930s, not only in its aspirations as a film that would export well to America, but also for its affinities to European cinema. This increasingly internationalist trend was already evident in the late 1920s when, for example, German director E. A. Dupont, came to Britain to direct *Moulin Rouge* (1928) and *Piccadilly* (1929), two prestigious productions, the latter starring Anna May Wong, the Chinese-American actress who also starred in Hollywood silent films. The greater internationalism of British cinema in this period and further discussion of Jessie Matthews is covered extensively in Bergfelder, Harris and Street (2007). Suffice it to note here that Matthews was a major box-office star and the films she was best known for featured narratives in which she played upwardly mobile young women who aspired to be stars. Production designer Alfred Junge used Art Deco sets for these musical extravaganzas which articulated an aspirational longing to break free from conventional structures of social connections and money.

Other British films dealt with 1930s concerns, for example, spy dramas, most famously Hitchcock's *The Thirty-Nine Steps* (1935) and *The Lady Vanishes* (1938) which anticipated the coming of war. Melodramas about social conditions, including *The Citadel* (King Vidor, 1938), *The Stars Look Down* (Carol Reed, 1939) and *South Riding* (Victor Saville, 1938), can be read as part of the 1930s pre-welfare state culture where, according to Marcia Landy, in British and American films

> characters and the social conflicts were polarized, the treatment of the social issues subordinated to the emotional conflicts experienced by the protagonists, and the conflicts often resolved through a populist bene-factor or through the efforts of an exceptional individual who overcame economic and social constraints in the interests of the community.
>
> (Landy, 1991: 433)

The overall vision celebrated in *South Riding*, a conservative adaptation of Winifred Holtby's popular novel set in a Yorkshire town, is of consensus, class harmony and national integration (see reading by Aldgate and Richards, 1983: 29–42). Such films were part of the hegemonic process which offered preferred, selective images of society which were, as a few films of the period demonstrate, only part of the story. The logic of most melodramas was to stress social cohesion and bourgeois hegemony, but it is interesting to note Landy's observation that a melodrama which does not do this, *They Drive By Night* (Arthur Woods, 1938), contains hybrid elements of film noir, working-class characters and a critical representation of the law (see Landy, 1991: 251–52). Films such as this were, however, the exception rather than the rule. Horror films were made in the 1930s but the BBFC's 'H' certificate, which existed from 1933–51, meant that producers tended to try to distance their films from an overt association with 'horror'. Instead, as Conrich has shown (in Chibnall and Petley, 2002: 58–70), they included horror elements in films that were otherwise marketed as melo-dramas, thrillers or comedies. Films most equating with horror during the decade include *Castle Sinister* (1932), *The Ghoul* (1933), *The Unholy Quest* (1934), *The Man Who Changed His Mind* (1936), *Dark Eyes of London* (1939) and *The Face at the Window* (1939).

THE SECOND WORLD WAR

The Second World War had a momentous impact on British cinema, momentous in critical, generic, ideological and stylistic terms. As with the First World War, British society was profoundly influenced by the demands of war, the most far-reaching development being the extension of state intervention in the economy, social welfare and culture. While it would not do to overemphasise the war's long-term impact, it is clear that there was 'a convergence of opinion towards the reformed capitalism and extended welfare provisions which formed the basis of the post-war consensus' (Stevenson, 1990: 460). As Antonia Lant has noted, the war context had an all-pervasive impact on film: 'the war caused every fiction, no matter how apparently remote from the crisis, to be understood in its terms' (Lant, 1991: 35). Critics believed that at last a national cinema was born, encouraged by the need to stress unity and in recognition of the importance of film as propaganda. Although this national cinema was identified and praised in rather narrow terms, privileging realism and documentary as the dominant form and aesthetic, the range and diversity of wartime British films extended far beyond those terms and was rooted very much in 1930s genre production. The result was a wide range of films, the most dominant genres being war films, focusing on life in the services/the male group, and the home front/women's contribution to the war effort; comedies; historical films; and costume melodramas.

Recent studies of wartime cinema have stressed the extent to which there was a consensus between the government and many film-makers to produce images which would create a sense of national collectivity. The films stressed pulling together in the face of national emergency, requiring individual sacrifice and a suspension of demands which conflicted with those of the state. The wartime notion of consensus was different from that of the 1930s, depending on a rhetoric which emphasised ordinariness in extraordinary times, an address to everyone to do their bit, however small or apparently insignificant, in the knowledge that their bit was, after all, for 'us', the nation. In the 1930s, consensus meant satisfaction with the status quo, but the wartime notion of consensus contained potentially more progressive elements in that it implied a resolve to extend many of the economic and social reforms into the post-war period.

At the popular cultural level, the wartime consensus involved promoting an overall image of Britain as a diverse but united community of interests. In so doing, however, the films ultimately fail to conceal the social contradictions involved in representing such an ideal picture of a unified nation at war. Class conflict is de-emphasised, but cannot be completely eradicated from wartime narratives. Similarly, women's experience of wartime work and the disruption of traditional family life and mores which was a necessary consequence of that experience, nevertheless resulted in conservative representations which tended to privilege the nurturing mother as 'the linchpin in conceptualising national unity' (Gledhill and Swanson, 1984: 36). The idea of nation as family depended on the ultimate reaffirmation of patriarchal values.

Films about the male experience of war focused on the bonding of men from different class and regional backgrounds and their training experiences, for example, *The Way Ahead* (Carol Reed, 1944) and *Journey Together* (John Boulting, 1945). Combat at sea and on land provided a ready source of drama, plots involving dangerous situations, mental and physical endurance, co-operation and heroism. They also provided a focus for flashbacks or parallel narratives of the home front. A film based on the wartime experiences of Lord Louis Mountbatten, *In Which We Serve* (Noël Coward, David Lean, 1942), exemplified the filmic notion of consensus where class differences are evident (but not presented as problematic), men are stoical and heroic and women know their place.

The film announces itself as the story of a ship, the HMS *Torrin*, which along with the war is the common factor binding its crew and their families.

Plate 2.5 A film industry at war. David Lean and Noël Coward on the set of *In Which We Serve* (1942). (Courtesy of Rank Film Distributors)

The narrative is a series of episodes from their various pasts, told in several flashbacks as the crew cling to a life-raft after the *Torrin* has been attacked and is slowly sinking in the background. The flashbacks show the happy and efficient crew responding in a cheerful and dedicated manner to their Captain, Kinross, played by Noël Coward. They also show scenes from their home backgrounds. The consensus ethos is particularly obvious in one flashback of three different Christmas celebrations – working- and upper class – which all mention the navy and the ship. The material differences between the classes are not commented upon but the women's common status, as loyal figures in the background who provide unquestioning love and moral support, is most clearly articulated by Alix, Captain Kinross's wife (played by Celia Johnson), who refers to the ship as a rival who must take precedence over other allegiances, 'wife, home, children, everything'. In this sense, the ship serves as a metaphor for class *and* patriarchal harmony in peacetime and in war. The peacetime scenes are particularly interesting for their implication that consensus preceded wartime conditions. When the ship finally sinks and the crew are rescued, Noël Coward

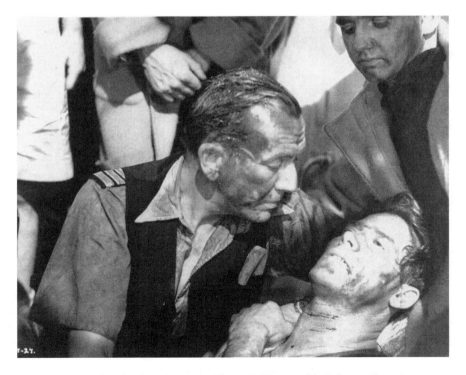

Plate 2.6 A united community at war: Captain Kinross (Noël Coward) assists a wounded sailor. *In Which We Serve* (1942). (Courtesy of Rank Film Distributors)

pays homage to them by saying that he would be happy to serve with any of the men again, implying an ongoing process of deference and service. The film begins and ends with documentary-style footage of ships being launched, men working to maintain them, the industrial processes of ship-building and with overhead shots of groups of sailors: a united community at war.

The box-office success *The Life and Death of Colonel Blimp* (Powell and Pressburger, 1943) deals with the notion of wartime consensus quite differ-ently: it frustrates generic expectations, introduces a complex relationship between past and present, offers sophisticated comment on national stereo-typing, and is shot in an unconventional style which tends to be viewed as part of Powell and Pressburger's overall output as auteurs. It was controver-sial on first release for its gentle critique of outmoded military values, and of gentlemanly rules of the game, epitomised by General Clive Wynne-Candy's (known as Candy, played by Roger Livesey) persistent plea for war-by-timetable, operated on a basis of unspoken codes of honour among gentleman-soldiers. The film proposes that these values are inappropriate when dealing with Nazism, making a clear distinction between war as a sort of sport for upper-class officers and war as a question of national survival.

The film opens in the Second World War with an arresting scene when a young army officer, Spud Wilson, and his men burst into the Royal Bathers Club, where Candy (an old man) is taking a steam bath. The sequence plays on the incongruity of the old bathers and the young soldiers who have inter-rupted their relaxation during some mock-military exercises.

After a comic tussle between Spud and Candy, the film goes into flash-back. Unlike *In Which We Serve*, Powell and Pressburger's flashback to the Boer War deals primarily with upper-class individuals, not representative communities/class interests united in the face of war. Instead of giving us little episodes, the flashback takes us chronologically through to the Second World War and is concerned with Candy and Theo. Theo (Anton Walbrook) is a German officer whom Candy befriends after a duelling inci-dent in Berlin just after the Boer War, a friendship which survives two world wars. Although theirs is the main relationship in the film, there are some nods to the idea of the new woman, represented in different ways by the two characters both played by Deborah Kerr, particularly Edith who rebels against her family, earning her living by becoming a governess in Germany, and Angela, Candy's respectful but gutsy driver who prefers to be called Johnny. Both characters are accorded considerable insight about human and international diplomacy, insight which (apart from Theo) eludes the men.

Despite its stylistic distinctions, its portrayal of the military establishment and its treatment of women, I would argue that *Colonel Blimp* shares some of the ideological preoccupations of documentary-narrative films like *In Which We Serve*. The notion of consensus is not entirely absent: it is possible to read Candy's capitulation to new ideas as the eventual achievement of

Plate 2.7 Candy (Roger Livesey) and Theo (Anton Walbrook), reunited after the First World War in *The Life and Death of Colonal Blimp* (1943). (Courtesy of Rank Film Distributors)

consensus (as opposed to difference) among generations. This has already been signalled by Theo's learning process as a member of the older German military establishment who reaches the conclusion that outdated methods will not work against Hitler, long before Candy's grudging enlightenment. Administrative divisions between diplomacy and soldiering are criticised, and Candy recognises the similarity between his behaviour at the end of the Boer War in defiance of his superiors and Spud's decision to accelerate his timetable for the military exercise.

Colonel Blimp refuses, however, to be an accommodating or straightforward film. There is, for example, something anarchic about the film's distinctive opening, its woven titles which symbolise a fascination with past and present, the arresting Technicolour photography (especially when so many Second World War films were shot in black and white), the artificiality of the military exercises, the bizarre exchange between Spud and Candy in the bathing room and, perhaps most striking, the almost Potteresque[11] dialogue which might break into song at any moment, particularly when 'War Begins at Midnight' has been repeated several times in staccato.

Colonel Blimp is a good example of a hybrid war film which conforms to notions of consensus but, at the same time, suggests a sort of anarchic abandon at its achievement, which in turn threatens the stability of that consensus.

In narrative and aesthetic terms, the desire to represent unity sometimes resulted in an interesting merger of documentary and melodramatic modes which diverged from classical Hollywood films in significant ways. Andrew Higson has compared two documentary-narrative melodramas, *Millions Like Us* (Frank Launder, Sidney Gilliat, 1943) and *This Happy Breed* (David Lean, 1944), which have their roots in the 1930s story-documentaries like *Night Mail* (Harry Watt, Basil Wright, 1936) and *North Sea* (Harry Watt, 1938). Higson's illuminating analysis shows that they are 'key texts in the formation of a relatively distinct British film genre, the melodrama of everyday life' (Higson, 1995: 262). The main features of this genre were a tendency to focus on varied groups of characters – often representing different classes, generations and regions – rather than on individuals; episodic narrative structures; an address to the spectator which invited him or her to identify as part of the collective national community; an aesthetic characterised by an iconography of the workplace and leisure activities, and montage editing (see Higson, 1984a: 22–26).

Millions Like Us dealt with the question of the mobile woman, that is, women conscripted for wartime work. The focus is on one woman, Celia, and her family's wartime experiences, although this is only one dominant strain of a narratively complex film. Although the film's overall theme is the celebration of community, it nevertheless articulates a specific lower-middle-class position (Celia's) and views women's wartime work and freedom as a temporary necessity, an ideological standpoint which is even more overtly conservative in *This Happy Breed* (see Higson, 1995: 176–271). Other contemporary melodramas were important in their address to women's experience. Although *Brief Encounter* (David Lean, 1945) is set in the late 1930s, its story of Laura Jesson's contemplated extra-marital affair, with accompanying contradictory feelings of excitement, temptation, agony and pain, spoke to many women who had similarly lived on the edge of that experience during the war. Families were split up, husbands were away for years, women went out to work and experienced new environments and temptations. *Brief Encounter* thus articulated a range of feelings about infidelity which invited easy identification, whether it involved one's husband, lover, children or country.

Comedy was a popular and prolific genre in the Second World War, comprising almost half the annual output of feature films. There were major continuities with the 1930s in terms of personalities (a notable exception being Gracie Fields)[12] and styles, but the war provided them with new comic situations and a shared sense of national responsibility to boost home-front morale by making people laugh at their worst fears and experiences. Typical situations were joining up, spy-catching, army life, the Home Guard and the trials and tribulations of life on the home front generally. George Formby was the most popular British film star until 1944 (when he was replaced by James Mason) and films like *Let George Do It* (Marcel Varnel, 1940) and *Turned Out Nice Again* (Marcel Varnel, 1941) enabled him to use the war to build on his already established repertoire and image as 'an icon of gullible naivety' (Murphy, 1989: 194). Other popular wartime film comedians were Arthur Askey and music-hall star Frank Randle who was popular in the north. Elsie and Doris Waters played Gert and Daisy, Cockney sisters who turned numerous home-front problems, which audiences were having to confront in their everyday lives, into hilarious situations. As Andy Medhurst has pointed out, variety artists performed the important wartime ideological function of 'reaffirming a notion of community' (Medhurst, 1986a: 179). After the war, variety played a less central role in British film comedy, although its traditions can be seen to operate in the work of Norman Wisdom and in the early *Carry On* films.

At the other end of the social and regional spectrum, there was an interesting cycle of comedies featuring rich upper-class characters and life-styles, for example *The Demi-Paradise* (Anthony Asquith, 1943), a film about a Russian engineer who comes to Britain in 1939 to develop a special ice-breaking propeller for ships. He is exposed to many varieties of Britishness, ranging from upper-class eccentrics to music-hall artistes. Against his initial negative preconceptions about the British he is later convinced that the war has encouraged 'more ideal national characteristics', summarised by David Lusted as showing Britain as a nation characterised by democracy, community, unity and plurality (Lusted, 1984: 28). *The Demi-Paradise* sketches an affectionate and uncritical portrait of the mythology of old England, a mythology which aimed to convince people that the certainties of pre-war values, particularly class distinctions, were sacrosanct and worth defending. Although the engineer falls in love with the granddaughter of the chairman of the shipyards, he returns to Russia without her, their failed romance symbolising that Anglo-Russian relations can only go *so* far. As Landy comments, this is typical of many wartime films which raise possibilities only to close them off at crucial moments:

> Its unwillingness to sanction a romantic relationship between the representatives of two different cultures is particularly revealing of the film's entrapment in a rhetoric that insists on traditional patterns of social life that obstruct the very changes that the film entertains.
>
> (Landy, 1991: 161)

The Demi-Paradise and other upper-class comedies therefore share many of the ideological contradictions which are evident in the 'melodramas of everyday life'. The introduction of the Russian factor, in conjunction with a defence of British traditions, anticipated Cold War narratives which polarised East and West.

Although historical films did well at the box office they did not form a high percentage of total output during the years 1939–45. The most popular included *Lady Hamilton* (Alexander Korda, 1941), *The Young Mr Pitt* (Carol Reed, 1942), *The Man In Grey* (Leslie Arliss, 1943) *Fanny By Gaslight* (Anthony Asquith, 1944) and *The Wicked Lady* (Leslie Arliss, 1945). Some historical films had official and unofficial backing from the Ministry of Information and the Foreign Office, which is evidence of the state's concern to use history as contemporary propaganda. MOI-supported *Henry V* (Laurence Olivier, 1945) is an obvious example of utilising the past for this purpose, with every speech, costume and setting reminding audiences of forthcoming victory. Despite criticism from American isolationists on the eve of America's entry into the war, the Foreign Office promoted Korda's box-office winner, *Lady Hamilton*, a film which included a fictitious speech by Nelson which could easily have been a contemporary call-to-arms. The film continued Korda's 1930s 'aristocratic–proletarian alliance' trajectory whereby 'the only real aristocratic leadership was one which symbolically represented popular aspirations' (Harper, 1994: 94). Reminiscent of *The Private Life of Henry VIII* (1933), *Lady Hamilton* made a deliberate appeal to female audiences by means of visual spectacle and the inclusion of Emma, a powerful and desiring central female character. This fascinating aspect of Korda's historical films was developed and elaborated upon by Gainsborough Studios during and after the war.

Since the early 1980s the study of Gainsborough melodramas has challenged dominant views about British cinema as being primarily informed by stylistic and thematic forms of realism that had become associated with notions of 'quality' and critical 'value'. On the contrary, the successful cycle of costume melodramas produced by Gainsborough in the 1940s used historical settings, escapist narrative formulas, opulent-looking costumes and sets that were created on small budgets to score a number of significant box-office successes that were generally dismissed by critics at the time and in subsequent critical discourse. As film historians such as Sue Harper (1994) and Pam Cook (1996) began to ask questions about the significance of these films to their contemporary culture, it became clear that this previously neglected sub-genre indeed has much to say about pressing issues of the time, particularly gender inequalities.

While Gainsborough was associated with a number of genres the first really successful costume melodrama was *The Man In Grey* (1943), set partly in the eighteenth century, starring Margaret Lockwood and James Mason. This film established the formula that was to inform later box-office hits, most notably *The Wicked Lady* (1945), set in Restoration England. These films were set in the past and featured feisty, wilful heroines who challenged the prevailing masculine order, even if in the end they did not succeed in completely overthrowing it. Studies of contemporary audience reaction to some of these films, completed by J. P. Mayer (1948), reveal that although the films were set in the past many people identified with the dilemmas facing the characters. In the context of the Second World War, when many people experienced temporary freedoms, extra-marital relations and travelled within and outside the country in an unprecedented way, the films tapped into contemporary dilemmas which explain their enormous box-office success.

A distinctive feature of the Gainsborough costume films is that they express much of their rebellious sensibilities through sets and costume. Although the films were released in a context of war and post-war austerity, they provided an opportunity for audiences to 'enter into a world of fantasy where freedom and pleasure were coterminous' (Harper, 1994: 131). One of the most significant designers to work on the films was Elizabeth Haffenden who exploited the arrival of the New Look fashions in historical designs that were anachronistic yet 'fitted' people's expectations of what was worn in the past. With its emphasis on an 'hour-glass figure' that accentuated the waist, chest and a fulsome skirt, the New Look was perfectly suited to emulation via the compelling heroines of the melodramas, as in *Caravan* (Arthur Crabtree, 1946). The films therefore celebrated excessive displays of femininity that, as has been argued by Sue Harper and Pam Cook, could encourage oppositional readings of films that relished transgressive, female desire at a time when the freedoms enjoyed during the Second World War were being curtailed. The heroines were often pitted against more conventional, conformist women who usually triumphed at narrative closure; nevertheless the feisty women were more appealing for their audacity and daring.

While the Gainsborough costume dramas can be related to gender issues they are also an important registers of the national psyche in other respects. Their fascination with exotic outsiders, particularly gypsies, in films such as *Madonna of the Seven Moons* (Arthur Crabtree, 1944), *Caravan* and *Jassy* (Bernard Knowles, 1947), signals an eclectic affinity with 'foreign' locations and styles that was typical of much of Gainsborough's output. This allowed art directors such as Andrew Mazzei to indulge themselves and their audiences with European-inspired decorative designs that ranged from rococo to expressionism. The critical acknowledgement of this aspect of Gainsborough was extremely important in signalling how *mise-en-scène* can constitute independent discourses that offer excessive visual pleasures to audiences and which stay in the memory as thrilling encounters with opulence as suggestive of sexual transgression.

The Gainsborough costume melodramas represented a high-point in the celebration of 'wicked ladies' in British cinema, which ended in 1950 when more docile stereotypes dominated the screen. Their resuscitation has had important consequences however for the analysis of British cinema generally since they highlighted aspects that had long been repressed: trans-national identities and fascinations; gender and sexuality; the questionable distinction between 'realism' and 'tinsel' and the importance of visual style. Although Gainsborough produced many different genre films, it was most renowned for its historical costume melodramas which were extremely popular at the box office. These escapist bodice-rippers addressed new sexual freedoms, providing 'a temporary imaginary location where marginal groups could experience that pleasure and confidence which were normally the prerogative of those who made the rules' (Harper, 1994: 185–86). This is all the more remarkable considering that they were scripted by middle-class writers who frequently punished deviant females like Hesther in *The Man In Grey* or Barbara in *The Wicked Lady*, 'in a rhetoric of disdain towards their working-class female audience' (ibid.: 126). While the melodramas could not, with their conservative narrative closures, be said to be progressive, they nevertheless provided their audiences with subversive pleasures to be found in their melodramatic plots' twists and turns; their shockability; their attractive rebels and their sumptuous costumes. Very often 'bad' characters were pitted against 'good' ones, the latter often being less alluring than the former. Occasionally, the audience is encouraged to identify with

Plate 2.8 Contrasting futures. Clarissa (Phyllis Calvert) and Hesther (Margaret Lockwood) have their fortunes told by a gypsy in *The Man In Grey* (1943). (Courtesy of Rank Film Distributors)

both, as in the case of Clarissa and Hesther in *The Man In Grey*, two school-friends who go on to live very different lives, Clarissa as a rich, unhappily married woman and Hesther as a poor, touring player who tells lies and schemes her way into Clarissa's household after they accidentally meet up. *The Man In Grey* and other melodramas' tales of transgression, excitement and escape fed into wartime conflicts between transient relationships vs. monogamy; emotional intensity vs. pre-war certainties; adultery vs. marriage; illegitimacy vs. traditional motherhood; austerity and rationing vs. plenitude and glamour. The context of material deprivation and the emotional upsets caused by separation of couples, mothers and children, must be measured against increased female participation in the workforce and greater sexual freedoms, travel and a general lifting of inhibitions. It is not surprising that the melodramas were so popular since on many of these levels they connected extremely well with the mood and experiences of wartime.

As noted above, the films' radicalism can be located in the work of Gainsborough's art directors, particularly John Bryan, who presented audiences with a transgressive visual discourse which privileged pleasurable looking, excess and exoticism. In this way, instead of reflecting the script-writers' middle-class concerns and fixating on their conservative narrative closures, the films instead provided an escapist fantasy which focused on the *pleasures* involved in the process of transgression. Margaret Lockwood's acting added sparkle to her spunky roles, most effectively in her portrayal in *The Wicked Lady* of bad, bored Barbara Skelton who steals her best friend's fiancé, becomes a highwaywoman, cheats and murders and has an extra-marital affair with highwayman Jerry Jackson (played by James Mason). Although she dies in the end, we remember the excitement of her rebellion and her charisma in comparison with duller characters who represent morality and goodness. Sue Harper has studied the function of costume in *The Wicked Lady*, revealing that Elizabeth Haffenden's designs celebrated sexual difference and sexuality by insisting on simple but crucial details. In a context of wartime rationing, the costumes displayed an extravagant flamboyance and symbolic fantasy which anticipated the arrival of the New Look in the post-war period (ibid.: 130–32 and see also Cook, 1996: 53–59, 78–79). Other more contemporary Gainsborough films, including *They Were Sisters* (Arthur Crabtree, 1945) and the major box-office hit of 1945, *The Seventh Veil* (Compton Burnett, 1945), can also be read in the context of the end of the war, and fears and aspirations for the post-war world (see Landy, 1991: 222–27).

CONCLUSION

Some conclusions can be drawn from the above survey of British genres to 1945. One of the most striking is the longevity of variety-based comedy from silent cinema to its place in boosting home-front morale during the war. The music-hall tradition provided such comedy with an extremely malleable and durable repertoire of situations, personalities and anarchic elements. Silent cinema allowed comedy to develop its visual dimensions, exploiting the idea of the cinema of attractions and spectacle. To some extent the arrival of sound reduced comedy's anarchic and critical potential, although there were clear continuities between characters like Squibs and Gracie Fields, and Will Hay's films were by no means conformist. New elements were however added, not based on conventional dialogue but instead on aural signifiers for particular personalities: Gracie Fields' voice and George Formby's singing and banjo-playing. It is arguable that these constituted a utopian address which did not feature in other aspects of their films. Comedy was to continue to develop quite differently from literary-based, documentary-influenced, quality films. Most comedy was domestically oriented, a factor which gave it a clear sense of Britishness and range of regional representation which did not predominate in other genres. More than any other genre, comedy put working-class characters on screen, the majority of them advocating a community of interests which was not necessarily at odds with the existence of other social classes. This consensual outlook found complete expression in the war when comedy was but one genre which sought to represent a united nation.

Another important trend was the costume/historical film which dominated in the 1930s and 1940s. These often included comic elements, for example, *The Private Life of Henry VIII* and *The Wicked Lady*, but for different ends than variety-based comedy. These ends were, perhaps much more specifically related to their own contemporary contexts: the genre did not continue to be popular in the 1950s and thus in this form can be seen to be very much tied to the 1930s and 1940s. The analysis earlier in this chapter of *The Drum* showed how much it was a product of 1930s concerns about the future of the Empire. The most successful historical films depended on striking a balance between coded allusions to contemporary anxieties and irreverent, escapist fantasy. It would appear that Korda and Wilcox's commitment to the genre in the 1930s established key precedents which were developed by Gainsborough in the 1940s. These drew on the popularity of historical novels and audiences' desire to see splendour and excitement on screen at a time of national crisis. From this point of view, the films' narratives and visual styles were influenced not only by previous popular historical films but also by their particular appeal in a wartime context.

The convergence of documentary realism and melodramas of everyday life displayed a similar relevance during the war. The ethos of community was therefore present across genres, although it is interesting to note the degree to which it was already in place during the 1930s. As explained above, the extent to which that community was, in fact, united, is questionable. While conflicts and instability can be detected in many of the films, their dominant narrative trajectories probably render alternative readings exceptional. It must be remembered that during the war cinema was not the only medium seeking to promote national solidarity: the need to maintain good morale meant that radio and newspapers also de-emphasised home-front problems. This overall official cultural context therefore militated against privileging the textual excess which was clearly there.[13] That it appears at all is, however, indicative of the paradox of many successful genre films: their ability to both contain and release utopian desires. One form of utopianism which was particularly immediate was the determination to convert the wartime communitarian spirit into post-war reform. The extent to which that occurred will be discussed in the following chapter.

Chapter 3

Genres from austerity to affluence

British cinema's eclectic base engendered a number of key genres which displayed considerable internal differences and emphases over the decades. While eclecticism was mostly founded on economic insecurity, it did, however, produce a variety of product which makes generic analysis a particularly useful way to assess the various representations of Britishness which competed for audiences' attention. While popular cinema is by no means the entire corpus of a nation's output, its ability to generate certain images at a mass level, particularly when cinema-going was at its peak in the 1940s, enables us to relate films to their political and cultural context. As we have already seen, particular genres represented notions of Britishness differently: while comedy was centred mostly on figures from outside London, historical films stuck very much to famous figures from history or on the expansion of Britishness under imperialism. To take the examination further, the following two chapters will assess the dominant and less dominant generic trends over the last half century of British cinema.

POST-WAR BRITISH SOCIETY AND GENRES, 1945–60

The wartime consensus in favour of the extension of state intervention in the economy and welfare services resulted in the establishment of the welfare state by Labour, a process which was not dismantled by the Conservatives in the 1950s, even though they were in office for the entire decade. The years 1945–60 were characterised by a range of other important social and political features: after the Suez debacle British nationalism became more inward looking in the post-colonial, anti-immigration context, and the Cold War created further impetus for questioning traditional international loyalties.[1] As immigration increased, race became a source of social conflict, demonstrated by riots in Nottingham and in Notting Hill, West London in 1958, when the local black communities were attacked by white Teddy Boys.[2] Despite the levelling intentions of wartime collectivism, class society remained intact. The election of a Labour Government in 1945 did not ensure that most positions of power were subsequently held by those who originated from the working-class or even middle-class backgrounds, and Britain remained a country characterised by class divisions. There was, however, some expansion of business and consumerism as post-war austerity evolved into affluence, especially for the middle classes, who took advantage of increased employment and opportunities provided by the mixed economy.

Regarding gender relations, the basic assumption was reinforced in all classes 'that girls would become wives and mothers, and therefore should be treated accordingly' (Marwick, 1990: 68). Women's total participation in the workforce fell after the war and the majority of jobs available to them were low paid, monotonous and part-time. The biggest change was an increase in employment of married women in part-time jobs, a trend caused initially by the post-war labour shortage but which has continued throughout the century (see Lewis, 1984: 148, 218–19). This caused anxiety about the quality of family life, a concern which became most pronounced in the 1950s, often placing emphasis on the family as a social institution under stress. It is not surprising in this context that many post-war narratives deal with complex and contradictory notions of the family. Divorce rates increased and the birth rate fell in the late 1940s, which caused anxiety about the traditional role of the extended family in British society which seemed in danger of being replaced by welfare provision and the ascendancy of the nuclear family.

The 1950s saw the emergence of youth problems, and the increasing visibility of disenchanted young men, particularly Teddy Boys, who were identified as potential young offenders. With unemployment at a relatively low level, many social reports expressed fears about affluent youths with money to spend who were associated with sexual immorality and violence.[3] Another facet of an increasing official tendency to identify and document social problems was concern about prostitution and homosexuality. Again, it is interesting to bear this context in mind when examining films of the 1950s which frequently allude to social problems, and which again and again reveal a crisis of masculinity. As a reflection of the male-dominated film industry it is not surprising that the foregrounding of a crisis in femininity was conspicuous by its absence.

In the cultural sphere, the 1950s was a significant decade when the 'angry young men' questioned the traditional literary canon. The angry young men were writers like John Braine, John Osborne and Alan Sillitoe who wanted to replace the upper-class drawing-room plays of Terence Rattigan and the formal experimentation of modernist writers like T. S. Eliot and Virginia Woolf with novels and plays which dealt with working-class themes and problems in a strident and accessible manner. The works of these writers contributed to the general interrogation of established cultural values, a trend which was taken up by film in the late 1950s and early 1960s when they were used as source material for the New Wave films. The notable incidence of social problem films in the 1950s, however, provides a useful link between the angry young literary backlash and trends which anticipated later filmic developments. The broad social contours of the 1960s will be described later, but there were clearly elements of continuity with the 1950s, especially in popular music with the ascendancy of American rock 'n' roll singers like Bill Haley and Elvis Presley who were important influences on 1960s British pop singers and groups, including Cliff Richard, the Beatles and the Rolling Stones. A general sense of liberalisation and recognition of youth culture was reflected in dress codes, ranging from the distinctive suits worn by Teddy Boys to leather-jacketed Rockers, mini-skirted young women, flower-shirted Mods and Afghan-coated Hippies. The late 1950s and 1960s were also associated with greater sexual freedoms and a desire to question, if not overturn, traditional political ideologies.

The fluctuating fortunes of 1950s British genres

The early post-war years and 1950s saw many significant developments in British genres, many of which reflected the wider changes mentioned above. In retrospect it would appear that social contradictions, which wartime films had attempted to conceal, could not always be contained in post-war genres. One of the most striking general thematic shifts was the retreat of narratives based on women's experience outside the home or specifically about women's desires and issues. During the 1950s there were more men on screen than women, more male actors played major protagonists and fewer women went to the cinema. When they were represented on screen, women tended to be firmly placed in marital and family situations, as a backdrop to the more complex analysis of male psychological, sexual, familial and generational problems which were the focus of so many British films in the 1950s. Overall, the period saw the decline of historical/costume films; the development of British comedy; a 1940s cycle of 'spiv'[4] films/British film noirs; the rise of Cold War films; science-fiction; horror; and the social-problem film.

Historical costume dramas and comedy

The historical costume film declined after the release of *Jassy* (Bernard Knowles, 1947) partly because there was a key change in production management at Gainsborough in 1946. Instead of continuing with the approach and style (historical romance, visual splendour and an appeal to female audiences), which had made Gainsborough's films so popular, the new Head of Production, Sydney Box, insisted on accuracy and realism. The result was films like *Christopher Columbus* (David Macdonald, 1949) which, according to Harper, 'has an elephantine pace, and is grimly silent on the key issues of popular culture and sexual pleasure' (Harper, 1994: 134). In the 1950s audiences had their desire for costume pictures satisfied by American historical spectacles (including *The Robe*, 1953; *The Ten Commandments*, 1956; *Ben Hur*, 1959 and *Spartacus*, 1960) and Italian 'peplum' cinema (lavish costume adventure epics, for example, *Ulysses*, 1954 and *Revolt of the Gladiators*, 1958). As Robert Murphy has noted, 'British producers seemed to have lost the knack' (Murphy, 1989: 145). It would also, however, appear to be the case that the decline of the costume film was related to the general decline in women's pictures, in itself a symptom of post-war conservatism about women's roles. As we have already seen in the previous chapter, Gainsborough's most popular melodramas spoke to female audiences who had themselves experienced transgression and a greater sense of freedom in the war. But it is also possible that many of the genre's most distinctive attributes and visual pleasures resurfaced in fascinating ways in Hammer horror films and in heritage cinema, indicating how genres mutate over time.

A genre which was very much subject to mutation was comedy. In different ways, late 1940s and 1950s comedies offer a critique of British institutions, institutions which serve as microcosms of British society as a whole. In this sense, the comedies of Norman Wisdom, Launder and Gilliat, Ealing Studios and the *Carry On* team have much in common, deriving their ideological impetus from fears about state power and a mistrust of bureaucratic structures in general plus the persistence of social class and a preoccupation with sexual repression. Norman Wisdom worked in the variety tradition, frequently playing 'little men', clumsy working-class characters who have no special charismatic qualities, but who nevertheless succeed in exposing upper-class hypocrisies and petty bureaucrats. Although many of these films can certainly be read to contain such critiques, an important caveat acknowledges that these were generally linked to a fear of 'modernising threats' which have been analysed by Geraghty who argues that 'If forced to choose between traditional and modern they [comedy films of the 1950s] opt for tradition' (2000: 56). Although Frank Launder and Sidney Gilliat had directed and written a wide range of British films since the 1930s, their 1950s comedies are particularly distinctive for their critical reappraisal of esteemed British institutions, which nevertheless contain some of these fears. An institution which was ripe for comic examination was the girls' minor public school, awash with eccentric teachers, senseless traditions, excessive sportiness, appalling facilities, poor academic results, sexually repressed schoolmistresses, sexually precocious schoolgirls and a headmistress who is Margaret Rutherford or, in the 1950s *St Trinian's* series, Alastair Sim in drag.

In the first of the school series, *The Happiest Days of Your Life* (Frank Launder, 1950), Alastair Sim plays Mr Pond, a headmaster who is forced to share his Nutbourne College for Boys premises with an evacuated girls' school because of a Ministry of Education error, which he later describes as 'a sexual aberration'. His initial meeting with the girls' tweed-clad headmistress, Miss Whitchurch (Margaret Rutherford), is mutually antagonistic, and much of the subsequent comedy is derived from the basic situation of two single-sex schools being forced to share facilities. Further complications ensue when both Miss Whitchurch and Mr Pond have to impress important visitors: in Miss Whitchurch's case some anxious parents, and in Mr Pond's the governors of a major public school he hopes will employ him as headmaster. The success of the visitations depends on parents and governors being given separate synchronised guided tours, each concealing the presence of pupils of the opposite gender! All proceeds well for a while, but the plan goes horribly wrong at the end when the parents and governors are greeted with the chaotic spectacle of collision: screaming, fighting boys and girls on the games field.

The Happiest Days of Your Life is set in the immediate post-war period, with mention of rationing and shortages giving it topical currency. Inefficient bureaucracy is the target of much of the humour, the Ministry of Education being responsible for the mix-up which Mr Pond initially blames on the nationalised railways. The traditional public school ethos with its absurdities, prejudices and anachronisms is also the subject of gentle satire. The visiting parents are concerned that their girls should not mix with 'other classes', an opinion presumably shared by Mr Pond and Miss Whitchurch. The failure of the two guided tours illustrates the film's concern with gender and class separatism: while Mr Pond and Miss Whitchurch secure their pupils' co-operation in the tours, tension builds up as synchronicity lapses and it becomes increasingly obvious that the awful truth will be discovered. Whereas the pupils are shown to relish cohabitation and new experiences, the older generation view them with horror. The pupils represent a youthful embrace of change, whereas Mr Pond and Miss Whitchurch can only look back in nostalgia. At the end of the film another school has been relocated to Nutbourne, this time a co-educational school which causes a horrified Miss Whitchurch to recommend to an equally horrified Mr Pond that they would both do better to seek posts teaching 'natives' in Tanganyika. This last point underlines the film's critique of outmoded educational institutions and their fear of 'new-fangled theories' of co-education and mixing classes. Presumably this refers to the 1944 Education Act's recommendations to extend secondary education to all pupils until they were aged 15, enabling a minority of working-class children who passed the 11-plus examination to go to grammar schools which usually led to better jobs and opportunities.

The film is also awash with innuendo and double-entendre, a technique which was exploited even more fully by the *Carry On* films. When Miss Whitchurch and her staff arrive at Nutbourne College, they are under the impression that they are joining another girls' school. After reading the school motto, 'Guard Thine Honour', their incredulous inspection of the staff common-room borders on high camp as they examine possessions

Plate 3.1 Shocking events at Nutbourne College. Miss Whitchurch (Margaret Rutherford), Miss Gossage (Joyce Grenfell) and Mr Pond (Alastair Sim) in *The Happiest Days of Your Life* (1950). (Courtesy of Lumière Pictures Limited)

that we know belong to the masters, but which they persist in interpreting as the property of strange female staff. Miss Whitchurch's comment, 'We are moving in a descending spiral of iniquity' gathers even more of a sexual connotation when they discover *The Memoirs of Casanova*, a book one of her pupils, Jessica James, had been caught reading 'in the closet'. As with many other films of this period, a retrospective camp reading can be used to add to the comedy but, even so, it is hard to imagine contemporary audiences not picking up on the high degree of verbal sexual banter. The casting of Margaret Rutherford (also in MGM's *Miss Marple* films and subsequently claimed as a camp icon) and Alastair Sim's portrayal of headmistress Miss Fritton in the *St Trinian's* films, elaborated much of this style of comic gender subversion.

Ealing comedies are probably the most celebrated subgenre in the late 1940s and early 1950s. The key films in the cycle are *Hue and Cry* (Charles Crichton, 1947), *Passport To Pimlico* (Henry Cornelius, 1949), *Whisky Galore!* (Alexander Mackendrick, 1949), *Kind Hearts and Coronets* (Robert

Hamer, 1949), *The Lavender Hill Mob* (Charles Crichton, 1951), *The Man In the White Suit* (Alexander Mackendrick, 1951), *The Titfield Thunderbolt* (Charles Crichton, 1953) and *The Ladykillers* (Alexander Mackendrick, 1955). While they could be said to share many common features concerning opposition to post-war restrictions and institutions, a cosy middle-class outlook and a nostalgia for wartime 'community', and a predominantly realist style with use of flashback, they are, as Charles Barr has shown, all quite different (Barr, 1977). Barr notes significant differences between mainstream Ealing comedies written by T. E. B. Clarke (including *Passport To Pimlico* and *The Lavender Hill Mob*) and more aberrant films, directed by Alexander Mackendrick (*Whisky Galore!* and *The Man In the White Suit*) and by Robert Hamer (*Kind Hearts and Coronets*). One should, however, be wary of rigid distinctions and of evaluating Ealing comedies only in terms of previous and subsequent Ealing production. As Robert Murphy has pointed out, Clarke's Ealing comedies resemble those produced by Gainsborough Studios, including *Holiday Camp* (Ken Annakin, 1947) and The Huggetts series (1948–49), although these have a more working-class focus than Clarke's scripts (Murphy, 1989: 214–18). The Huggetts were a working-class couple (played by Jack Warner and Kathleen Harrison) first featured in *Holiday Camp* and whose exploits were followed up in *Here Come the Huggetts* (Ken Annakin, 1948) in which Diana Dors plays the Huggetts' glamorous visiting niece, causing mayhem along the way. *Vote for Huggett* (Ken Annakin, 1948) deals with local politics with Joe Huggett as a popular borough councillor while the next Huggett film, *The Huggetts Abroad* (Ken Annakin, 1949), takes them to South Africa, a move which turns out to be disastrous when they become involved with a diamond smuggler. Their plucky attempt to seek a better life is thus thwarted and they return to Britain, grateful for normality after their hairy experiences.

Barr calls Clarke's mainstream comedies 'daydreams' of 'timeless, seamless communities' where England is a united family. A prime example is *Passport To Pimlico*, a film about the discovery of an ancient document which proves that Pimlico belongs to the Duchy of Burgundy and is therefore independent from London and post-war restrictions. The film explores the consequences of freedoms gained by independence, particularly the release from rationing. But these freedoms are not presented as uniformly desirable: one character, the publican Garland, epitomises the worst elements of the brutal free market which the film ultimately rejects. Garland sees the abandonment of restrictions as a signal for ruthless competition ('every man for himself'), giving the go-ahead to a market economy operated by spivs. But instead of promoting freedom from restrictions as the ideal future, the film's fantasy is a return to wartime solidarity which the Burgundian crisis has provoked. As Charles Barr has argued, this 'fantasy' represents Ealing's refusal to confront the challenges and problems of post-war society: 'The sadness is that there should be so deep a compulsion to dream of consensus, to shy away from the conflicts that come up in an "open" society rather than to follow them through clear-sightedly' (Barr, 1977: 106).

By contrast, an Ealing comedy like *Whisky Galore!* presents a very different image of how a community might react to a sudden reversal of fortune, in this case the discovery of a cargo of whisky in a sinking ship off the Scottish coast. Barr argues that the dynamic impact this incident has on the community, encouraging resourcefulness, survivalism and toughness, is quite different from the 'nice, wholesome and harmless' response of most of the inhabitants of Pimlico when their ancient document is discovered. Instead of fearing corruption, the community in *Whisky Galore!* grasps its opportunity with both hands, even resorting to ingenious subterfuge by replacing local tap water with the whisky! According to Barr, films such as *Whisky Galore!* can be more accurately described as dreams than day-dreams in the sense of 'playing out, in compressed or symbolic forms, of conflicts as they in fact are' (Barr, 1977: 117). *Passport To Pimlico* looks backwards in nostalgia whereas *Whisky Galore!* signals optimism about how society can deal with the problems and challenges of the postwar world. Tony Williams' reading of *Passport To Pimlico* has also stressed its horror of the market economy and desire to repress darker aspects of British post-war society, but Williams prefers to view this scenario as closer to a nightmare than Barr's daydream idea, creating a link between *Passport To Pimlico* and the films of Hamer and Mackendrick. This nightmarish undercurrent of repressed fantasies and sexual tensions forms a surprising connection between Ealing and Hammer Horror (see Williams, 1994: 95–106).

Two other Ealing dreams/nightmares are worth mentioning: *Kind Hearts and Coronets* and *The Man In the White Suit*, films which in different ways subvert mainstream Ealing norms. *Kind Hearts and Coronets*, an intensely verbal black comedy, deals with questions of sexual repression and class society at a much deeper psychological and symbolic manner than previous Ealing comedies. Louis Mazzini's revenge against his aristocratic relatives for dispossessing his mother, a duke's daughter, when she married his father, a penniless opera singer, involves him exposing the cold hypocrisies of aristocratic values while at the same time using them in an extreme manner to murder his way to his title. With elegance, style, coldness and laconic humour (factors which make his crimes more acceptable to the audience), Louis murders six of his relatives who stand between him and the dukedom. The fact that Alec Guinness plays all of Louis' relatives works to heighten the black comedy as well as detracting from the reality of mass murder. Once his goal has been attained, an ironic twist of fate leads to Louis' arrest for a murder he did not commit. He is acquitted, but on leaving prison remembers that he has left his memoirs in his cell, memoirs which detail each of the murders he did commit! A further irony of the film is that by means of his voice-over narration, which we assume is the text of his memoirs, the verbal precision and elegance he has used throughout to persuade us of his superiority and rightful position as duke, will ultimately condemn him, his cleverness being finally outwitted by his own irrepressible egotism.

With its story of a man, Sidney Stratton (Alec Guinness), who invents an indestructible fabric, *The Man In the White Suit* explores the question of the common and conflicting interests in capitalist economies. While it adheres to Ealing's general realist style and theme of the individual battling against institutions, it unpicks complex facets of contemporary life from which the mainstream comedies shied away. Stratton's fabric causes consternation when its mass production is funded by his employer, prompting anxiety about potential unemployment in the textile industry and a reduction in profits if people no longer had to replace their clothes. Made in the same year that a manufacturer's cartel opposed the production of long-life light bulbs, *The Man In the White Suit* is an inventive social comedy which addresses the conflict between technical invention and traditional commercial interests: the scientist is forced to recognise that progress is not a question of brilliance in the laboratory, but of recognising the tenacity of economic, social and bureaucratic obstacles.

It is interesting that Ealing films have been most persistent in the popular conception of late 1940s and early 1950s Britishness, particularly in America. Michael Balcon's confessed aim to represent the British character on screen probably has much to do with this, as well as critics' praise for Ealing's realist style. Despite the films' differences, their most recurrent feature seems to be nostalgia for the wartime community, a nostalgia which does not reflect the conflicts and compromises on which that community and consensus were based. Ealing declined in the late 1950s: the nostalgic mainstream ethos was no longer appropriate in a period of rapid social change and when the film industry was adapting to competition from television while developing old and new generic themes. Ealing had little appeal for the youth audience who were increasingly drawn by films which celebrated their own experiences and culture. Films which attempted political satire did so at a more direct level than Ealing had attempted. *I'm All Right Jack* (John Boulting, 1959) and *Left, Right and Centre* (Sidney Gilliat, 1959) both reveal a profound disenchantment with notions of community and are suspicious of collective organisation in any form, particularly trade unions and political parties. The Ealing style of comedy, however, has resurfaced on several occasions, for example, Bill Forsyth's *Local Hero* (1983) which like *Whisky Galore!* features 'a familiar interweaving of eccentric, isolated communities and national pride' (Michie, 1986: 268), or Chris Monger's *The Englishman Who Went Up a Hill, But Came Down a Mountain* (1995), 'that Welsh Ealing Comedy the Balcon Boys didn't get around to making' (French, 1995).

The 1950s comic focus on British institutions is also evident in two popular series – the *Doctor* films (directed by Ralph Thomas: *Doctor In the House*, 1954, *Doctor at Sea*, 1955 and *Doctor at Large*, 1957) and the notorious *Carry On*s (Gerald Thomas, 1958–78, 1992). At a subtextual level, the *Doctor* series, starring Dirk Bogarde, was concerned with male adjustments to the welfare state ethos with the nuclear family as its backbone. From this perspective, it can be argued that the welfare state and a reduction in family size threatened traditional male responsibilities. In his discussion of the relevance of horror films to this social theme, Peter Hutchings has made perceptive remarks about the similarly pertinent *Doctor* films: 'while the "Doctor" films can accommodate a 1950s "new man", they work to trivialise and diminish him through humour and ridicule' (Hutchings, 1993: 45). Thus, Bogarde plays Simon Sparrow, an awkward, powerless character who is petrified by women and frustrated by the institutions within which he works. Similarly, the *Carry On* series poked irreverent fun at key British institutions, including the army, the police force, the medical profession, the education system and film genres like the western, James Bond and horror. The successful comic formula bore close resemblance to crude seaside-postcard humour and to music-hall sketches. It involved stereotyping (particularly of women), exaggeration, a plethora of puns and sexual double-entendres executed with lewd professionalism by a team of character actors and actresses, including Sid James, Hattie Jacques, Kenneth Connor, Kenneth Williams, Charles Hawtrey, Barbara Windsor, Joan Sims and Jim Dale.

While censorship was still fairly strict, and overt sexual behaviour was relatively rare on screen, the *Carry On*s thrived in a sexually repressed context as 'a suite in the key of impoliteness' (Medhurst, 1995: 2). Their impoliteness gave the lie to the notion that to be British meant that you were middle class, reticent and well mannered: people in *Carry On* films are generally represented as stupid, sexually unattractive, haughty and selfish. But the humour is more gentle and observant than biting. *Carry On Nurse* (1959) comments on the privileges of private hospital patients. Cosseted in a private room, the Colonel (Wilfred Hyde-White) appears to be a perfectly healthy rascal, obsessed with horse racing and continually interrupting the nurses for trivial requests. At the end of the film, Matron (Hattie Jacques) is amused to see how the nurses have got their revenge by inserting a daffodil into his rectum instead of a thermometer!

Spiv films, film noir and war films

An important series of films dealt with the underworld, crime and corruption: spiv films and British film noirs. Spiv films dealt with criminal activity, particularly that arising out of wartime restrictions. The black market provided opportunities for petty crime rackets and British gangsterdom.

Important films in the post-war cycle of spiv films were *Waterloo Road* (Sidney Gilliat, 1945), introducing greasy Ted Purvis, 'the screen's first fully fledged spiv' (Murphy, 1986: 293); *They Made Me a Fugitive* (Alberto Cavalcanti, 1947), featuring a gang leader called Narcy, 'a truly rotten working-class hero' who 'almost succeeds in proving that the civilized rules of society have not survived the war' (Murphy, 1989: 153); *Brighton Rock* (John Boulting, 1947), an adaptation of Graham Greene's tale of Brighton low-life with tormented protagonist Pinkie, a sadistic Catholic gangster; *It Always Rains on Sunday* (Robert Hamer, 1947), Ealing's portrayal of a spivvish escaped convict who uses his ex-lover to hide from the police; and *The Third Man* (Carol Reed, 1949), with Orson Welles giving his celebrated performance as Harry Lime, racketeer *par excellence*. Lime takes the image of the spiv to extremes: his crime (selling diluted penicillin) is far more horrendous than flogging silk stockings or watches on the black market; whereas many spiv characters are incidental, Lime dominates the film even though he is hardly on screen; the *idea* of Lime as a fondly remembered rascal who has fallen to the depths of materialist corruption, offers a critique of the slippery slope *logic* of spivvery, even linking it with totalitarian ideology. When Lime explains his black-market activities to his friend, Holly Martins (Joseph Cotton), while they are riding high above the city on a Ferris wheel, he invites Martins to contemplate how easy it was for him to commit a horrendous crime when he felt personally distanced from it – if one of the dots (the milling people) below them suddenly stopped, would he care? This makes allusion to the contemporary debates about Nazi responsibility for war crimes when many Nazis claimed that because they were operating according to a strict chain of command, they did not feel personally responsible for the atrocities they committed. This is particularly interesting in terms of the film's address to Britishness, implying that Lime's un-British, proto-fascistic behaviour was something alien to the British character, his penicillin racket being explained to Martins by British Major Calloway (Trevor Howard) as a despicable scheme, the underlying implication being that any spiv activities are dangerous, unpatriotic *and* un-British.

Film noir is a notoriously heterogeneous subgenre, encompassing elements of melodrama, the thriller and even horror, but many British films, particularly in the 1950s, could be said to display the classic, thematic, icon-ographic and stylistic characteristics of American film noir in a British context (see Miller, 1994: 155–64). *The Third Man* and *Brighton Rock* are often referred to as British noirs, with their low-key lighting, troubled male protagonists and focus on corruption and low-life. Marcia Landy has detected 'a respectable number of films that feature a male protagonist victimized by a femme fatale in claustrophobic settings that highlight the instability and paranoid atmosphere of the environment' (Landy, 1991: 266–67). *Daybreak* (Compton Bennett, 1946) featured the infidelity of the femme fatale and *The October Man* (Roy Baker, 1947) involved paranoia and fear of insanity. Looking at their origins in pre-war adaptations of Edgar Wallace novels, Robert Murphy argues that British noirs can best be described as a 'morbid' cycle of films which became increasingly preoccupied with psychology and neurosis in the 1940s (Murphy, 1986: 304).

Many of these anticipated the increasing obsession with male problems and crises of masculinity to be found in 1950s film narratives. *Odd Man Out* (Carol Reed, 1947) features an Irish gunman, Johnny (James Mason), who is wounded after a robbery to raise funds for 'the organisation'. Throughout most of the film Johnny is an outlawed man, hunted by the police until the tragic ending when he dies in a heavy snowfall, with his lover, against a background of high iron gates. Noir stylistics abound: his disorientation is initially conveyed by blurred images and tilted camera angles, and when he is hiding in an air-raid shelter the harsh lighting contrasts convey his mental confusion in Expressionist style to such an extent that he lapses into a dreamlike state, mistaking a child, who has run into the shelter after a runaway ball, for a friend. Most critics applauded the film's realism, Basil Wright going so far as to claim it a 'masterpiece' by 'one of the finest artists the screen has produced in any country' (Wright, 1947). For Edgar Anstey, however, its vision was too bleak, inappropriate in a period of post-war austerity when he felt that people should 'not too readily accept the view that the defeat of all humanity's aspirations is not only inevitable but aesthetically admirable' (Anstey, 1947).

War films returned as a notable genre in the 1950s, but with significant differences from wartime predecessors. Whereas films featuring war subjects, especially at the peak of their production in 1940–43, were concerned with mobilising the 'people's war' which demanded the co-operation of all classes, 1950s war films did not demonstrate the *process* of achieving consensus; instead they simply privileged the middle class and its values unproblematically. As Neil Rattigan has put it: 'This time Britain would not be winning-by-not-losing but be simply winning; and without the awkward (from the dominant ideological point of view) need to draw attention to the contribution required and attained by the working class' (Rattigan, 1994: 150). Instead, the focus of interest in these films is a questioning of heroic values and issues of male identity, most notably in *The Bridge On the River Kwai* (David Lean, 1957) and *The Cruel Sea* (Charles Frend, 1953), 'the closest that British 50s war films came to making an anti-war statement' (Medhurst, 1984: 36). Although the top box-office film *The Dam Busters* (Michael Anderson, 1955) did not question the heroism of war to the same extent, it is a key film in the perpetuation of certain images of the Second World War which have become entrenched in the popular imagination: the ingenuity of British boffins; the romance and superiority of British aircraft; the camaraderie of male groups who fight the enemy in a spirit of sacrifice and professionalism.

Plate 3.2 Barnes Wallis (Michael Redgrave) and Guy Gibson (Richard Todd) plan the *Dam Busters* raid (1955). (Courtesy of Lumière Pictures Limited)

The locales were all-male environments: ships, planes, prisoner-of-war camps; women and the home front were seldom featured. Although *The Dam Busters* is set primarily at home, it rarely strays away from the air-base, except for the opening scenes where inventor Barnes Wallis works at home on plans for a bomb designed to destroy dams in the Ruhr Valley. Combat is never shown, except for the secret mission which the film gradually moves towards, delayed by a series of obstacles which work to create emotional tension as well as suspense. Unlike the episodic, multi-protagonist narratives of many films made in the war, *The Dam Busters* uses a linear narrative punctuated by pauses, setbacks, lulls and a spectacular climax. At first Barnes' tests fail and it looks as if the experiments will have to be abandoned. He faces numerous bureaucratic barriers before the go-ahead is given for his invention, which is sanctioned in the end only because of support from the Air Chief Marshal and intervention from Downing Street. The bombing of the dams can only take place on a specified date when conditions are exactly right. The men chosen for the job are an elite squadron who are not told the full details of the plan until just before the mission.

And so the obstacles, barriers and expectations dominate the mood of the film to such an extent that the pace only slackens in the immediate build-up scenes before the mission. These in turn create even more suspense as the men appear to be waiting for their great moment with cheerful anticipation and suppressed excitement. We are denied the full spectacle of the dams bursting until the last bombs have been dropped.

Exchanges between the men are inarticulate as far as emotional matters are concerned, but the film is certainly not devoid of emotion. This is created via secondary devices, like Guy Gibson's tender affection for his dog, Nigger, whom the other men also love and care for. When he learns that the dog has been run over he blinks awkwardly, says nothing, but later arranges for the dog to be buried at the same time as the squadron takes off for their mission. The distinctive 'Dam Busters' theme music is also used for emotional effect throughout the film, as well as cosy shots of barrack life, the men interacting like pent-up, high-spirited schoolboys in a single-sex environment. Women hardly feature in the film except as cheerful canteen waitresses, handmaidens to heroes. The plan and its evolution dominates everything: when Guy is watching dancing girls at a show he has a brilliant lighting idea which could solve targeting difficulties. His friend mistakes his transfixed expression for lustful glances at the girls! The relationship between Guy and Wallis is characterised by an emotional tension which is never articulated at a verbal level. Wallis' plan soon becomes theirs and the film ends with the two men sharing in the sadness of having lost some of the airmen but also because the project, and presumably their collaboration, has finished. This strategy of raising expectations, dashing them, configuring them differently and so on, has a similar emotional impact as the narrative strategies employed in melodrama. The spectator is left wanting the narrative to continue, hoping that the same conflicting but fascinating sensations of emotional deprivation and gratification will be repeated slightly differently in another film.[5]

Films using a Cold War backdrop sought to demonstrate a rigid polarisation between East and West and were anti-Communist, including *High Treason* (Roy Boulting, 1951), *The Man Between* (Carol Reed, 1953) and *The Young Lovers* (Anthony Asquith, 1954). *The Young Lovers* is the story of an affair between Ted, an American working for the American Embassy in London, and Anna, the daughter of a diplomat from an unnamed Communist country. They are forced to part when their romance is discovered, but Ted runs away with Anna when he finds out that she is pregnant. The American Embassy cannot believe that their romance is not a cover for espionage. The couple are eventually chased to the south coast where a wrecked boat is discovered, leading to the conclusion that the couple drowned in a storm while trying to escape. But the film's final image is of Ted and Anna huddled together in their boat, clearly having survived the storm.

The rigid Cold War ethos is obvious to the point of heavy-handedness throughout *The Young Lovers*: Anna talks of there being no 'third place' to shelter in the conflict between East and West; in Anna's father's house there is a stolid-looking henchman who follows her and listens to her telephone conversations; the American Embassy interprets all Ted's calls to Anna as enemy codes; Anna's unborn child is referred to as 'subversive'. Although the film highlights the problems of such strict opposition between East and West, it offers no real optimism or alternative vision. The lovers are simply presented as unfortunate individuals who were born in the wrong place. Communism is depicted as a force which obliterates individuality: Anna says to her father 'I am not millions, I am me'. Anna wants to defect from her country whereas Ted is loyal to the USA. The final image of them on the boat hardly suggests compensatory optimism: they have each other but nowhere to go.

Science-fiction and horror

Science-fiction films like *Seven Days to Noon* (Roy Boulting, 1950) also related to Cold War themes and, in particular, expressed fear of new technology and the nuclear arms race. A professor who has been working on the atomic bomb is so worried about its potential usage that he threatens to blow up London unless further experiments are halted. In classic suspense formula, he is stopped just in time before the protest bomb explodes, creating an exciting climax. In the process the film nevertheless raises wider questions about the dangers of atomic power.

Science-fiction films were outnumbered by horror, a genre which was especially imaginative and pertinent regarding contemporary social themes. The most commercially successful studio in the late 1950s was Hammer Horror, the key territory in the lost continent of popular British cinema which has been rediscovered by film historians as a crucial component of the national output. The reasons for horror's popularity during this period (and into the 1960s) concern censorship, film industry trends, Hammer as a creative and economic enterprise, and the contemporary social and political context. Censorship restrictions prevented horror films from being made in significant numbers before 1955. The arrival of the 'X' certificate in 1951 encouraged companies to use horror to attract an increasingly younger audience, during a decade when cinema admissions were declining in the face of competition from television and other popular amusements. In just a decade Hammer became an efficient, productive and highly successful studio, thanks to astute management by Anthony Hinds. Although other companies including Amicus, Tyburn and Anglo-Amalgamated made horror films, Hammer produced by far the most popular and distinctive variations of British horror. Although Hammer had been in existence since 1947 it was not until 1955 that it decided to concentrate on the horror genre.

While Ealing's *Dead of Night* (Alberto Cavalcanti, Charles Crichton, Basil Dearden, Robert Hamer, 1945) is a significant British horror film, it did not lead to the generic vitality which was provided by Hammer ten years later. Peter Hutchings has argued that combined with film industry experience, centralisation at Bray Studios and links with an American distributor, Hammer's technical and artistic personnel were particularly attuned to exploit youth-market possibilities (Hutchings, 1993: 39–41). The team of director Terence Fisher and actors Christopher Lee and Peter Cushing provided a style of film which became synonymous with British horror. As well as the quality of the team at Hammer, the studio was unwittingly assisted in its development during the 1950s by having to enter into an agreement for distribution with the American company Robert Lippert Films. The NFFC had ceased funding smaller companies in 1951 which necessitated the arrangement with Lippert for mutual distribution of films in the US and the UK. This required Hammer to alter their style in such a way that had the following effects: 'Hammer's earlier fixity in class and gender matters was radically destabilised. It made a whole tranche of films with its American friends in which the old certainties about pleasure and probity were exploded' (Harper and Porter, 2003: 151). The distinctive use of both Eastmancolor and Technicolor was a key trait of Hammer films, as was the employment of some American actors including Zachary Scott for 'B' features when the tie-in with Lippert had been forged. Gothic themes were favoured at Hammer and an important place was accorded to set design, which was responsible for much of the budget for each film.

Although many of the horror films were set in the past they nevertheless touched on contemporary issues. In his study of the Britishness of Hammer productions 1956–64, Hutchings has identified several trends which related to contemporary themes in an imaginative manner. Whereas American horror and science-fiction films of the period tend to configure the monster, the 'Other', as relating directly to the 'Red menace', i.e. Communism, the British generic variation is slightly different. The unidentified, more amorphous alien threat in the *Quatermass* films (*The Quatermass Experiment*, Val Guest, 1955 and *Quatermass II*, Val Guest, 1957) can, for example, be interpreted as an allusion to Britain's decline as an imperial power: a victim of the international power struggle where the origin or nature of the enemy is not altogether clear (Hutchings, 1993: 41–42). In both these films the unknown force causes terror by unleashing disfiguring fungi which attack the human body, similar to later films in the genre which deal with issues of body horror. *The Quatermass Experiment* features an unknown substance which transmutes flesh into a horrifying fungal form, while *Quatermass II* concerns a fungal growth, again attributable to a mysterious force, which embeds itself into the human face. These films are interesting in the context of anti-nuclear protests in the mid-to-late 1950s, particularly the formation of the Campaign for Nuclear Disarmament (CND), launched in 1958.[6]

Plate 3.3 Britain as the centre of an amorphous threat. Richard Wordsworth in *The Quatermass Experiment* (1955). (Courtesy of Hammer Film Productions)

Another feature of contemporary relevance in Hammer films concerns a more domestic matter. A striking feature of the classic phase of Hammer horror directed by Terence Fisher, including *The Curse of Frankenstein* (1956), *Dracula* (1958), *The Hound of the Baskervilles* (1959) and *The Mummy* (1959), is that the films all contain professionals as major protagonists (doctors, detectives, professors, etc.). The figure of the professional can be related outward from the working ethos of Hammer studios to the rise of the modernising middle class, which was epitomised by Harold Wilson's electoral success in 1964 (ibid.: 60–66).[7]

It seems that the crisis of masculinity which was such a striking feature of many British films of the 1950s was also at the heart of horror. Allied to this, as Harper argues, is a preoccupation, at a symbolic level, with female sexuality. As evident from the *Quatermass* films, the monster can be related to male fears about a mysterious, engulfing alien organism. On the other hand, the *Dracula* films locate sexual pleasure as something to be experienced by the female victims (Harper and Porter, 2003: 145–50). In Hammer horror narratives it is therefore not surprising that the professional's role is to restore order to the chaos which has resulted from a breakdown of patriarchal authority: the repressed surfaces as a nightmare vision of violence and sexuality which must be controlled. This pattern is consistent until *The Gorgon* (Terence Fisher, 1964) when the professional fails to restore order: 'a radical shift is thereby accomplished away from questions of masculinity and male subjectivity to a broader concern with sexuality and gendered society in general' (Hutchings, 1993: 83). Although *The Gorgon* was a box-office failure, the key ideological shift indicated the way forward for subsequent horror films.

No account of horror in the 1950s would be satisfactory without mention of Michael Powell's *Peeping Tom* (1960), panned on release but subsequently claimed (by Martin Scorsese among others) as one of the greatest British films ever made. *Peeping Tom* concerned filmic self-reflexivity which had never been a dominant strain of classic Hammer horror. Along with two other horror films produced by Anglo-Amalgamated – *Horrors of the Black Museum* (Arthur Crabtree, 1959) and *Circus of Horrors* (Sidney Hayers, 1960) – *Peeping Tom* picks up on a fascination with its own vision/look which was evident to a lesser degree in *Dead of Night*. In this sense, the spectator is implicated as a participant observer of the horrors depicted on screen, which perhaps accounts for its hostile critical reception. As Hutchings has pointed out, *Peeping Tom* is riddled with 1950s pornographic iconography, shot in garish colour and with women as its major victims (ibid.: 88). In a literal and metaphoric sense, the technology of photography and film are used as murderous weapons. The narrative is a chilling story of a photographer who films women while he murders them with a spike on the end of his tripod. The victims' expressions are particularly terrified because as they die they can see their distorted reflection in a fish-eye lens he has placed on the front of the camera. It is not difficult to detect problematic male sexuality and fear of independent women as the major reactionary dynamic at work in *Peeping Tom*. In that sense, it is very much a film of its period. In a disturbing way, as Marcia Landy has pointed out,

> sexuality is taken out of the closet and exposed to sight. ... Sex is portrayed as threatening, as aligned with institutional power. The patriarchal family is seen as a reproducer of socially and personally repressive forces, but so is the practice of clinical science, and, for that matter, the cinema.
>
> (Landy, 1991: 430)

These concerns are also evident in British social-problem films of the 1950s and 1960s.

Social-problem films, kitchen sink dramas and Free Cinema

The liberalisation of censorship encouraged films which broached taboo subjects. These were often marketed for their X-rated shockability factor, but this time realism rather than horror or escapism was the order of the day. The industry's concern over declining box-office attendance created a receptive climate for new themes and independent companies which were prepared to take risks. When these paid off, for the first time British film-making received substantial sponsorship from American backers, although it should be stressed that dollars primarily backed top box-office James Bond and the Beatles' films rather than kitchen sink dramas (see Murphy, 1992: 256–75). The critically praised New Wave films of the early 1960s had their roots in a number of earlier films, including *It Always Rains On Sunday* (Robert Hamer, 1947), *The Blue Lamp* (Basil Dearden, 1950), *Yield To the Night* (J. Lee Thompson, 1956) and *Victim* (Basil Dearden, 1961), which aimed to expose and explore issues such as criminality, juvenile delinquency, capital punishment and homosexuality. These tended to reinforce dominant concerns about social developments in a period when an increasing number of investigations, official reports and surveys revealed the state's anxious and confused response to social change. A similar ideological perspective can be discerned in cultural documents, including films. Fears which were articulated most consistently at textual and subtextual levels concerned the consequences of consumerism, greater class mobility, more women in the workforce, sexuality, and disaffection between the generations.

Although a genre of films which could be labelled 'social problem', dealing with some elements of working-class life and issues, did exist before 1956 (see Landy, 1991: 432–82), the distinctive 'kitchen sink' cycle which lasted until about 1963 is historically specific and consolidated the genre's visibility and critical reputation in important ways. Realism was given a poetic imperative by Lindsay Anderson, Karel Reisz, Tony Richardson and other practitioners of 'Free Cinema' documentaries, first shown at the National Film Theatre, London, 1956–59, which provided them with training and credibility before they ventured into kitchen sink features. The term Free Cinema referred to the belief shared by the documentarists that cinema should be freed from commercial constraints and look back for inspiration to Grierson's documentary movement of the 1930s (this will be discussed in Chapter 7). Imbued with a critical spirit of auteurism and in a tradition of benevolent middle-class humanism, Anderson's group wanted films to be personal statements, giving the director total control to celebrate what they called 'the poetry of the everyday'. Like the French *nouvelle vague*, the films were connected with critical writings in magazines like *Sequence* and were particularly concerned to present themselves as opposed to 'the pressures of conformism and commercialism' (Free Cinema programme notes) in mainstream film-making, particularly associated with Rank. In many ways the New Wave was janus-faced: it looked back to realist traditions but at the same time aimed to broach controversial subject matter. Studio sets were rejected in favour of location shooting and colour replaced by black and white, often grainy images. The Free Cinema films resembled Humphrey Jennings' wartime documentaries in their celebration of working-class community and focused on the lives of particular groups of working people: Lindsay Anderson made a film about a Margate amusement arcade called *O Dreamland* (1953) and his *Every Day Except Christmas* (1957) was about the people who worked in Covent Garden market. Reisz's documentary about a London youth club, *We Are the Lambeth Boys* (1959), prompted him to explore the working-class individual in a fictional context with Alan Sillitoe's screen adaptation of his novel *Saturday Night and Sunday Morning* (1960). This shift is indicative of the films' general indebtedness to plays and novels written by a new generation of working-class authors in the 1950s, angry young men like John Braine, Alan Sillitoe and David Storey, and other writers including John Osborne and John Wain, who were primarily in revolt against literary modernism (see Ritchie, 1988).

The New Wave and the 1960s

Historian Arthur Marwick (1996: 9) has argued that the upheavals of the 1960s had a profound impact on British society, an impact which from many different perspectives was as significant as the upheavals wrought by the Second World War. But it is also important to note that the 1960s saw an accentuation of many of the trends which were already under way in the 1950s: the expansion of youth culture; consumerism; official concern about morality; permissiveness; and the persistence of class and racial conflict. A Labour Government was elected in October 1964, with Prime Minister Harold Wilson representing the future of technological change and demonstrating that ex-grammar school boys from the north of England could reach the highest positions of political office.[8] But, as with the post-1945 period, the existence of a Labour Government did not mean that class divisions were eroded, and many sections of the working class still experienced profound economic difficulties despite the media's obsession with affluence and the 'swinging sixties'. Indeed, the concept of the 'swinging sixties' emphasised certain trends (the expansion of boutiques, fashion photography, the permissive society, drugs and pop culture) at the expense of others which were of equal, if not more, significance.

There were many contradictory developments in the 1960s which the ebullient image of rampant hedonism rather overlooked. Many issues which went on to become polarised sites of social and political conflict were clearly gathering momentum. On the one hand, the often racist, anti-immigration sentiments of the 1950s persisted while, on the other, there was support for legislation against racial discrimination.[9] The decade was also somewhat confused about the relationship between regionalism and metropolitan centralism: there was an active revival of the Scottish Nationalist movement and a pronounced cultural awareness of regionalism, while the ethos of 'swinging London' dictated that aspiring youngsters could only explore their destiny in London, as the world's most exciting capital city. In this context, the films of the period can be read as cultural expressions of the decade's oscillation between optimism and pessimism, certainty and uncertainty.

As in the 1950s, the traditional family unit continued to be threatened by rising divorce rates. A social survey carried out in 1969 showed that despite the availability of the contraceptive pill, two-fifths of couples did not use birth control. The pill tended to be used by better-off married women and even though the permissive society was often used as a description of the sexual behaviour of young people, 'sexual permissiveness was far from rampant in the late sixties' (Marwick, 1996: 170). The stigma of unwanted pregnancy was certainly a very real fear for many women in the early 1960s, as many of the films indicate.

The New Wave and mainstream cinema

The 1960s was an exciting period for British cinema, producing critically applauded New Wave films as well as more popular genres at the box office, which will both be examined in this section. Indeed, the decade can be described as a period when there were 'a greater number of significant and exciting films made in Britain than at any time before or since' (Murphy, 1992: 278). The coincidence of timing between the British New Wave and French *nouvelle vague* might invite comparisons on an aesthetic level, assessing to what extent the British example constituted a break with past themes and cinematic traditions. As already indicated, realism was an already established cinematic tradition which these films simply took further in their concern to provide cultural authenticity in the period's spirit of sociological enquiry. Obtrusive cinematic devices were not a feature and most films employed broadly classical narrative structures. Occasionally, however, sound and image were integrated in an extremely sophisticated manner, as in the Goose Fair sequence in *Saturday Night and Sunday Morning* when Arthur Seaton (Albert Finney) is being chased by the angry husband of a woman with whom he has been having an affair, and the husband's army mates who are also close on Arthur's heels. The sequence relies on the juxtaposition of fluid and static camera-work, editing for suspense, low-key lighting and a soundtrack almost entirely without dialogue which is matched to the images at significant points, ranging from traditional fairground music, jazz, pop music and silence. Writing in 1960, Charles Barr called this sequence 'perhaps the best ten minutes in any British film', arguing that Reisz, 'free to take his time, and to assert his personality as a director . . . has moved successfully from documentary to fiction' (Barr, 1960). The director assumed an accentuated role in the marketing and critical reception of these films. Location shooting was another distinctive element, with many sequences totally given to displaying the industrial landscape, revealing authorial rather than narrative motivation (see Higson, 1984b; Hill, 1986: 129–32). There was an emphasis on working-class characters as central protagonists and a concern, particularly in films like *Saturday Night and Sunday Morning* and *This Sporting Life* (Lindsay Anderson, 1963), to probe their inner motivations. Despite Joe Lampton's bitter protestations that 'it's old-fashioned, all that class stuff', some attempt was made in *Room at the Top* (Jack Clayton, 1959) to present the class question on a more sophisticated level than in previous films, exposing the fallacy that Britain was an increasingly classless society.

John Hill (1986), however, has argued that the New Wave films of 1956–63 by no means reveal a progressive image of society in that period. Although new themes were introduced to the cinema screens, they were presented in such a way as to reveal an intensely traditional and conservative bias. Many of the films concern the problems of young men who feel trapped by a provincial and class background, in search of an affluent lifestyle which will enable them to forget all about class barriers and marital obligations, move to London and become successful. But this scenario is shown to be fundamentally flawed, even dangerous: in *Room at the Top*, Joe Lampton's (Laurence Harvey) ruthless attempt at class mobility by marrying the boss's daughter leaves him utterly miserable and is achieved at the expense of a woman he really loves and who is the moral force of the film; *A Kind of Loving* (John Schlesinger, 1962) ends with the young man trapped in marriage, and in *Billy Liar* (John Schlesinger, 1963) the young man never does escape to London, preferring to live in his own fantasy world. The depiction of women in most of the films is dismissive: they are shown as the new consumers of television sets and washing machines, out to trap men into marriage by becoming pregnant, and often possessing little intelligence. In *Look Back In Anger* (Tony Richardson, 1959), Jimmy Porter (Richard Burton) is a particularly misogynistic character and indicative of the film's general tendency to vaunt social discontent and masculinist anxieties regarding women and effeminacy. But it is important to bear in mind, as Robert Murphy suggests, that although women in the kitchen sink cycle suffer to a great degree, several of the key female characters 'have a seriousness, an emotional weight, altogether lacking in the pathetically trivial roles women had to play in most 1950s British films' (Murphy, 1992: 33).

A notable example is *A Taste of Honey* (Tony Richardson, 1961), an adaptation of Shelagh Delaney's first play, written in 1958. Tony Richardson was keen on making maximum use of location shooting (Manchester, Blackpool) and used Walter Lassally, cinematographer on some of the Free Cinema documentaries. Authentic location work was a hallmark of the New Wave films, as was the employment of young, untried actors, in this case Rita Tushingham who had been picked from a Liverpool repertory company in 1960 to perform in *The Knack* at the Royal Court. Unusually for the kitchen sink cycle, the focus is on Jo, a young woman, and her relationships with several key characters: her mother, Helen, and Helen's young lover, Peter; Jimmy, a black sailor with whom Jo has a transient relationship resulting in pregnancy; and Geoff, a homosexual who wants to take care of her and her baby.[10] Not much affluence is evident in *A Taste of Honey* as the characters roam a sparse industrial landscape punctuated by canals, docksides and bleak hillsides. Helen and Jo's first flat is squalid and all the characters struggle to survive material hardship and emotional crises: Helen's insecurity around Peter; Jo's fears for herself, her baby and the future in general; Geoff's presentation of himself as an outcast who desperately wants to be involved with Jo and her baby. As John Hill has pointed out, the ending of the film is deeply ambivalent: Jo chooses her mother over Geoff in her time of crisis as she is about to give birth. He is excluded by dint of his sexuality and mother and daughter are reunited as 'second best' in the absence of a father and 'proper' family relations(Hill, 1986: 167). *A Taste of Honey* is therefore a film which probes female subjectivity to a further degree than most of the New Wave films, but nevertheless at narrative closure subscribes to a similar conservative ideological trajectory. But it is important to remember that while Geoff's effeminacy is criticised, he nevertheless plays a key role in Jo's development, offering her friendship when she is at a low ebb, pregnant and alone: a far cry from the angry young man of other social realist films. Also, as Lovell argues (in Higson, 1996: 172–77), the film is distinctive in the sense that it contains feminine sensibilities on many levels, and not just regarding the female characters. The result is a film in which generation role-reversal occurs (between Jo and her mother Helen) as well as Jimmie and Geoff being worlds away from the 'Angry Young Men' of other films taken to be representative of the cycle. Indeed, as Taylor (2006) has demonstrated, much is to be gained by looking at the films of this period discretely rather than assuming that they can only be analysed as a coherent cycle. Analyses which proceed on an individual basis reveal many intriguing formal patterns within each film which may or may not relate to social problems of the time or to 'new wave' cinema as a critical construction.

This points to certain cycles of film often obtaining an excessive amount of attention in film histories at the exclusion of others which may have been more popular with audiences. Indeed, according to *Kinematograph Weekly's* box-office surveys for the 1960s, most of the New Wave social-problem films did not make as much money as *Carry On*s, pop musicals, the James Bond cycle, horror or big-budget adventure spectacles. In 1960, for example, the top box-office winners were *Ben Hur* (US, MGM), *Can-Can* (US, Twentieth-Century Fox), *Doctor In Love* (UK, Rank), *Sink the Bismarck* (US, Twentieth-Century Fox) and *Carry On Constable* (UK, Anglo-Amalgamated). British films which scored highly in subsequent

Plate 3.4 Shooting *A Taste of Honey* (1961) on location in Manchester.
(Copyright MCMLXI Woodfall Films Ltd. All Rights Reserved)

surveys were – 1961: *Saturday Night and Sunday Morning**; 1962: *The Young Ones* and *Dr No*; 1963: *From Russia With Love, Summer Holiday* and *Tom Jones*; 1964: *A Hard Day's Night* and *Goldfinger*; 1965: *Those Magnificent Men In Their Flying Machines, Help!, A Shot In the Dark* and *Carry On Cleo*; 1966: *Khartoum, The Blue Max, Thunderball, Alfie, Born Free* and *The Great St Trinian's Train Robbery*; 1967: *A Man for All Seasons, You Only Live Twice, The Family Way*, Casino Royale* and *One Million Years BC*; 1968: *Half a Sixpence, Far From the Madding Crowd, 2001: A Space Odyssey, Up the Junction*, Poor Cow*, Here We Go Round the Mulberry Bush** and *Carry On Doctor*; 1969: *Oliver!, Chitty Chitty Bang Bang, Where Eagles Dare, Battle of Britain, Carry On Camping, Half a Sixpence, Oh! What a Lovely War* and *Carry On Up the Khyber*. Although many of these films had American backing, they were registered as British and reflect the dominant generic trends of the 1960s. Out of a total of the 42 films listed above, only five (marked *) could be described as social problem or New Wave.

American musicals did very well at the box office, most notoriously *The Sound of Music* (1965), *My Fair Lady* (1964) and *Mary Poppins* (1964), all top box-office hits of 1965. By 1970 American musicals were still big money-spinners: *Paint Your Wagon* (1969) and *Hello, Dolly!* (1969). Although *Oliver!* (Carol Reed, 1968) and *Chitty Chitty Bang Bang* (Ken Hughes, 1968) indicated British involvement in the revival of traditional musicals, the British contribution was more notably concentrated in the subgenre of the pop musical, starring Cliff Richard (*Expresso Bongo*, Val Guest and Wolf Mankowitz, 1959, *The Young Ones*, Sidney J. Furie, 1961, *Summer Holiday*, Peter Yates, 1962 and *Wonderful Life*, Furie, 1964); the Beatles (*A Hard Day's Night*, Richard Lester, 1964 and *Help!*, Richard Lester, 1965) and the Dave Clark Five (*Catch Us If You Can*, John Boorman, 1965). These capitalised on the British pop invasion which began in the early 1960s, the increasing visibility of youth culture and concerns about generational conflict.

Although Richard Lester's films were the boldest in terms of stylistic innovation, they frequently utilised familiar themes from the musical genre. *A Hard Day's Night* conveyed what it felt like to be a Beatle at a key point in the group's career when they were on the verge of becoming international pop stars. The pseudo-documentary style shows them at work and at play, working-class lads who use their wit and talent to survive the ruthless media and pressures of Beatlemania. Like the 1930s backstage musicals, *A Hard Day's Night* asserts the superiority and revelational qualities of its medium: cinema. Lester's camera exposes the relentless hounding of 'the boys' by the middle-class media, particularly journalism and television. As the essential audience, the fans are not subject to a similar critique. Instead, the film reaffirms the tradition of showmanship and vitality residing in the relationship between performers and audience, albeit frantic and sexual in this case (see Ehrenreich, Hess and Jacobs, 1992). Escape is an important theme in *A Hard Day's Night*: to get away from fans and the media the Beatles flee from a fire escape at the back of a television studio. The sequence then becomes a musical number ('Can't Buy Me Love'), punctuated by Lester's jump-cuts, with the Beatles at last appearing to be free and happy. As soon as the song is over they are reprimanded for being on private property, a narrative device which marks the song off as a brief non-naturalist interlude when the *cinema* audience alone is privileged to enjoy what Lester promotes as the essence of the real Beatles: they *are* their music. This performs the dual commercial function of addressing the cinema audience *and* the record-buying public who have come to see the film partly to hear the songs.

Related to the pop musicals were the Swinging London films, films which embraced elements of pop and youth culture and examined different facets of metropolitan affluence and the myth of the permissive society. As Robert Murphy has pointed out, key films in the cycle – *The Knack* (Richard Lester, 1965), *Alfie* (Lewis Gilbert, 1966) and *Georgy Girl* (Silvio Narizzano, 1966)

– reflected ambivalent attitudes towards the supposed excitement of living in London in the 1960s (see Murphy, 1992: 139–60). *The Knack* opens with a startling sequence when country girl Nancy (Rita Tushingham) is introduced to the sexual mores of the big city. Sex is a commodity as girls queue up to satisfy Tolen (Ray Brooks), who is proud of his reputation of having the knack of attracting girls. Instead of succumbing to Tolen's sexual reputation Nancy falls for a gawky, wimpish teacher (Michael Crawford), a choice which represents the film's critique of the permissive society and the commodification of sex. Nancy's rebellion against Tolen includes her crying 'Rape!' repeatedly to advertise the fact that he is not sexually irresistible, and she also bursts the tyres of his motorbike, a symbol of his masculine and sexual prowess. These veiled critiques of 'Swinging London' resurfaced more obtrusively later in *Up the Junction* (Peter Collinson, 1967) and *Poor Cow* (Ken Loach, 1967), films which depicted London life as materially and emotionally desolate. According to this logic, Billy in *Billy Liar* was wise not to follow Julie Christie to London, retreating into his safe world of inner fantasy amid provincial conservatism. Yet the startling sequence of Christie, swinging her bag past C & A with not a care in the world, stays with us as representative of the dreams many had, and still have, of what it means to escape to the big city of bright lights and false promises.

The fantasy of independence and escape manifested itself in other films which can be interpreted as complex offshoots from both the Swinging London genre and pop musicals. *Blow-Up* (Michelangelo Antonioni, 1967) and *Performance* (Donald Cammell and Nicolas Roeg, 1970) were set in London. Both dealt broadly with the theme of image and reality and could be said to operate in a rapidly emerging postmodern environment of blurred geographic boundaries and shifting sexual identities.[11] The critique of the media is evident in *Blow-Up* as Thomas, a successful fashion photographer (modelled on David Bailey and Donald McCullin), tries to make sense of material he has accidentally shot, possibly of a murder in a park. His search for truth is, however, thwarted, conforming to the film's general depiction of 'a society paralysed by its own distractions' (Walker, 1974: 327), unable to make meaning of its existence. *Performance* takes the element of masquerade implied by its title to extreme proportions when the film's two central characters, Turner (Mick Jagger), a retired pop star and Chas (James Fox), a gangster on the run, appear to assume increasingly interchangeable identities when Chas hides out in Turner's house. In a famous sequence, Chas' violent criminal activities are intercut with scenes from an Old Bailey trial, implying that gangsterdom and the law are similarly corrupt. The relationship between Chas and Turner (Chas looking increasingly like Turner towards the end of the film) and the bisexuality of Turner's female companions, calls into question boundaries of gender and sexuality. As Peter Wollen has commented: 'Chas surrounds himself with an armour of masculinity to deny his own femaleness. Turner surrounds himself with a cocoon of femininity to deny his maleness, his violence' (Wollen, 1995: 23). As the Rolls-Royce drives off at the end of the film it seems as if its occupant has shed both protective armour and nurturing cocoon. *Performance* can also be usefully related to the sub-genre of the 'underworld' crime film analysed by Chibnall and Murphy (1999). This sub-genre has roots in earlier films including *They Made Me a Fugitive* (Alberto Cavalcanti, 1947), *Brighton Rock* and *Night and the City* (Jules Dassin, 1950). These demonstrate that 'noir' was evident in non-US films, constituting many 'B' films of the 1950s in particular. Chibnall has argued that these films continued to be significant in the 1960s and have been overshadowed by social realist films of the period. Yet 'underworld' films such as *The Frightened City* (John Lemont, 1961) and *Hell Is a City* (Val Guest, 1960) similarly relate to 1960s concerns such as 'cultural vulnerability, commercial reorganisation and moral deviation' (Chibnall and Murphy, 1999: 108). *Get Carter* (Mike Hodges, 1971) was a significant film in this regard, set in Newcastle on the theme of a gangland killing and showing that distinctive evocation of place was not confined to the 'New Wave'.

One of the most popular 1960s genres was the James Bond cycle which began with *Dr No* (Terence Young, 1962), a new Bond film being released practically every year until *You Only Live Twice* (Lewis Gilbert, 1967), after which the pace abated somewhat when Sean Connery decided to step down as Bond until his brief reappearance in *Diamonds Are Forever* (Guy Hamilton, 1971). British and made at Pinewood, these films were backed by American dollars (United Artists) as the major component of the Hollywood, England trend – dollars which kept flowing into Bond films long after American capital was withdrawn from the rest of the British industry at the end of the decade. Like other successful British genres (Gainsborough melodramas, Ealing comedies, Hammer horror and the *Carry On*s), a secure production-base provided a long-serving technical and creative team who worked towards perfecting the Bondian formula. This involved exotic foreign locations; gadgets/special effects; huge sets; elaborate and exciting action sequences which are defused after their climax by comedy; the basic Bond persona developed by Sean Connery and elaborated somewhat in later incarnations; an unknown leading girl who has a bit more to her than the film's other women, whose function is primarily for sexual titillation; suspicious foreigners out to destroy the world and whose characterisations border on the racist; a memorable title song for each film which is woven around the original Bond theme; a distinctive pre-credit sequence; a big budget and a high-profile marketing campaign.

In terms of ideology, the Bond films were not escapist aberrations. They can be related to other British films of the period with their stress on technology and its potential to serve and destroy. Bond's globe-trotting and proven success with women reveals another, fantasy aspect of the social realist films' masculine nightmare of being trapped in the provinces with a wife and family. In keeping with British films which displayed anxiety about female sexuality, the only difficult, easily expendable women in Bond films are lesbian and/or in the service of the villain. With the retreat of the Cold War the Englishness of Bond betrayed a concern to insert a comforting national stereotype (particularly with Roger Moore's Bond) into a world which is increasingly governed by international forces and threatened by an unidentified enemy. They created a sense of nostalgia for imperialism and an optimistic faith in Anglo-American co-operation, themes which relate very much to their time of release. As I have argued elsewhere, they also relate to Anglo-American relations, as well as to the figure of Bond as an individualist figure who, particularly via the casting of Connery, a Scottish actor, 'represented "Britishness" of a meritocratic rather than a class-based nature'; Connery's Bond did not possess the same class inflections as his superiors (Street, 2002: 189).

American investment resulted in a variety of British films which looked back to past genres and anticipated new developments. *Tom Jones* (Tony Richardson, 1963) was a lavish costume picture in the Korda and Gainsborough mould, but which included even more eroticism and visual pleasure. Its rich colour photography and sumptuous sets anticipated Ken Russell's period dramas including *Women In Love* (1969), which in turn influenced art film-makers like Derek Jarman. Anti-war films, particularly *The Charge of the Light Brigade* (Tony Richardson, 1968) and *Oh! What a Lovely War* (Richard Attenborough, 1969) anticipated the sentiment of anti-Vietnam War films. Looking at the 1960s from a British generic perspective is complicated by the internationalisation of the industry, not only in financial terms but also because of the plethora of foreign directors who worked in Britain, including Roman Polanski, Michelangelo Antonioni, Stanley Kubrick and Joseph Losey. It is often argued that they were particularly well placed to examine Britain with their critical outsider insight, a strategy utilised by Losey in his collaborations with Harold Pinter, *The Servant* (1963) and *Accident* (1967), and his 1970 adaptation of L. P. Hartley's novel *The Go-Between*.

While *The Servant* dissects the upper-middle class with a degree of astute observation, it is perhaps most notable for its cinematography by ex-Ealing Douglas Slocombe and its premiere in November 1963, just after the news broke of the Profumo affair.[12] The film's major protagonist, Tony (James Fox), is an upper-middle-class ex-army officer who buys a smart London house and employs Barratt (Dirk Bogarde) as his servant, whom he treats like a batman. Barratt gradually assumes control over Tony's life by establishing domestic control, alienating Tony's girlfriend Susan (Wendy Craig) and making Tony emotionally dependent on him by encouraging his homosexual tendencies. Tony represents upper-middle-class weakness in a civilian world where military boundaries are no longer tenable but it is tempting to interpret the film's confused and chaotic ending, with Tony

Plate 3.5 Mirror images: master–servant, servant–master? Barratt (Dirk Bogarde) and Tony (James Fox) in *The Servant* (1963). (Courtesy of Lumière Pictures Limited)

having sunk to the lowest depths at the hands of the manipulative, evil Barratt, as a reactionary plea *for* the certainties of class boundaries. If the servant becomes master, the film argues, the result is chaos.

Far more radical was Lindsay Anderson's *If . . .* (1968) which critiques a world ordered by elitism, hierarchy, discipline and tradition. Anderson takes a public school as a metaphor for Britain, particularly the codes and conventions of its ruling class, with rebel boys led by Mick (Malcolm McDowell) taking direct action at the end when they bomb and machine-gun dignitaries, governors and masters on Founder's Day. Like *The Servant*, the film had topical currency, coinciding with the student revolts of 1968. Unlike Barratt's sinister conquest of Tony, the boys' rebellion in *If . . .* is represented as a utopian triumph for youth over a nonsensical world which is crumbling under its own absurdity and obsolescence. The sense of actual triumph is, however, ambivalent, as Anderson has pointed out: 'I was surprised that young people cheered that ending when it first came out. Perhaps they didn't look beyond the end, because it's very difficult for me to imagine that Mick is going to win' (interview with Anderson by Friedman and Stewart, 8 June 1989 in Dixon, 1994: 167). While notable for its inclusion of surreal elements, the film is distinctive in a formal way but this again perhaps militates against it as a radical text since its codes of insurrection are consigned to the imaginary realm of possibility rather than practicality.

If . . . shares thematic similarities with other 1960s films which were politically conscious from completely different generic perspectives, including *Privilege* (Peter Watkins, 1967) which dealt with a pop star who is manipulated by a repressive government in league with the Church, and *Kes* (Ken Loach, 1969), a sensitive study of Billy (David Bradley), a young boy from Barnsley whose success at training a kestrel is achieved against the odds of a repressive and unenlightened school background. One exceptional teacher, played by Colin Welland, shows an interest in Billy and his kestrel, suggesting a glimmer of hope in an otherwise grim picture of new schools built to cater for children from housing estates, whose teachers govern by bullying and corporal punishment. When Billy visits the employment office he is offered little hope for the future, fearing that he will become a miner like his brother, who kills Billy's kestrel out of revenge after a family squabble. The death of the kestrel is symbolic of Billy's desperate position in an adult world which has more or less failed to communicate with him. He tells Welland that he admires the kestrel because of its independence and individuality – qualities which are hardly encouraged in Billy.

Appearing ten years after the first New Wave films, *Kes* is listed as a 'money maker' in *Kinematograph Weekly's* annual survey of 1970, along with a handful of horror films, musicals, a James Bond and a *Carry On*. It is another example of a film which draws on previous generic trends but incorporates new elements. Like many films in the early 1960s it was based on a novel, made on a very low budget (£157,000), produced by Woodfall Films and financed by United Artists. *Kes* is similar in its regional locale and working-class characters to the New Wave films of the early 1960s. Billy's brother, Jed, is a miner who displays much of the angst of the angry young men of the earlier films. Like Arthur in *Saturday Night and Sunday Morning*, his life is governed by strict divisions between work and leisure time and on his nights off he is 'on the pull' for girls. The film also shares the same uncertain sense of the future that was a feature of so many New Wave dramas. But *Kes* is different in several important ways. The location shooting trend is taken to an extreme and shots of the industrial landscape are integrated with the narrative by including the kestrel as an important narrative and symbolic feature. Shot in colour (invested with a realist ethos), it frequently juxtaposes background shots of the pit with nearby countryside, high- and low-angle shots of the kestrel as it swoops over fields and trees. Rather than dwelling on the pit, the changing face of the landscape is also a key feature: terraced houses, new housing estates, Billy's ten-year-old school and the town centre are suggestive of the co-existence of different values, different generations and destinations. By focusing on Billy, an adolescent, rather than on Jed, *Kes* defuses the focus on male anxieties, although Jed tells Billy that he needs to be more of 'a man' to go down the pit and his schoolteachers frequently comment on his waif-like appearance. Masculine values are satirised throughout the film. In a comic sequence of a football match, Billy's Physical Education teacher struts and shouts at a group of less than enthusiastic boys who realise that the game is being played more for his benefit than theirs. Women are not presented as the root of the problem: Billy's mother is a sympathetic character who shows him some sensitivity and stands up to her son Jed when he tries to posture as the man of the house. From this perspective it can be argued that *Kes* draws on some of the established generic codes of social realism but, at the same time, prefigures the films of Terence Davies which appear in part to draw on that heritage.[13] In many ways the legacy of the New Wave and Sixties cinema was therefore janus-faced, looking back to notions of poetic realism but at the same time anticipating some of the diverse and contradictory trends which characterised British film production in the 1970s and beyond.

Chapter 4

Genres in transition: 1970s to 1990s

THE 1970s: A SOCIETY AND A FILM INDUSTRY IN DECLINE

British society had not undergone a fundamental transformation in the 1960s, the class system remaining broadly intact with the 'permissive society' being somewhat of a misnomer (see Marwick, 1990: 154, 170). There was a sense, however, that 'life was lived with greater gusto than ever' (ibid.: 152), despite many of the fears expressed in 1960s cinema regarding the consequences for class, consumerism and particularly female independence. Yet these concerns reverberated well into the 1970s when social conditions had deteriorated and particular conflicts, which had been brewing under the surface in the 1960s, became acute. These conflicts primarily concerned industrial relations, race and gender, a volatile melting-pot of issues which were symptomatic of Britain's more fundamental malaise.

The 1970s was a decade of economic contraction blighted by industrial strife. The most notorious incidences were the bitter miners' strikes in 1972 and 1974, which led to the defeat of the Conservative Government. And, in turn, widespread strikes during the 'Winter of Discontent' of 1978–79 brought down James Callaghan's Labour Government. Economic insecurity, unemployment and deteriorating industrial relations provided the general background to a growing division between the north and the south of Britain: the north being depressed and in decline while the south remained relatively prosperous. Affluence had done little to reduce the historic geographical divide, which was exacerbated by Britain's protracted industrial decline. Although class conflict showed no sign of disappearing, and powerful positions continued to be dominated by the upper classes, there was nevertheless some blurring of the distinctions between classes (Marwick, 1996: 209–10). On the other hand, race was developing into one of the most acutely divisive issues in Britain in the 1970s, with the racist National Front frequently attacking ethnic minorities and their supporters. Post-1970s changes will be described later in this chapter, but it is important to signal the persistence of racial conflict, a stark continuity with previous decades. There was also considerable anti-Irish feeling as 'the Troubles' in Northern Ireland escalated and the Irish Republican Army instituted a terrorist campaign in Britain.[1] As far as gender relations were concerned the second wave of feminism, which was becoming increasingly vociferous, exacerbated masculinist anxieties about women in the workforce and the erosion of traditional family values.[2] These broad social and economic conditions formed the backdrop of British genre production which continued to offer a pertinent guide to shifts in social anxieties and behaviour, if not as obviously as in previous decades when more films were made and there was greater continuity of production.

After the popular and critical success of British cinema in the 1960s, during the following decade the film industry was undergoing a period of stagnation. As American finance was withdrawn and with minimal state support for British films, the industry was left in a vulnerable position, the total number of feature films produced falling from 98 in 1971 to 36 by 1981 (Wood, 1983: 143). Cinema admissions were declining at the same time as the popularity of television and other amusements increased, a trend the arrival of multiplexes in the mid-1970s could not reverse. Cinema-going was no longer *the* mass entertainment of the British population and many film producers attempted to carve some sort of a niche for themselves in an ever-shrinking market. Surveys showed that the British audience was very young, a consideration which therefore influenced the direction of many genres. New formulas were sought, as traditional genres struggled to keep up with technological change and competition from television, latching on to ideas like the television spin-offs described below, or to the exploitation of stars in the popular music industry. As we shall see, some of these strategies were more successful than others. Overall, the 1970s were interesting years when producers either reacted defensively to the difficult economic context in which they were forced to operate, or they thought big, gambling recklessly against the odds. It is paradoxical that during this period of decline in the film industry trends nevertheless emerged which contributed to the industry's revival in the 1980s, inaugurating developments in the heritage/costume genre, the action film and hybrids which exploited film as film spectacle, not as a poor relation to television or to popular music.

Horror, science-fiction and comedy

Horror continued to be a significant genre well into the mid-1970s when it entered a period of stagnation and decline, along with the rest of British film production. In the 1960s there were significant developments which drew on conventions established by Hammer yet at the same time incorporated new stylistic trends and reflected contemporary anxieties. As Peter Hutchings has pointed out, during the years 1964–66 the major changes concerned formal innovations (including stylised dream sequences, colour cinematography and slow motion), and after 1967 there was an increasing thematic preoccupation with male insecurity which we have observed in other genres. *The Sorcerers* (Michael Reeves, 1967), *Witchfinder General* (Michael Reeves, 1968) and *The Devil Rides Out* (Terence Fisher, 1968) 'all articulate a situation in which a securing of a fixed male identity depends upon a violent objectification of the women that previously in the genre had been taken for granted' (Hutchings, 1993: 156). The profitability Hammer had experienced, largely influenced by American connections forged in the early 1950s, had abated by the late 1960s. After the box-office failure of *Taste the Blood of Dracula* (Peter Sasdy, 1970) the studio did not recover, transferring its sponsorship to TV spin-off films by the early 1970s. Directors such as Pete Walker with a background in exploitation cinema, were able to experiment with horror. Walker's films *House of Whipcord* (1974), *Frightmare* (1974) and *House of Mortal Sin* (1975) featured graphic depictions of violence that Chibnall (1998) argues relate to the 1970s for their attacks on the hypocrisy of establishment authority figures such as judges, priests or matriarchs while at the same time highlighting the ineffectualness of youth and counter-culture. Walker worked outside conventional studio structures, financing and directing the majority of his films.

Hammer was not the only studio producing horror films in this period. Another prolific producer of films was Amicus, a British company founded by two Americans living in the UK. Hutchings has argued that Amicus has been relatively neglected in surveys of British cinema because they do not easily fit into accounts that locate Gothic as a primary influence on horror (Hutchings in Chibnall and Petley 2002: 131–44). Amicus-produced horrors featured stars who were known actors in the genre, including Christopher Lee and Peter Cushing, and they adopted the narrative model of different stories, some of them connected by a key event or location. Some were linked by a 'master of ceremonies' host figure, such as the *Dr Terror* films (for example *Dr Terror's House of Horrors*, 1964). As Hutchings points out, many of the films can be related to their time of production and to their British origins since they 'feel very British, not just in terms of their casts and settings but also in their attention to and familiarity with the minutiae of British life' (Hutchings in Chibnall and Petley, 2002: 142). Other important horror films of the period include those which have acquired cult status: *Witchfinder General* and *The Wicker Man* (Robin Hardy, 1973), films which deal with the occult, pagan worship, witchcraft and, as observed above, male angst.

Independent women are the chief targets of these films: they are punished and murdered for their sins, until the fascinating figure Carmilla, lesbian vampire, offers a compelling portrait of a strong, sexual and powerful woman in *The Vampire Lovers* (Roy Ward Baker, 1970). Although she featured in two subsequent horror films, *The Vampire Lovers* went the furthest in representing her as the driving force of the narrative, although it should be noted that her power was usually checked by the films' apparent affirmation of the male gaze. Along with the strong maternal figures in several films, including *Countess Dracula* (Peter Sasdy, 1970) and *Blood From the Mummy's Tomb* (Seth Holt, 1971), Carmilla represents 'a definite rupture within British horror, a moment of potential change, a partial moving away from an objectification of the female, which is quickly closed down' (ibid.: 183). In Carmilla's case, the repression of this potential in *The Vampire Lovers* involved suggesting a male omniscient presence (the narrator Count Karnstein) who controls the look and ultimate objectification of all the female characters (ibid.: 164). Although Carmilla is powerful, as Andrea Weiss has shown her exploits are geared towards gratifying male heterosexual fantasy in a pornographic manner. With the relaxation of censorship restrictions and in the struggle to revive flagging cinema attendance, 'lesbian sexual behaviour had become graphically depicted, another titillating, exaggerated characteristic of the excessive B-movie genre' (Weiss, 1992: 88). This male-oriented representation 'is an articulation of men's sub-conscious fear of and hostility towards women's sexuality' (ibid.: 103). In *Lust for a Vampire* (Jimmy Sangster, 1970) Carmilla is a much weaker character altogether, with a suggestion that her lesbianism is perverse. As David Sanjek has commented: 'the eventual destruction of the villainous women allowed audiences implicitly to condemn at one and the same time vampirism and lesbianism, equating the two as crimes against nature' (Sanjek, 1994: 200). For lesbian audiences, the only saving grace of these films lies perhaps in readings which emphasise camp, but at the expense of negating their dominant generic attribute: horror (Weiss, 1992: 106).

Nicolas Roeg's *Don't Look Now* (1973, UK–Italian co-production), based on a short story by Daphne du Maurier, was a more sophisticated blend of horror and thriller with Italian locations, starring Julie Christie (Laura) and Donald Sutherland (John). Usually discussed in terms of Roeg as an auteur with its theme of strangers in a strange land, *Don't Look Now* has also acquired a reputation as quality horror, a variation on the genre which certainly paid off: it was the top grossing British film of 1974 (*Cinema TV Today*, 21 December 1974). Laura and John go to Venice to recover from the death of their daughter and meet a psychic woman who claims that the child is trying to contact them. Laura is desperate to reach her daughter whereas John is opposed to dabbling into the other world of psychic forces which he knows exists but is determined to resist. Restrained in tone and functioning as a sort of mosaic-puzzle which unfolds in a cumulative but not necessarily revelationary manner, *Don't Look Now* is renowned for Roeg's editing (particularly the opening sequence when the child's death by drowning is intercut with her father's psychic premonition) and cinematographic skills rather than the campy kitsch and sexploitation which characterised many horror films of the 1970s. The tension between its horror and thriller elements also creates suspense, climaxing with the exposure of the full horror of a small red-hooded figure who has been prefigured through symbolic imagery throughout the narrative. A distraught John follows the figure, believing that it is his daughter, only to discover that it is actually an aged dwarf who has been murdering people in Venice, a fate which John is destined to suffer when the dwarf stabs him at the end of the film. Although *Don't Look Now* was a critical and box-office success, it is interesting that it did not result in more quality horror projects which might have saved the genre from decline during this period.

Science-fiction was not as prevalent as a genre in the 1970s as horror, but there were a few key futuristic films, including *A Clockwork Orange* (Stanley Kubrick, 1972), *The Man Who Fell To Earth* (Nicolas Roeg, 1976) and *Alien* (Ridley Scott, 1979), which incorporated some horror elements, pointing the way to the international revival of both genres in the 1980s. These films, particularly *Alien*, are examples of generic mutation where the future of horror became more and more tied to hybridity with science-fiction narratives. *A Clockwork Orange* was a *cause célèbre* of the campaign against screen violence. Rather like the adverse reaction to *Peeping Tom*, Kubrick's film was accused of glamourising violent thuggery and gang rape. Its British setting made the viewer particularly uncomfortable as the main protagonist, the 'monster' Alex (Malcolm McDowell), went on the rampage, raping a woman to the soundtrack of *Singin' in the Rain*, in anticipation of Quentin Tarantino's notorious use of popular music during scenes of extreme violence in *Reservoir Dogs* (1993). Alex's incarceration and treatment was equally unsettling for the viewer, presenting a pessimistic vision of a reactionary, repressive, state apparatus. Kubrick withdrew the film from UK distribution after a succession of alleged copycat violent incidents. For an overview of British science fiction cinema during this period and others, see Hunter (1999).

The Man Who Fell To Earth starred David Bowie as an alien who visits earth (USA) on a mission to save his planet from dehydration. The film was largely sold on its casting of Bowie, in 1976 one of Britain's most popular rock stars and whose off-screen image as Ziggy Stardust, the title of one of his albums, was decidedly futuristic. In auteurist terms, the film continues Roeg's fascination with placing individuals in foreign environments. In so doing, it passes pessimistic comment on American society from the view of an outsider (the alien assumes a British identity and Bowie is British, London accent intact) who ends up being trapped on earth. The nightmare scenario of US corporate imperialism as represented in *The Man Who Fell To Earth* connects with continued concerns about Britain's decline as a world power and it also articulates a critique of the use of new technologies to serve capitalist ends.

Ridley Scott's *Alien* also contained a critique of 'the corporation' and made clear the commercial imperatives which determined missions into space but, unlike *The Man Who Fell To Earth* which blatantly targeted American capitalism, it did not locate them as nationally specific. *Alien* did extremely well at the box office and was largely responsible for the horror/science-fiction revival in the 1980s, particularly in the United States. Many of its conventions derived from classic suspense thrillers. Its success can also be attributed to the everyday imagery of the spaceship, to H. R. Giger's Academy Award-winning designs, to delicate juxtapositions of the familiar and unfamiliar and to Sigourney Weaver's excellent performance as Ripley. The film exploited the simple idea of an alien on board a spaceship which, in a celebrated scene, explodes from inside a man's stomach where it has been incubating. The film employed the traditional technique of locating horror in the everyday: the crew are having a quiet meal when the alien creates chaos by bursting onto the scene.

Many other science-fiction films were not so successful, particularly as the trend for big-budget spectacle and complicated co-production financial arrangements became the norm. Two sequels to *Alien*, released in 1986 and 1992, were American films – a corporate tendency which was indicative of the way Hollywood cornered the market for horror/sci-fi blockbusters with hits like *The Shining* (1980), the *Friday the Thirteenth* series (1980–82, 1984–86, 1988, 1989), *Robocop* (1987 and 1990) and the *Terminator* films (1984, 1991 and 2003). Big budgets and spectacle were also the hallmark of British disaster films which appeared intermittently and sank without trace throughout the 1970s: *Zeppelin* (Etienne Perier, 1971), *Juggernaut* (Richard Lester, 1974), *Avalanche* (Frederic Goode, 1975) and *S.O.S. Titanic* (Billy Hale, 1980). The disaster movie was an interesting attempt to incorporate some of the techniques of the classic suspense thriller with the horror of natural disasters. But the British examples failed to match the ingenuity and terror of *Airport* (1970), the American film which instigated the trend, or *The Towering Inferno* (1975), one of the most successful disaster movies ever made. Ironically, the genre did not recover after the box-office success of *Airplane!* (1980), an American comic spoof of the disaster film genre which employed all its conventions but this time for laughs rather than screams.

The climate of retrenchment and liberal censorship had a profound impact on comedy in the 1970s, particularly in the direction of collapsing the traditional boundaries between sexploitation and comedy. There were six broad types: *Carry On*s and British comedies which relied on verbal innuendo rather than on explicit sexual situations; sex and sexploitation-comedies; spin-offs from successful television series; star-based comedies (the *Pink Panther* comedies); surreal and anarchic satire (Monty Python), and light/observational comedy (the films of Bill Forsyth). The *Carry On* team continued to make about one film a year until box-office failure *Carry On Emmanuelle* (Gerald Thomas, 1978), ironically a parody of the porn film business: *Carry On* films were increasingly out of kilter with the perceived demand for nudity and sexual explicitness. As Andy Medhurst has put it:

> The films' jokes about sex had been premised on a giggling naughtiness that looked increasingly dated in the era of permissiveness. Once Barbara Windsor's breasts had broken free in *Camping* (1969), where was the humour in suggesting such a thing might happen?
>
> (Medhurst, 1995: 3).

Such a thing did happen, frequently, in the *Confessions of . . .* series starring Robin Askwith, 1974–77, which contributed to the demise of *Carry On*. Askwith progressed from sexual encounter to sexual encounter in different milieux: as a window cleaner, a pop star, a driving instructor and at a holiday camp. The first, most successful film in the series, *Confessions of a Window Cleaner* (1974), was directed by Val Guest, former horror director, while the rest were directed by Norman Cohen whose experience was in comedy. Although they retained some of *Carry On*'s irreverent traditions, the emphasis on an individual rather than a team of stock characters, and the preoccupation with nudity rather than sexual suggestion, were important departures. Yet at the same time they were related to the work of television character-comedians such as Benny Hill, and devices like the speeding-up of sex scenes indicated an irreverent attitude towards representations of sex. There were many sex-comedies in the *Confessions . . .* mould including the *Adventures . . .* series directed by Stanley Long and Derek Ford – *Commuter Husbands* (1973), *Keep It Up Jack!* (1974), *Diary of a Space Virgin* (1975) and *What's Up Nurse* (1977) – films with salacious titles designed to titillate dwindling audiences with their suggestion of breaking taboos. The films also took advantage of the relaxation of censorship in a desperate attempt to grasp a market opportunity by showing what television was banned from transmitting.

Television and film comedy

A striking generic development was the number of television comedy spin-offs, films which repeated the characters and formulae of successful television situation comedies. Again, this can be explained by the industry's dire financial problems and the need to attract audiences for whom television was their primary screen entertainment. Hoping that popular television characters would entice telly addicts back into cinemas, as a defensive strategy producers wanted to back safe bets, proven successes in other media, with the assurance that any marketing campaign did not have to work too hard at attracting an audience already familiar with the comedy's major features. But therein lay a huge problem: the audience expected their favourite television moments to be recreated, leaving writers and directors very little room for character or situation development. The segmented half-hour television format allowed for continuity with previous episodes and a basic comic situation which could be explored on a discrete basis each week. Placing characters in spectacular situations or involving them in incredible capers in order to fill a 75-minute screen slot was no substitute for the acutely observational, small-scale familiar situations which formed the basis of successful television situation comedy. While in the first instance audiences could be lured to see a spin-off, the poor box-office takings at a sequel reveals how far audience expectations were not met. *Steptoe and Son* (Cliff Owen, 1972) scored high box-office takings whereas its successor, *Steptoe and Son Ride Again* (Peter Sykes, 1973) did badly. *On the Buses* (Harry Booth, 1971) was the highest grossing British film of 1971, second only to *The Aristocats* (Disney, US, 1970); a year later *Mutiny On the Buses* (Harry Booth, 1972) did not do so well. Many other TV spin-offs were produced including *Dad's Army* (Norman Cohen, 1971), *Bless This House* (Gerald Thomas, 1973), *The Likely Lads* (Michael Tuchner, 1976) and *George and Mildred* (Peter Frazer Jones, 1980).

Big-budget, star-oriented comedy was also a feature of the 1970s. After the success of *The Pink Panther* (Blake Edwards, 1964) British comedian Peter Sellers was persuaded by television-turned-film producer, wannabe movie-mogul Sir Lew Grade to appear in three more *Pink Panther* films, also directed by Edwards: *The Return of the Pink Panther* (1975), *The Pink Panther Strikes Again* (1976) and *The Revenge of the Pink Panther* (1978). These were targeted at the international market and did well at the box office, relying heavily on Sellers' well-developed, distinctive character Inspector Clouseau, who fitted well into incredible scenarios, as opposed to the main characters in the sit-com spin-offs who were ordinary and difficult to write into fantastic situations in a convincing manner. Similarly successful, and in contrast with the majority of televison spin-offs, were the Monty Python films which extended the boundaries of their surreal television comedy traditions. Perhaps because their trademark was unpredictability, originality and satire, they transferred to the big screen well with their grandiose themes and irreverent, shockable subject-matter contained within a narrative framework in *Monty Python and the Holy Grail* (Terry Gilliam, Terry Jones, 1975) and *Monty Python's Life of Brian* (Terry Jones, 1979). They appealed to the important youth market and capitalised on relaxed censorship as a means of extending the range of risqué comic subjects which could only be suggested on television. Gilliam and Jones were free to develop ideas in the knowledge that audiences of Python films did not always expect a repetition of famous sketches, funny walks and dead parrots, but an extension of the satirical comic mode itself.

In anticipation of the revival of domestic-oriented comedy in the 1980s there were two significant low-budget films directed by Bill Forsyth: *That Sinking Feeling* (1980) and *Gregory's Girl* (1981). *That Sinking Feeling* draws on Ealing's concern for the importance of community during hard times with its story of unemployed Glaswegian youngsters who steal ninety stainless steel sinks from a plumber's warehouse. *Gregory's Girl*, set in the outskirts of Glasgow, is a romantic comedy which highlights the awkward emotional growing pains of an adolescent who finds it difficult to do the things boys are supposed to do well: play football and attract girls. Both films used young, untried actors and managed to combine colloquialism with traditional themes, a formula which was repeated with success by Forsyth in subsequent films. They also were notable for their revival of regional humour, continuing the tradition of non-metropolitan comedic representations of Britishness which had been particularly evident in the 1930s and 1940s.

The music industry and musicals

The musical continued to be profoundly influenced by rock/pop/punk culture in the 1970s and the form in its classical sense was on the wane. Many of the most successful involved rock stars: David Essex in *That'll be the Day* (Claude Whatham, 1973) and *Stardust* (Michael Apted, 1974); Roger Daltry, Elton John, Keith Moon and Eric Clapton in *Tommy* (Ken Russell, 1975); Sting in *Quadrophenia* (Franc Roddam, 1979), a film whose soundtrack was written and performed by Pete Townshend and The Who; and Roger Daltry in *Lisztomania* (Ken Russell, 1975). A number of films featured live performances, including *Rory Gallagher's Irish Tour* (1974) and *Exodus – Bob Marley Live* (1978), and some drew on the style of television's *Top of the Pops* but also anticipated pop-promo videos with their usage of soundtrack and/or performance by the original artist in a fictional setting, including John Lennon's *Imagine* (1973) and the 'two-tone' group Madness in *Take It or Leave It* (1981).

Punk rock was represented in three very different films: *Jubilee* (Derek Jarman, 1978), *Rude Boy* (Jack Hazan and David Mingay, 1980) and *The Great Rock 'n' Roll Swindle* (Julien Temple, 1980). In *Jubilee* Jarman dispensed with conventional narrative, placing Queen Elizabeth I in an impressionistic collage of images of contemporary Deptford where she witnesses urban chaos, the anarchic and fascistic elements of punk, plus violence, deprivation and the commercial exploitation of the punk rock movement by mercenary entrepreneurs. This latter theme was also explored in *The Great Rock 'n' Roll Swindle*, a film which blurred the boundaries between documentary and fiction in an extraordinary account of the Sex Pistols' exploitation by the record industry and media. *Rude Boy* made many of Jarman's political points more explicit, juxtaposing the optimistic Thatcherite[3] vision of Britain with the realities of unemployment, racism and urban decay as a context for the appeal of punk culture to fans of The Clash, one of punk's most important groups. The increasing mutually beneficial tie-ins between film and popular music provide an interesting example of how, during this period, the music industry in many ways shored up the ailing film industry to gain more exposure for its rock and pop stars. But from the 1980s the popularity of short pop-promo music videos made feature films less attractive as a major publicity exercise for most pop and rock stars. The film industry had taken temporary advantage of its capacity to fill the visual culture gap which was evident in the representation of music stars on film. While television programmes like *Top of the Pops* gave rock and pop stars some exposure, the performance of their hit records was rarely accompanied by imaginative films, a situation which was to change radically in subsequent years.

Other musicals adopted more traditional themes and styles: Dickens' *Scrooge* (Ronald Neame, 1970) and Ken Russell's homage to Busby Berkeley in *The Boy Friend* (1972), starring Twiggy. Apart from *Tommy* (1975), Russell's other major musicals of the decade were *Mahler* (1974) and *Lisztomania* (1975), both extravagant biopics which are very much auteur works featuring Russell's controversial tendency to disrupt audiences' conservative preconceptions about the reception of classical music, often using revered pieces as soundtrack for sexually explicit and violent scenes. Alan Parker's NFFC-backed box-office hit musical *Bugsy Malone* (1976) was a novelty in that it used children in an adult story of gangsterdom in Prohibition Era USA. This experience was instrumental in securing backing for Parker's next musical project with teenagers, *Fame* (1980), which he made for MGM and which is registered as an American film. With their American settings and Parker's much publicised frustration with the British film industry and the film critic establishment, it was no surprise that he moved to Hollywood for most of his subsequent ventures.

Crime, thrillers and costume dramas

Crime/thriller films divided into four general categories during the 1970s: British gangsterdom; police films; Agatha Christie adaptations; and spy thrillers, including James Bond. *Get Carter* (Mike Hodges, 1971) starred Michael Caine as a tough London gangster who travels north to avenge his brother's murder. The film was a co-production between MGM and EMI, as was another British gangster film, *Villain* (Michael Tuchner, 1971), a veiled portrait of the Krays starring Richard Burton.[4] *The Long Good Friday* (John Mackenzie, 1981) owed much to these earlier films for generic inspiration but inflected its East End gangster (Bob Hoskins) with a harsh capitalist mentality which is pitted against his gangland rivals and the IRA. The private-eye formula was adapted to a Liverpool setting in Stephen Frears' *Gumshoe* (1971), and there were successful adaptations of TV-crime series with *Callan* (Don Sharp, 1974) and *Sweeney!* (David Wickes, 1977). Interestingly, these did not suffer the fate of the sit-com spin-offs: their narratives were well plotted, longer versions of successful television drama formats and the central detectives provided a familiar focus for audience identification.

Agatha Christie's novels provided source material for a spate of lavish thrillers with a comic and period touch and with a view to the export market: *Murder On the Orient Express* (Sidney Lumet, 1974), *Death On the Nile* (John Guillermin, 1978) and *The Mirror Crack'd* (Guy Hamilton, 1981), generally big-budget affairs with all-star casting and international appeal. In the context of an unsettled society, their popularity can in part be explained by the nostalgic desire for the more ordered world depicted in Agatha Christie's detective stories where crime does not pay, poverty and deprivation do not exist and narrative closure is always assured with devastating aplomb. A similar desire for escapism was also reflected in the continuing popularity of the James Bond films, which also managed to inject a degree of product differentiation with the temporary return of Sean Connery as Bond in *Diamonds Are Forever* (Guy Hamilton, 1971), and his subsequent replacement by Roger Moore's incarnation with all his laconic panache in *Live and Let Die* (Guy Hamilton, 1973) and *The Spy Who Loved Me* (Lewis Gilbert, 1977). *The Day of the Jackal* (Fred Zinnemann, 1973), *The Thirty-Nine Steps* (Don Sharp, 1978) and *The Eye of the Needle* (Richard Marquand, 1978) were other notable spy thrillers of the period.

Historical/costume films were predominantly based on the lives of royalty, political figures and classical composers. *Henry VIII and His Six Wives* (Waris Hussein, 1972), *Young Winston* (Richard Attenborough, 1972), *Mary, Queen of Scots* (Charles Jarrott, 1972), *Hitler: The Last Ten Days* (Ennio de Concini, 1973), *Luther* (Guy Green, 1976) and *Winstanley* (Kevin Brownlow, Andrew Mollo, 1977) – all of these participated in a revival of the genre which had in part been provoked by successful television historical series. Ken Russell's *The Music Lovers* (1971) combined auteurist exuberance with a semblance of historical detail, while *Barry Lyndon* (Stanley Kubrick, 1975), *Joseph Andrews* (Tony Richardson, 1977) and *The French Lieutenant's Woman* (Karel Reisz, 1981) also provided renowned directors with ambitious themes and sets.

Several strategies had been attempted in the struggle to win back audiences. It was very much a case of trial and error, the least successful being the move to replicate television and the most promising the promotion of cinema as a specific form of entertainment, working alongside television, borrowing some ideas and adapting them in an imaginative way for the big screen as with Monty Python comedies, private-eye films and historical dramas. But, overall, the 1970s were difficult years for British film genres which were plagued by extreme financial insecurity, uncertain marketability and artistic direction, providing a sharp reminder of the fragility of the industry's base – a reminder that was all too quickly forgotten in the optimism surrounding the 'British Are Coming – Eighties Revival'.[5]

Thatcherism, heritage and beyond: 1980s–1990s

Ironically, the years of Thatcherism provided the political–cultural background to the revival of British cinema in the 1980s. While Thatcher's commitment to the market economy offered little assistance to film producers, as we have seen in Chapter 1, a fortunate combination of temporary tax incentives, the multiplex boom and the international success of heritage costume films saved the industry from extinction. Of particular note is how the market-dominated ethos of the Thatcher government left the film industry to resort to dependence on television, particularly Channel 4. The public service remit of Channel 4 meant that many lower-budget films were funded that were critical of Thatcherism. As Hill has noted, 'The economic policies of the Thatcher government, when applied to the film industry, actually helped to stimulate the production of films which, at an ideological level, were typically hostile to Thatcherite beliefs' (Hill, 1999: 30). Lester Friedman (1993: xv) has argued that Thatcher's decade produced an intriguing range of films which directly and indirectly critiqued its harsh extremities, its unerring pursuit of the market economy and declared opposition to state intervention in industry and welfare. Some film-makers were galvanised by their desire to provide cultural opposition to the Conservative Party's disturbing right-wing tendencies and to expose the harsh realities of life experienced by many under Thatcherism. Margaret Thatcher's attempt at charismatic leadership provided an obvious focus-point for opposition, although political critique was not always as explicitly evident in mainstream films as it was in the defiantly oppositional art cinema of Derek Jarman (to be discussed in Chapter 8). On the other hand, as the case of the heritage genre demonstrates, while not being entirely without relevance to the Thatcher years (see the discussion of heritage films below), some films made during this period harked back to earlier periods in history, ignoring contemporary problems.

Contemporary problems concerned an accentuation of many of the polarisations between the haves and have-nots which underscored British society in the 1970s. Thatcher's political opportunism during the Falklands Crisis of 1982 enabled her to distract attention from domestic problems by exploiting British nationalism.[6] The most acute domestic problems were explosive industrial relations, unemployment and poverty, racial conflict, and law and order. In 1981 a succession of riots broke out in London (Brixton, Finsbury Park and Southall), Liverpool (Toxteth), Manchester (Moss Side), Bristol and Leicester. A public enquiry into the riots revealed that the police had in part provoked the violent outbursts and that the underlying causes were the recession and unemployment which hit the black community particularly hard. The Troubles in Northern Ireland continued, although some relief came in 1994 (during the premiership of John Major, Margaret Thatcher's successor) when the Irish Republican

Army agreed to a temporary ceasefire. As far as class divisions were concerned, despite Margaret Thatcher's notorious grocer's-daughter, middle-class background, the basic divisions were still very much in operation. There was however some evidence of upward mobility, particularly amongst the much publicised working-class and lower-middle-class yuppies who made quick profits from buying property and shares, gaining an entrée into the hitherto middle- and upper-class dominated world of business and finance. For the unemployed and the sick, however, the Thatcher years offered increased impoverishment and insecurity.

The continuation of Conservative policies under John Major in the 1990s, albeit less extreme than Thatcherism, did not, arguably, cause such a cultural backlash as was evident in the 1980s but, as we shall see in the following discussion of cinema in recent years, British genres and hybrids continued to demonstrate a fascinating relationship with both social trends and their own historic and stylistic generic imperatives. Ironically, the advent of New Labour resulted in films perhaps less critical of the establishment than was evident in those produced under Thatcher when, as Friedman (1993) aptly titled his edited collection about cinema in this period, 'Fires Were Started'. While New Labour's film policy attempted to encourage a range of representations that might be appropriate to the diversity of the UK, as shown in Chapter 1, these have not necessarily produced innovatory modes of film-making, or launched a sustained and effective challenge to the domination of Hollywood.

History as spectacle

The film which marked the recovery of British cinema in the early 1980s was *Chariots of Fire* (Hugh Hudson, 1981), a period film based on the true story of rivalry between two runners, Harold Abrahams and Eric Liddell, who eventually won places on the British team for the 1924 Olympics. The film had many of the hallmarks which typified subsequent historical films: precise and loving photography of sites of national heritage (in this case, Cambridge University), a focus on male rivalry and bonding, and a nostalgic view of the past. *Chariots of Fire* heralded the ascendancy of the most dominant British genre for the following decade: quality historical films often referred to as heritage, including *Heat and Dust* (James Ivory, 1984), *Another Country* (Marek Kanievska, 1984), *A Passage To India* (David Lean, 1985), *A Room With a View* (James Ivory, 1986), *Maurice* (James Ivory, 1987), *Howards End* (James Ivory, 1992), *Shadowlands* (Richard Attenborough, 1993) and *The Remains of the Day* (James Ivory, 1993). These were box-office successes in Britain and America, continuing the profitable export of films which offered a particular construction of, in this case, Englishness.

Andrew Higson (1993) has identified other common stylistic and thematic features of the genre as it developed: the display of history as spec-

Plate 4.1 Lucy (Helena Bonham-Carter) as heritage tourist in *A Room With a View* (1986). (Courtesy of Merchant Ivory Productions)

tacle via a pictorialist camera style; the primacy of *mise-en-scène* over narrative; a fascination with upper-class life; the use of classic literature as source texts, especially E. M. Forster; and a consistent use of particular actors including Helena Bonham-Carter, James Wilby and Anthony Hopkins. Higson places these films in a political context of Conservatism, particularly Thatcherism, interpreting the heritage genre as symptomatic of a middle-class denial of present-day social conflicts. He argues that the films' visual style privileged heritage space at the expense of highlighting elements of irony and social critique which were evident in many of the source novels:

> The novels explore what lies beneath the surface of things, satirizing the pretentious and superficial, and especially those who are overly concerned with keeping up appearances rather than acting according to the passions of the heart. The films, however, construct such a delightfully glossy visual surface that the ironic perspective and the narrative of social criticism diminish in their appeal for the spectator.
>
> (Higson, 1993: 120)

By contrast, Alison Light (1991a) has argued that social conflicts and the struggles of outsider groups, particularly homosexuals and the lower classes, are not diminished by alluring photography. I would take this position further and suggest that much of the social critique to be found in Forster's novels *does* surface in the films. As well as the high production values, the viewer of *Maurice* (1987) remembers the cross-class homosexual relationship between Maurice and the gamekeeper and the choice Maurice makes in favour of that relationship at the expense of his social position and career. In *A Room With a View* (1986) Lucy Honeychurch's visit to Italy exposes English insularity, fear of the other and sexuality. Leonard Bast's disastrous attempt at class mobility in *Howards End* (1992) highlights the hypocritical norms of the upper-middle class. In *The Remains of the Day* (1993), butler Stevens' unquestioning support of Lord Darlington is linked with uncritical attitudes towards the appeasement of fascism in the 1930s: both stances are presented as disastrous in personal and political terms. It would therefore appear that rather than operate as closed texts, the films do offer a complex variety of spectator positions and pleasures that do not necessarily support a reading that demarcates them as unremittingly conservative (Monk in Monk and Sargeant, 2002).

Fascination with the past featured in another dominant genre: the biopic. These were concerned with more recent history than the classic heritage films but displayed the same attention to period detail. *Dance With a Stranger* (Mike Newell, 1985) was based on the Ruth Ellis case (the last woman to be hanged in Britain); *Sid and Nancy* (Alex Cox, 1986) was about punk rocker Sid Vicious; *Prick Up Your Ears* (Stephen Frears, 1987) dealt with homosexual playwright Joe Orton; *The Krays* (Peter Medak, 1990) followed the exploits of London's gangsters; *Scandal* (Michael Caton Jones, 1989) was based on the Profumo affair; *Backbeat* (Ian Softley, 1993) focused on the Beatles' early years in Germany; *Tom and Viv* (Brian Gilbert, 1994) dealt with the turbulent relationship between T. S. Eliot and his first wife; and *The Young Poisoner's Handbook* (Benjamin Ross, 1995) with the case of Graham Young, who poisoned his family and workmates.

Most of these films featured neurotic characters, the narratives' focus being on individual struggles rather than on wider social issues. But it is possible to read into that hysteria a fear of the other, a fascination with difficult moments in the national past which indicate contemporary fears. The nostalgic elements were therefore invested with an uneasy contemporary gloss which co-existed with the familiar visual pleasures offered by period spectacle. Fears about homosexual relations and non-conformist women were evident, for example, in several key films in the subgenre. For all its 1960s panache and Ortonesque humour, *Prick Up Your Ears* portrays Joe Orton's relationship with Kenneth Halliwell as obsessive, unhealthy and destructive. Miranda Richardson's Ruth Ellis is hysterical, as is her portrayal of Eliot's wife in *Tom and Viv*: Ruth is hanged and Viv is consigned to lunacy. *The Young Poisoner's Handbook* presents Young as a clever scientist who poisoned his parents, persuaded his psychiatrist that he was cured but after being released from a psychiatric hospital proceeded to poison his workmates. The audience is encouraged to be fascinated with Graham's cold, calculated, fatal experiments, containing many misogynist moments in the process when female characters are presented from Graham's point of view, as deserving to die.

Hybrid films

The next grouping of films dealt with recent/contemporary social problems in an overt manner: issue-based films that encompassed several generic elements from comedy to thriller. Many such hybrid films do not fall into distinct generic categories, but I group them together here in an attempt to convey the extent to which contemporary issues have been addressed in films including *The Ploughman's Lunch* (Richard Eyre, 1983), *My Beautiful Launderette* (Stephen Frears, 1985), *High Hopes* (Mike Leigh, 1988), *Sammy and Rosie Get Laid* (Stephen Frears, 1988), *A Letter To Brezhnev* (Chris Bernard, 1985), *Bhaji On the Beach* (Gurinder Chadha, 1993) and *The Crying Game* (Neil Jordan, 1992). *The Ploughman's Lunch* is the most overtly political, dealing with an attempt by James (Jonathan Pryce), a BBC news editor, to write a book on the Suez crisis at the same time as the Falklands crisis is going on around him. His search for the truth about the past is as tortuous as the contemporary events which surround him. The broad issues raised by the film concern the falsification of the past through established historical discourse, with obvious parallels being made regarding the falsification of Falklands reportage and the staging of the 1982 Conservative Party Conference.[7] The characters in the film appear at the Conference, fiction meeting fact in an extraordinary behind-the-scenes sequence which deconstructs the theatricality of modern politics. The film eschews conventional character identification, maintaining an ironic distance from its subject matter with interesting results, as Sheila Johnston has observed: 'The film works on the principles, not of harmony, but of cacophony, not consensus but dissent' (1985: 108). Of particular interest in this connection is James, who is both attractive and repellent: we want to identify with him but are left feeling cheated by his self-centred pursuit of the truth. The film is unusual in its interweaving of fictional narrative events with their contemporary historical context: the micro-level is James' quest about Suez, while the macro-level is undoubtedly Thatcherism. The viewer is therefore encouraged to arrive at political conclusions about the film's many dissenting elements: its portrayal of consumerism (the title alluding to the manufacture of the past), the world of television journalism and the Conservative Party under Thatcher. As one critic put it, *The Ploughman's Lunch* 'was about the exploitative, fraudulent, manipulative skills of the

Eighties' (Walker, 1985: 264). John Hill has labelled films such as this as 'state-of-the-nation' films, including other such examples as *Britannia Hospital*, *Hidden Agenda* (Ken Loach, 1990) and *The Last of England* (discussed in Chapter 8). He argues that while they were indeed symptoms of profound disquiet with the Thatcher regime they were lacking in providing 'an alternative social vision which appeared to be capable of either challenging it effectively or winning a place in the popular imagination' (Hill, 1999: 165).

My Beautiful Launderette also has a Thatcherite context and is about the experience of being Asian and British. Against a background of racism and the market economy, Omar, a young Pakistani man, has a relationship with Johnny, a white punk. Omar manages his uncle's launderette and together with Johnny, transforms it from a broken-down wreck into a sparkling, successful venture. Its success becomes a symbol of Omar and Johnny's enduring relationship, but also of their vulnerability when it is attacked by racist punks. *Bhaji On the Beach*, the first feature film to be directed by an Asian woman in Britain, deals with the theme of being Asian and British from a more overtly comic perspective as it follows a group of Indian women from Birmingham on a trip to Blackpool. The trip brings out their

Plate 4.2 Tradition meets tradition. Ambrose Waddington (Peter Cellier) and Asha (Lalita Ahmed) in *Bhaji On the Beach* (1993). (Courtesy of Film Four International and Christine Parry)

pasts, their anxieties and how they relate to each other. A contrast is made between the young women, one of whom discovers that she is pregnant, and the aunties, the older women who find it difficult to adjust to change. The film also deals with the issues of inter-racial relationships and domestic violence. Chadha wanted her film to join other representations of British-ness, illustrating the diversity implicit in such a notion: 'What I'm trying to say is that Britain isn't one thing or another. It isn't just *Howards End* or *My Beautiful Launderette*. There are endless possibilities about what it can – and is – already' (Chadha quoted in Stuart 1994: 27).

Youth problems and race are also addressed in *Sammy and Rosie Get Laid*, and *A Letter To Brezhnev* offers an unusual focus on two young Liver-pudlian women whose lives are changed when they meet some Russian sailors who are visiting the port. Mike Leigh uses satirical comedy to comment on contemporary class/working-class issues, for example in *Grown-Ups* (1980), *High Hopes* (1988) and *Life Is Sweet* (1990) where 'to be English is to be locked in a prison where politeness, gaucheness and anxiety about status form the bars across the window' (Medhurst, 1993: 11). Leigh's film *Naked* (1993) is a less comic, dark, meandering narrative about Johnny, a man from Manchester on the streets in London. *Naked* presents a particularly bleak and at times misogynistic account of poverty and depriva-tion in contemporary Britain. Johnny is a sexually violent, at times bigoted character whose long speeches betray an angry, frustrated intelligence which also prevents him from committing himself to anything or anyone. The film presents him as a sort of modern-day prophet whose observations on other people's lives and ambitions are painful for both the characters and the audience. No solutions are offered in this disturbing film where patient, loyal characters like Johnny's on-off girlfriend Louise is abandoned by him at the end, a fellow Mancunian, lost and lonely in London, but rejected by the man who asks the right questions but has none of the answers.

Northern Ireland has been dealt with in a number of films, including *Angel* (Neil Jordan, 1982), *Cal* (Pat O'Connor, 1984) and *The Crying Game*. Most films focus on how the Troubles affected people who would not ordi-narily choose to be violent: *Angel* shows how a saxophone player becomes a gunman to revenge the killing by Protestants of a deaf-mute friend; *Cal* portrays the IRA as exploitative of young people when a young man is pres-surised into terrorism. Brian McIlroy (1993: 107) has argued that box-office successes such as these tended to play down the political conflicts in favour of character development: 'these films repress history and politics for fear of distancing the non-Irish audience'. *The Crying Game*, an extremely popular film at the box office, is an interesting example of this argument.[8]

In *The Crying Game* an IRA group take a black soldier, Jody (Forest Whitaker), hostage, threatening to shoot him in three days if he cannot be exchanged for an IRA member who has been arrested. One member of the IRA group, sensitive and apparently non-violent Fergus (Stephen Rea),

Plate 4.3 Jody (Forest Whitaker) being held hostage by Fergus (Stephen Rea) in *The Crying Game* (1992). (Courtesy of Artificial Eye Film Company Ltd)

befriends Jody while keeping watch over him and Jody makes him promise that he will look after his girlfriend, Dil (Jaye Davidson), in London. Fergus allows Jody to escape when he has been ordered to shoot him, but as Jody runs away he is hit and killed by an army vehicle on its way to attack the camp where Jody has been held hostage. Fergus escapes and goes to London where he meets and is attracted to Dil. He is shocked when he finds out that Dil is a transvestite, a revelation which occurs just before Fergus' IRA 'friends' Maguire (Adrian Dunbar) and Jude (Miranda Richardson) track him down and threaten to harm Dil if Fergus does not agree to shoot a judge, an almost certain suicide mission. Fergus, confused over his relationship with Dil, cuts Dil's hair and dresses him as a man in an attempt to stop the IRA from harming him. Fergus confesses to Dil his involvement in the IRA and his role in Jody's kidnapping and death. Dil ties him to the bed, preventing him from carrying out the mission, and shoots Jude when she comes in search of Fergus after Maguire has been killed assassinating the judge when Fergus did not appear to do the job. Fergus takes the blame for Jude's death and Dil visits him in prison, clearly wanting to continue their relationship, though there is some doubt (on Fergus' side) as to whether this will be a sexual one.

The Crying Game does not have much political punch beyond its initial setting in Armagh and subsequent IRA suspense plot. The details of the conflict in Northern Ireland are not discussed at any length, merely serving as a backdrop to the relationship between Fergus and Jody and then between Fergus and Dil. Fergus is portrayed as more caring and sensitive than Maguire and Jude, who are fanatical and ruthless in their pursuit of him in London and in their commitment to the cause. Both Fergus and Jody are men who have almost accidentally become involved in the conflict, and who are depicted as outsiders, victims who would have been friends in different political circumstances. In this way the film operates as a tense and effective thriller, a love story with a gender twist but not as a drama which deals in any depth with the Troubles in Northern Ireland.

Some films which might have started generic trends do not appear to have done so. *Brazil* (Terry Gilliam, 1985), a fantasy/satire on bureaucratic society, and *The Company of Wolves* (Neil Jordan, 1984), a Gothic horror fairytale, remain more or less isolated casualties of the 1980s boom, eventually ousted by the more robust, bankable longevity of heritage films.[9] Other genres, particularly the thriller and the road-movie, are in transition. *The Cement Garden* (Andrew Birkin, 1992) and *Shallow Grave* (Danny Boyle, 1994) indicate a darker slant on the thriller, exploring the impact of death on young people and the apparent callousness with which they can ignore it. *Butterfly Kiss* (Michael Winterbottom, 1994) similarly deals with overt violence in a bleak depiction of two women on the road in the north, murderous gays who appear to have no qualms about killing whoever gets in their way. *Shopping* (Paul Anderson, 1993) is a British action film about joy-riders in the London docklands. Rather than being a 'hard-hitting dystopian drama', *Shopping* has been accused of being 'so obsessed with its own hipness that it ends up being totally embarrassing' (Ben Thompson in *Sight and Sound*, July 1994: 55). These films are similar to *Naked* in that they refuse to offer solutions to the problems raised in their narratives, arguably part of a postmodern condition which suspends judgement on societal issues, instead presenting a range of positions within a context of generic hybridity. On the other hand, they could be indicative of anxiety about the arrival of the twenty-first century, their pessimistic narratives revealing a crisis of national, social and sexual identities.

The heritage genre has spilled over into representations of Englishness which are not necessarily set in the past. The top British film at the box office in 1995 was *Four Weddings and a Funeral* (Mike Newell, 1994) which bears a relationship to the heritage films in several important ways: it stars Hugh Grant who was moulded as a heritage star from *Maurice*, and it displays a fascination with the upper classes, featuring numerous ceremonies at which they, their clothes and possessions are on full display. Yet in *Four Weddings* there is little sense of the underlying social contradictions and rifts which were suggested in many of the heritage films of the 1980s. As we shall see, *Four Weddings* inaugurated a trend of more contemporary romantic comedies with a heavy slice of modern heritage, geared towards the American market. As Nick Roddick has argued: *'Four Weddings* certainly exports a view of British life which is much more like the rest of the world wants it to be than it actually is' (1995: 15).

Two films released in Britain in 1996 were exemplary illustrations of the then dominant strands of British cinema: *Trainspotting* (Danny Boyle) and *Sense and Sensibility* (Ang Lee).[10] *Trainspotting*, based on a novel by Irvine Welsh, concerned a group of heroin addicts in Edinburgh. In a rare exploration of the habit from the drug-taker's point-of-view, the film uses voice-over narration to convey the pleasures and pains of both shooting-up and of kicking heroin. Instead of using a realist style, Boyle and scriptwriter John Hodge opted for an episodic, comedic and at times surrealistic approach, particularly in one celebrated scene when the narrator, Renton, plunges his hand into a excrement-filled toilet bowl in search of drug-laced suppositories which he has evacuated. In the novel this scene is almost unbearably realistic, but the film goes on to show Renton actually disappearing down the toilet, emerging into an underwater scene where he dives for the tablets as if they were precious pearls at the bottom of the sea. While this provides a degree of relief from being revolted by the realistic elements of the

Plate 4.4 Begbie (Robert Carlyle) intimidates Renton (Ewan McGregor) in *Trainspotting* (1995). (Courtesy of Figment / Noel Gay / Channel 4 / The Kobal Collection)

sequence, the sea-diving fantasy nevertheless communicates Renton's desperate idea of the value of his search and is in keeping with the film's juxtaposition of two contrasting ideas and styles: poison or pearls, reality or fantasy. *Trainspotting* not only deals with drugs but also with poverty and squalor, the 'other Scotland' from the Edinburgh Festival and the 'other Britain' from the sumptuous hues of heritage.

Sense and Sensibility, adapted for the screen by Emma Thompson, features heritage star Hugh Grant as Edward Ferrars and a host of other actors who have appeared in costume films. The novel's concern with patrimony and the strains it placed on women are well communicated in the film, and Ang Lee's direction utilises heritage stylistics to perfection: pictorial framing with a *mise-en-scène* which functions as 'a rigorous exercise in drawing straight lines around the emotionally distraught, sexually hungry, and therefore potentially ruinous women characters' (Fuller, 1996: 22). The film has an ironic quality which is implicit in many other heritage films, but especially so in this one, making it strangely modern and, at times, extremely comic. Although humour and satire function differently in *Sense and Sensibility* and *Trainspotting*, its usage might provide a common attraction for audiences with divergent tastes. As Claire Monk has put it: '*Sense and Sensibility* might just be the heritage movie that girls who like boys who hate heritage movies will get away with taking those boys to see' (1996: 51). At the end of the twentieth century, picturing the past was very much in generic flavour, even if claims to authenticity were growing increasingly dubious.

Chapter 5

Contemporary British cinema

HERITAGE, NOSTALGIA AND THE TRANS-NATIONAL

The UK Film Council, the Government-sponsored body responsible for allocating public funds to film-making, declared in 2006 that 'Cinema is an immensely powerful medium at the heart of the UK's creative industries and the global economy. Cinema entertains, inspires, challenges and informs audiences. It helps shape the way we see and understand ourselves and the world'. Yet the task of examining the extent to which British cinema encourages us to 'see and understand ourselves and the world' is not entirely straightforward, since as this book demonstrates, British cinema is, and always has been, a complex site of representation. Additionally, the cinema audience for British films is relatively small since as noted in Chapter 1, US films continue to dominate the box-office and DVD sales; many British films do not get released or only reach art-house audiences, while some are broadcast on television. There is also the complicating issue of classification which persists in spite of the 'cultural test' for films to qualify for tax credit. Indeed, as we have seen, most analyses tend to begin with a preamble about how difficult it is to define a British film, especially since much of current production is funded by a variety of sources originating from several countries. The debate generally considers the amount of British 'cultural content' which may or may not be reflected in its personnel, locations and subject-matter. Yet it is clear that many films engage with the multifarious aspects of living in Britain and that, as John Hill (in Vitali and Willemen, 2006: 110–11) has observed, 'while British cinema may depend upon international finance and audiences for its viability this may actually strengthen its ability to probe national questions'. Indeed, the need to differentiate products in the global market provides an economic rationale for displaying 'British' themes and identities on screen in an attempt to carve a niche in territories such as the United States, a market that is particularly difficult for foreign films to access. In addition, as the films discussed in this chapter demonstrate, the increasingly trans-national production context for British films can sharpen their critical perspective on many aspects of British life and culture.

The sentiment behind Hill's comment is therefore far from being concerned purely with economics. A long-standing imperative to reflect contemporary issues is revived with the desire for British films to probe 'national questions'. The critical acclaim of the social-realist 'New Wave' dramas produced by the 'Angry Young Men' in 1958–64, including *Room at the Top*, *Saturday Night and Sunday Morning* and *A Kind of Loving*, provides an example of how British films have been appreciated primarily for their ability to comment on issues of their time, in this case class and gender. More recently, the success of Mike Leigh's *Vera Drake* (a UK–French co-production, 2004) at international film festivals and at the box office attests to the continuing interest in British films that seek to probe social issues, even if these are represented via narratives set in the past. The persistence of the realist imperative might also take other forms, for example the national and international success of *The Full Monty* (1997), a film about six unemployed steel workers in Sheffield who form a successful male striptease act that ironically gives them back their self-respect and revives a sense of local community, was based on its ability to address a social issue in a comedic fashion. Even so, in this case it is not so much the *fact* of a film representing an 'issue', but *how* this has been done that has attracted critical comment. It has been argued that *The Full Monty*'s sentimental populism in fact masked a Blairite fantasy whereby self-help can alleviate social deprivation and conceal the persistence of deeper-seated ethnic and class divisions (Dave, 2006: 70–71). In this way contemporary British cinema comments on (or ignores) a range of complex themes that are relevant to 'national questions', even if their ostensible intention is to suggest otherwise. This chapter will explore the range of representations that typify contemporary British cinema according to the following themes, some of which have already been introduced in previous chapters as well as newer themes that have emerged as being important in recent years: nostalgia – 'heritage' past and present; youth culture – matters of life and death; experiences of ethnicity and asylum, and place, space and identity.

Nostalgia – 'heritage' past and present

From many perspectives British culture is steeped in nostalgia. As we have already seen in Chapter 4, the 'heritage' industry's ability to evoke nostalgic responses for times not directly experienced by its consumers is similarly reflected in films that mobilise affective regimes set in both the past and the present. Whatever stance one wishes to take in response to the well-known academic debates outlined earlier that have focussed on 'heritage' cinema since the 1980s, there is no doubt that the style or genre has had a profound impact on the ways in which British films are seen to offer cultural commentary about the contemporary mobilisation of the past. I would agree with Monk (2002: 117–91) however that in analysing the broad impact of heritage cinema it is necessary to consider films set in both the past and the present, since the latter in particular offer an exclusive, reactionary version of Englishness, represented by films such as *Four Weddings and a Funeral* (1994) and *Bridget Jones's Diary* (2001), that is arguably more marked than in heritage films set in the past.

The heritage film has diversified considerably since being identified primarily with adaptations of Forster novels such as *A Room With a View* (1985), *Howards End* (1992) and *Maurice* (1987) that can be described as 'intimate epics of national identity played out in a historical context . . . melodramas of everyday bourgeois life in a period setting' created by a non-British, Merchant–Ivory production team but featuring British themes and actors (Higson, 1996: 233). As we have seen, the 'museum aesthetic' of these films has attracted critical attention in so far as their *mise-en-scène* is considered to be either too distracting and seductive to foreground any social or ironic critique that the films' narratives might otherwise offer, or, conversely, a key site of pleasure for a diverse range of audiences and as an example of how a melodramatic *mise-en-scène* can offer a complex, often contradictory commentary on the mores of class society. One might argue, for example, that in films such as *The Remains of the Day* (1993) *mise-en-scène* actually *becomes* the focus of critical commentary about the bizarre operations of domestic service in a large country house. In one scene an elderly servant has become ill on a staircase and uncharacteristically left his dustpan and brush in full view. This lapse causes anxiety because it becomes the focus of suspense when the objects need to be removed out of sight of the master, a ridiculous situation in view of the gravity of the servant's illness. The timely removal of the offending items demonstrates another servant's professionalism while at the same time deploys *mise-en-scène* as an active element and means of demonstrating the human cost of a social system based on inequality and privilege.

The heritage film can therefore be seen as a typical example of the ways in which many British films have become hybridised as generic forms, capable of conveying a range of complexities that centre on narrative, setting and *mise-en-scène* that defy reductive or generalised categorisation. In this way films such as *Elizabeth* (1998) mobilise a heritage theme of royalty while at the same time incorporating an eclectic, postmodern style that resonates with other British films that revive older generic forms, such as the gangster film in *Sexy Beast* (2000) and *I'll Sleep When I'm Dead* (2003). These films pay homage to *Get Carter* (1971) which has become a cult classic in the British gangster genre, and *The Long Good Friday* (1980), demonstrating that 'heritage' can in fact be loosely used as a means of describing generic homage with reference to particular regimes of visual representation that have been developed more in relation to cinema than to history. It functions as a palimpsest upon which narratives about aspects of British life – past and present – can be inscribed.

Thus while Mike Leigh (2006: 12) claimed he was not influenced by films of the 1950s for *Vera Drake* it is clear that the film draws on a cinephilic sensibility that demonstrates an awareness of the heritage aesthetic described above. Set in 1950, about Vera (Imelda Staunton), a working class woman whose family is unaware that she performs backstreet abortions 'to help out young girls', the film displays the past with sets that are evocative of a 'heightened realism', establishing a verisimilitudinous address that encourages us to recognise the period even if we have not experienced it directly. The minutiae of detail, from domestic crockery and wallpaper to clothes, is convincing, acquiring narrative weight as the film progresses from its opening shots which capture Vera in the kitchen, shot from outside the door as her family walk in and out of the frame when she busily attends to the cooking, humming a cheery tune. This technique – of holding a shot while allowing the actors to move in and out and for a clear view of the decor and props – is repeated on different occasions, acquiring a pictorial resonance that demonstrates the dynamic elements of the film's *mise-en-scène*. Later, when Vera is cleaning a rich woman's house we see her again from outside the doorway, but this time the items on display are similar to the contents of the affluent properties in heritage films. Yet the nostalgia, the cosiness, is reserved for Vera's house, since it is there that we experience a sense of belonging, of a small, interdependent community whose unity is threatened when Vera is arrested.

The film contains a class critique as social inequalities form its major theme. Again, *mise-en-scène* is a key visual register when, for example, Vera crouches on the floor to clean Mrs Fowler's fender, a small figure dwarfed by the magisterial marble fireplace as her employer nearly steps on Vera when reaching for a card on the mantelpiece (see Plate 5.1). When Vera visits a young West Indian woman to perform an abortion, the room is dark, bare and minimally furnished. The harshness of the surroundings accentuate our perception of the woman's evident fear and ignorance about what to expect once Vera has gone. By contrast, a rich young woman who has become pregnant can pay to go to a clinic after being referred by a psychiatrist because she has been told what to say to convince him to make the recommendation. She is housed in a comfortable room, the deed is done and she returns home afterwards with her problem neatly solved. Each set has a pristine quality that illuminates the set designer's achievement while displaying items that ironically have acquired a heightened commercial value in a contemporary culture interested in vernacular china and antique kitchen appliances.

Indeed, these items are invested with economic and symbolic status in visual, virtual and print culture that similarly promote commodities from the past, or designs that are imitative of the past, to constitute significant

Plate 5.1 Imelda Staunton as Vera, dwarfed by the fireplace in *Vera Drake* (2004). (Courtesy of Fine Line Features / The Kobal Collection / Simon Mein)

indicators of taste and identity. In *Vera Drake* this sensibility acquires an additional generic function that produces an ironic comment on this changed, contemporaneous value of the *mise-en-scène*. When we see the kitchen of Frank (Adrian Scarborough), Vera's brother-in-law and his wife Joyce (Heather Craney), who have recently moved to a house, the same camera positioning is used to contrast the more modern, brighter, sparser setting with the few cramped rooms Vera shares with her family. Although the film does not relate to the majority of British films of the 1950s it does share resonances with the 'new wave' films' critique of materialism and its association with female characters, whereby Vera's complete lack of interest in making money is contrasted with Joyce's incessant desire for the latest domestic appliances and a television, a caricature that is exaggerated to the extent of her appearing to use becoming pregnant to get her husband Frank to buy her what she desires. As soon as Vera is disgraced Joyce, with her socially mobile aspirations, takes the opportunity to persuade Frank to distance himself from his brother's family with whom she would rather not identify.

Other films are similarly influenced by an aesthetic awareness of heritage sensibilities, but from a different perspective, as with Pawel Pawlikowski's

My Summer of Love (2004). This film is not set in the past, and draws on a broad range of influences that evoke a sense of the 'northern pastoral' rather than the more usual industrial settings associated with the British 'new wave' films of 1958–64, or the post-industrial north of *The Full Monty* or *Brassed Off* (1996). It nevertheless shares some of the themes and stylistic traits of 'the new wave' including 'That Long Shot of Our Town From That Hill', a term used by Higson to describe characters viewing the industrial landscape from a hill that can be seen as an expression of the director's authorial, outsider commentary (referred to by Lovell in Higson, 1996: 171). While this observation is generally taken to indicate a middle-class perspective on working-class culture, its use in *My Summer of Love* is rather generic shorthand to indicate a locale that this particular narrative assumes is familiar to the audience. *My Summer of Love* features a cross-class romance that takes place between two young women in rural Yorkshire. The masculine angst of the 'new wave' has been reversed with these characters who inhabit an uneasy relationship with their class background. Tamsin (Emily Blunt) lives in a mansion while Mona (Natalie Press), an orphan, lives in a pub with her brother, a born-again Christian who is converting the pub into a religious centre. Our first view of Tamsin is in an ironic shot that frames her with her white horse, a statuesque figure seen from above as Mona lies on the grass beneath her. She is subsequently identified with an iconography of class including classical music that she plays badly on the cello, or a stylised bohemianism that pervades her parents' mansion. Similarly, Mona is depicted at odds with her surroundings, without a home, in a somewhat liminal state as the two young women appear to be most free when riding on an old motorbike over the hills, accompanied by non-diegetic music that recalls a *nouvelle vague* sensibility.

While very different from *Vera Drake*, the film similarly adopts some visual strategies more usually associated with the stylistics of 'classic' heritage films. These pictorial compositions are ravishingly beautiful shots of the countryside, of blue and pink skies, of Tamsin's family mansion and of the exotic, idyllic summer she spends with Mona, who is seduced by the hedonistic, bohemian life she discovers with Tamsin. As in *Maurice*, or even television's *Brideshead Revisited* (1981), the pleasures of homoerotic attraction are explored through visual sumptuousness. Combined with elements of quirkiness that are reminiscent of Terrence Malick's *Badlands* (1973), Tamsin and Mona enjoy a brief time of intimacy, acting out a fantasy life listening to Edith Piaf records in the rambling mansion, dressing-up and defying convention in public. The film has a dreamy quality that reflects this experience while at the same time introducing the themes of pretence and betrayal that bring the summer and the relationship to an end. Mona's trust in Tamsin is shattered when she discovers that she has been used for idle amusement, as erotic distraction for a rich girl who has lied about having a sister who died and who will return to boarding school rather than run off

Plate 5.2 Robbie (James McAvoy) and Cecilia (Keira Knightley) reunited in fiction in *Atonement* (2007). (Courtesy of Focus Features / The Kobal Collection / Alex Bailey)

with Mona. The film's visual and thematic intensity is accentuated by the temporal notion of 'summer', of an idyllic time that will inevitably pass. Similarly, Tamsin and Mona's young age marks them as being open to new experiences, another theme of many contemporary British films that also deal with aspects of youth culture (see next section below).

Atonement (Joe Wright, 2007), a US/UK/French co-production (Working Title) based on Ian McEwan's novel, makes similar use of heritage-influenced *mise-en-scène* and a theme of youth, betrayal and misunderstanding. It centres on a child's (Briony Tallis, played by Saoirse Ronan) false accusation of a young man, Robbie (James McAvoy) who she names as the rapist of her fifteen-year-old cousin Lola. In making this claim, Briony is influenced by witnessing her elder sister Cecilia's (Keira Knightley) attraction to Robbie and of his similar feelings for her. Robbie asks Briony to deliver a note to Cecilia which Briony reads and is shocked to find that it is far from a prosaic love-note but in fact the wrong, smuttier version that Robbie wrote in fun and meant to consign to the waste-paper basket. She builds up a false picture of him as a 'sex maniac' and her bewilderment at her sister's love affair contributes to her 'naming' of Robbie as the rapist in order to end a series of events she has found disturbing. The accusation has tumultuous consequences for Robbie who did not commit the crime (the rapist was her brother's friend who was staying at the house). Robbie is imprisoned and then joins the army in the Second World War, when he is reunited with Cecilia who is working as a nurse. Briony plans to finally tell the truth so that Robbie can be exonerated. At the end of the film we learn that this conclusion was invented by Briony who wrote down the tragic story of her youth in a novel, giving Robbie and Cecilia a happy ending in fiction that was not the case in real life since they were both killed in the Second World War. The surprise of McEwan's novel is therefore retained in the film: we are witnessing a true story with an embellished ending which has been created to give the author, Briony, some sense of atonement for the dreadful thing she did as a child. The film's cinematographic style wallows in heritage visuals, particularly in the first section which takes place in the manor house where Briony encounters the young lovers. The camera style is however reminiscent of more recent films which favour a roving camera and crisper editing style than that which is associated with 'classic' heritage films. Briony's first, confused sighting of the lovers flirting with each other is, for example, communicated via editing which plays with point-of-view as we see the child witnessing the scene through an open window in the house. In many ways this film epitomises the prestige-associated high-end of contemporary British cinema with its heritage visuals and themes; adaptation from a prestigious literary source by an eminent British author; use of big box-office actors such as Knightley; and numerous Oscar nominations. Youth culture is indeed examined but apart from the film's general observation about the power of misunderstanding that comes out of ignorance, and a child's confusion about the 'adult' world of sexual attraction, this is a narrative about the past. At the same time another strain of contemporary cinema probed a very different social milieu.

Youth culture: matters of life and death

Trainspotting (1996) was undoubtedly the film that ensured that the most frequent cinemagoers, aged between fifteen and thirty-four, became increasingly the major focus of representations on screen. Its strident critique of bourgeois living and depiction of drug abuse amongst the Scottish 'underclass' established a trend of films that were similarly innovative in terms of style and theme. For while *Trainspotting*'s content was bleak, its style was visually and aurally energetic, incorporating surrealist elements, Brit-Pop soundtrack and featuring a striking, ironic voice-over narration by the lead character Renton (Ewan McGregor). The '*Trainspotting* effect' reverberated in films such as *Twin Town* (1997) and *Human Traffic* (1999), that sought to reflect the Welsh experience by being set respectively in Swansea and Cardiff. While these films are aimed at a younger audience than *Vera Drake* or even *Atonement* they nevertheless present a similar preoccupation with notions of community, in this case young people drawn together by drugs, a shared lifestyle and self-consciously occupying an outsider status in relation to the older generation. While the locales of Swansea and Cardiff might have promised to deliver a regional insight into these problems, the 'generational conflict' theme tended to limit the scope of both films' ability to invoke a specific Welsh address to little more than a perfunctory degree. Rather, *Human Traffic* explores outsider status by focusing on club culture in a formal attempt to duplicate the 'rave' experience that some critics found unsuccessful (see Brooks, 1999: 47). The film borrows from *Trainspotting* the frenetic aesthetic that moves in and out of characters' consciousness as thoughts are immediately reproduced as surreal events on screen. In terms of relevance to the traditions of British cinema, this technique pre-dates *Trainspotting*, since it was used distinctively in *Billy Liar!* (1963), another example of a British 'new wave' precedent informing a contemporary film. Also, *Human Traffic* takes place over a weekend, as its leading character Jip (John Simm) declares: 'Forget work, forget your family, forget your latest insecurity – the weekend has landed!', a premise that resonates with Arthur Seaton (Albert Finney) being 'out for a good time' in *Saturday Night and Sunday Morning* (1960) as well as with Renton's 'choose life' speech in *Trainspotting*. The forty-eight hour escape from dead-end jobs for the characters in *Human Traffic* provides an interlude of freedom, a similarly structured temporal technique as in *My Summer of Love*.

Friendship between five people is the major theme of *Human Traffic*, with each character being introduced via voice-over, as in *Trainspotting*.

The love of verbal dexterity is a trait these films borrow from Tarantino but in a starkly different context. *Human Traffic* does not seek to pronounce on the drug issue, but its style allows it to articulate different opinions, contrasting the friends' enthusiasm with inter-cut shots giving dire warnings, often in a caricatured fashion. The dead-end job is tolerated so the weekend's highs can be paid for, the film providing in one of its ironic intercuts an account of how drugs are circulated in clubs, their managers aware of what is happening and profiting from the transactions. The contrast between the intense excitement and build-up to going to the club with Sunday's 'low', when the friends are dispersed and have awkward conversations with their parents, communicates a sense of the fragility of their experience of friendship, based as it is on a mutual desire to have a good time during the brief period in their lives when they need not make other plans; the concept of a life on hold is one that reverberates in many youth culture films. *Human Traffic* is a sensitive exploration of 'the chemical generation' in scenes such as Jip's desperate attempt to talk his way into a club so one of their group without a ticket can join them for the long anticipated night out. As noted earlier, this trope of contrasting the working environment as mundane and endured for enabling the weekend 'event' to happen, harks back to the theme of *Saturday Night and Sunday Morning*. In this and other respects there are clear continuities between older and contemporary cinema culture.

Even darker issues are addressed by *28 Days Later* (2002), another film aimed primarily at the younger, core cinema-going audience. Produced by the same team as *Trainspotting*, *28 Days Later* is a hybrid genre film (including horror, thriller, science fiction) that explores the theme of total devastation caused by a deadly virus known as 'the rage' that is spread after animal rights activists release an infected monkey from a research facility in Cambridge. In twenty-eight days the virus spreads, killing all but a few survivors including Jim (Cillian Murphy) who awakes in hospital from a coma to discover that the virus has claimed thousands of lives, with news of it reaching Paris and New York. The unfamiliar sight of London devoid of cars and people is conveyed by digital technology, one of the first major British feature films to use the format. This grainy aesthetic adds to the film's 'grunge' effect which is also evident in the costuming and serves the additional function of heightened realism. Jim explores the post-apocalyptic world which is spectacular for its strange emptiness, familiar London landmarks such as the London Eye and Big Ben acquiring a sinister appearance as he wanders through the empty streets. Eventually Jim meets other survivors, Selena (Naomie Harris), and then Frank (Brendan Gleeson) and Hannah (Megan Burns), a father and daughter. Together they form a sort of family and leave London in an abandoned taxi to locate a military encampment of other survivors outside Manchester. The sequences of their journey north are like a road movie as they drive through beautiful countryside and survive further attacks from 'the infected'. At the end of their journey Frank is however contaminated by the virus and shot by one of the soldiers. The encampment is a large country house which is an ironic usage of a location more usually reserved for heritage films. Rather than finding temporary security, Jim, Selena and Hannah find that the soldiers are ruthless in their terror of becoming infected, their own worst enemies as the film develops a devastating exploration of human nature in crisis. Jim, Selena and Hannah eventually escape and try to attract the attention of a plane that gives them hope that they will be rescued. Yet we do not know at the end of the film whether the rest of the world is in a similar state of devastation or, indeed, whether they will be saved.

The sense of community which is confined to older teenagers and 'twenty-somethings' evident in the previous films discussed is not demonstrated in *28 Days Later* as the catastrophe brings disparate people together and communicates respect for the older generation who are not caricatured as in *Trainspotting* and *Human Traffic*. Indeed, the characters who are most threatening and 'uncool' in *28 Days Later* are the young army officers who have become brutalised by the crisis. By contrast, the tender feelings Jim has for his dead parents when he finds that they have committed suicide rather than be infected by the 'rage', is another example of how this film's different generic mix and dark theme works against creating 'youth' as an autonomous and idealised grouping.

A nightmare scenario that is rooted in realism is the result of genre hybridity combined with location shooting. An eerily empty supermarket provides a momentary sensation of security, as familiar habits of pushing shopping trolleys and picking favourite foods creates a nostalgic sense of the past for the survivors, a memory of 'normal' life. The film tapped into contemporary fears about techno-science, genetic engineering and AIDS with its critique of experiments on animals in the opening sequence when we see monkeys as victims of the 'rage' tests. The virus is carried in the blood which has connotations with fears about AIDS, as well as the appearance of new infections that in this case are the result of human intervention.

Despite the terrifying scenario the stylistic energy that was evident in *Trainspotting* was repeated and the cast included Christopher Eccleston as the military commander. Eccleston had also starred in director Danny Boyle's successful thriller *Shallow Grave* (1994), and was associated with other 'revival' British films such as *Elizabeth*. These aspects contributed to the film's box-office success in Europe and the USA, representing the transnational appeal of much of recent British cinema. In addition it shares with *Human Traffic* and *My Summer of Love* a stylistic foregrounding of place with its shots of the city and the rural landscape that have the effect of combining a local address with a more global sensibility. While each film has its particular locale which may or may not be familiar to audiences, their basic topographies could also be identified with other cities and landscapes,

Plate 5.3 The end of London as we know it. Cillian Murphy in *28 Days Later*
(2002). (Courtesy of DNA / Figment / Fox / The Kobal Collection / Peter Mountain)

evoking a kind of shorthand familiarity that opens up these films to international audiences. A sequel was released in 2007, *28 Weeks Later*, but this
was not as successful as the original, even though it continued with the
theme of spreading infection, 'the rage' and indications of global disaster.
Danny Boyle was executive producer rather than director, and a new cast
featured in the sequel. This example demonstrates the difficulty of genre in

that repetition does not always result in box-office success. The novelty of *28 Days Later* was absent from its successor; what had appeared as a new and exciting formula turned out to be restricted to its first appearance.

Ethnicity and asylum

As the previous films discussed have challenged any homogeneous notion of British film culture, those that reflect the experience of different ethnic groupings similarly work to broaden a sense of how cinema is capable of engaging with changing social and economic realities. The comedy genre, as Mather points out, has been a particularly significant genre in this respect since

> the comic mode, when effectively mixed with dramatic and compelling explorations of ethnicity in 'everyday' British society, is . . . particularly well suited to depictions of 'hybrid' groups and communities, who may be involved in the process of formulating new identities and priorities, but do not necessarily wish to forget or deny the emotional, spiritual and cultural journey which they have undertaken, en route towards a new future, spiritual home or 'promised' land.
>
> (2006: 112)

Since the decline of the independent film workshops of the 1980s which produced some innovative, experimental films detailing Black British experience (see also Chapter 8), including *Passion for Remembrance* (1986), *Handsworth Songs* (1986) and *The People's Account* (1988), more populist forms have been successful at the box-office, produced by film-makers from the Asian, African and Caribbean diaspora. While operating in different generic contexts, comedy has tended to dominate the output of directors such as Gurinder Chadha whose most notable films have been *Bhaji On the Beach* (1993) and *Bend It Like Beckham* (2002) which examine the experience of multiculturalism in Britain and the inter-generational conflicts that can result from the tension between tradition and hybrid identities which can be described as 'British-Asianness'(Malik in Higson, 1996: 213). *East is East* (1999), adapted from a stage play by Ayub Khan-Din, explores the clash between first and second generation Pakistani immigrants in Salford in the 1970s. George Khan (Om Puri) is married to Ella (Linda Bassett), a white English woman, but is determined to bring up his children as traditional Muslims. They rebel and refuse to accept the wedding plans Khan hatches with other Asian families, which are a source of comedy as well as an acute observation of the strains on family life wrought by cross-cultural identities and allegiances. As Malik has commented, *East is East* is predicated on the deployment of a classic 'culture clash' discourse in which 'the struggle to acquire "Black Britishness" or "British-Asianness" . . . is typically attributed to the supposedly irreconcilable differences between an antiquated tradition of religious or cultural fundamentalism and a modern, enfranchised, secular lifestyle' (Malik, 2002: 97).

In this respect the film can be compared to *My Son the Fanatic* (1997), scripted by Hanif Kureishi, which presents the opposite scenario in which the father, rather than the son, is at odds with tradition. It is a darker comedy in which Parvez (Om Puri), a Pakistani-born man who works as a taxi driver in Bradford, sees his son reject western values in favour of religious fundamentalism and is shocked to see him participate in violent Muslim action against prostitutes who Parvez knows through the taxi service. The only solace he finds is with Bettina (Rachel Griffiths), one of the prostitutes with whom he develops a relationship that is presented as loving and outside of the stressful conflicts that dominate the rest of his life. As Dave has commented, in both films

> the desire for pure, unitary, cultural identities based on traditional certainties is pitted . . . against the wishes of those for whom identity is irretrievably caught up in the 'cultures of hybridity' which have arisen as a result of diasporas created through post-war, post-colonial migration.
>
> (Dave, 2006: 13)

Unlike his son, Parvez cannot extricate himself from the life and tastes he has acquired in Britain, and can see through the hypocrisy of a Muslim teacher from Pakistan, who stays in his house at the request of his son to give religious instruction, but whose real agenda is to emigrate to Britain. On the other hand, the world of prostitution and night-clubs that Parvez comes to know through his job is depicted as violent, racist and exploitative, lightened only by his friendship with many of the women and their culture of mutual support. No easy solutions are given in a film that explores the fractured relationships experienced by men such as Parvez whose job places him in the position of contemplative observer, a situation that the film depicts by containing many shots of him looking out of his car, much as Travis Bickle does on the streets of New York in Scorsese's *Taxi Driver* (1976).

Last Resort (2001) and *Dirty Pretty Things* (2002) focus on more recent experiences of immigration from Eastern Europe. Pawel Pawlikowski's *Last Resort* is about Tanya (Dina Korzun), a Russian woman who comes to Britain with her son in search of her English fiancé who never appears. She decides to apply for political asylum, beginning a process that leaves her in bureaucratic limbo, detained in a holding area in 'Stonehaven' which was filmed in the seaside town of Margate. This jaded environment of amusement arcades and bleak housing is the background for exploitation by men out to profit from immigrants by involving them in the internet porn business. Wanting to return to Russia but desperate for cash, Tanya becomes

Plate 5.4 Dina Korzun and Paddy Considine as Tanya and Alfie in *Last Resort* (2000). (Courtesy of BBC / The Kobal Collection)

friendly with Alfie (Paddy Considine), an arcade manager, who eventually helps Tanya and her son escape from Stonehaven. Much of the film focuses on the degradation experienced by asylum seekers who are virtual prisoners while they are caught up in the bureaucratic mire of detention.

The film exploits the irony that this takes place in an environment designed for pleasure, and many shots capture the resort's faded glory in heritage fashion as pictorially constructed shots of the bay, seafront and iconic 'Dreamland' amusement arcade (featured in Lindsay Anderson's short film of 1953), contrast with the grim tower block which is Tanya's temporary home. Familiar or comforting notions of place are challenged as the setting exaggerates her loneliness and isolation, shot in a de-saturated palette of greys and other muted colours. The bleak apartment she shares with her son has paper peeling off one wall which ironically is patterned with palm trees. Alfie paints it blue, provides them with furniture and a television and offers kindness which develops into love for Tanya who nevertheless still wants to return to Russia.

The uprooting of Tanya and her son is conveyed visually through shots which are resonant of a bleak iconography of the Eastern Bloc with its grey concrete tower blocks. At the same time, the place is recognisable as Margate, producing a sort of visual short-hand for environments of displacement and alienation that are not necessarily confined to a single location. Massey's observations about the negative impact of 'time–space compression', in which people on the move like Tanya have little control over a process which generally exaggerates unequal power relationships, are pertinent to this film (Massey, 1993: 239). In this case the new technologies are used to exploit the refugees in Stonehaven for the internet porn business. Ironically, more basic technology such as the telephone is difficult to access as we see queues of immigrants outside one seafront box, frustrated by the process and language. On the other hand, as pointed out by Roberts, the telephone box

> provides a focal point around which the asylum seekers and refugees gather. The exilic and diasporic spaces of London or other possible transnational connections permeate the the experiential and geo-political borders of Stonehaven . . . The phone box becomes a transnational space by which a metonymic 'last resort' of parochial, historically contingent England is steadily undone.
>
> (Roberts, 2002: 83)

From another screen perspective *Last Orders* (2001), adapted from Graham Swift's novel, uses Margate jetty as the final destination for spreading the ashes of Jack (Michael Caine), whose friends journey there by car from London. Their memories of Jack are recalled in flashbacks along the way, with Margate functioning in this instance as a seedy, but nevertheless fondly remembered holiday destination, representing in this case 'parochial, historically contingent England', rather than the more desolate representations offered in *Last Resort*.

Yet seaside resorts are not only traumatic for immigrants, as shown in artist Tracey Emin's loosely autobiographical film *Top Spot* (2004), which documents the home-grown sexual exploitation of teenage girls born and brought up in Margate. Even this film, with its poignant and harrowing accounts of teenage experience, contains shots of great symbolic beauty, using a combination of formats and techniques such as Super 8 footage and slow-motion cinematography. Emin intended the film to be a 'universal story' rather than its imagery and narrative relating solely to Margate. The film's focus on six adolescents, their fantasies and traumatic experiences including rape and suicide, uses Margate as a place that is seductive but also the background from which they wish to escape. One of the characters, for example, dreams of going to Egypt: we see shots of Margate intercut with Cairo, which has its own version of 'Dreamland'; on another occasion we see Cleopatra's Needle in Ramsgate (near Margate) as the background to one of the girls eating chips. This suggestion of a local–global imagination is consistent with other films' usage of location as a graphic and symbolic means of visualising the impact of globalisation.

Place, space and identity

Homi Bhabha has written about some of the key differences between 'diversity' and 'difference' which can be usefully applied to British cinema. He argues that while celebrating cultural diversity involves a desire to return to fixed, 'pre-given cultural contents and customs . . . that live unsullied by the intertextuality of their historical locations, safe in the Utopianism of a mythic memory of a unique collective identity', cultural difference, on the other hand, is more of a dynamic process which recognises cultural exchange and interaction (Bhabha, 1994: 34). I would argue that the films I have discussed in this chapter attempt to represent the latter as explorations of the places, spaces, specificities of, and interactions between, many co-existing identities that relate to the global/local realities of modern society. There are other films, however, for which the latter is more problematic. The successful cycle of romantic comedies tends to present a more hermetically sealed world in which difference is largely ignored in favour of using London as a site of a 'fairy-tale' existence for the mostly affluent characters in films such as *Notting Hill* (1999), *Bridget Jones's Diary* and *Love Actually* (2003). In these films the characters' quest is towards the attainment of romantic fulfilment and the environments in which they live display a *mise-en-scène* of contemporary privilege that in particular is represented through property, for example, the large period houses of *Notting Hill*. American actors often feature as major characters, emphasising a cross-cultural dimension that can be seen to relate to their production companies' aspirations for overseas distribution, as well as to the funding structures behind the films which frequently involve American financial participation. In this case 'national questions' are hardly probed, but perhaps in their exclusion of 'difference' the films nevertheless reveal, as Dave has argued, 'the insecurities of the middle class' (2006: 46).

The London featured in the romantic comedies is indeed a world away from its depiction in Gary Oldman's *Nil By Mouth* (1997) or in Michael Winterbottom's *Wonderland* (1999). The latter depicts one working-class family's experiences over four days within a cityscape which is marked by a fractured and uncertain sense of time and space. The postmodern city is represented by time-lapse shots, slow-motion and speeded-up images which suggest the trans-national experience of travelling in tube trains, of crowded city streets, of people entering and leaving pubs and, from the view of one character's high-rise flat, of iconic London landmarks such as St Paul's Cathedral. The four days in the life of the family are thus inserted within a much larger canvas which conveys the pace, fluidity and alienating space of contemporary city life. In an approach that is similar to some of the strategies deployed in the social-realist British film, *Wonderland* includes shots of the landscape which are not necessarily related to the advancement of the narrative. This 'realistic surplus' of shots of the characters walking along the street which are interspersed with speeded-up or slowed-down shots of the cityscape, allows bodies and *mise-en-scène* to become part of Winterbottom's expression of the complex 'reality' of urban living.

A range of other disparate images of London can be observed in films including *Lock, Stock & Two Smoking Barrels* (1998), *Croupier* (1998) and *Bullet Boy* (2004). In these films the criminal underworld engulfs the characters, as perpetrators or victims. For Dave, the notion of the 'urban pastoral' developed by Stallabrass is instructive in understanding *Lock, Stock & Two Smoking Barrels* for its nostalgic preoccupation with images of a glamorous, criminal, masculine 'underclass' that is evocative of the 'retro' culture of contemporary 'New Lad' magazines (2006: 84). The representation of violence and guns is reminiscent of Tarantino's style that parodies and celebrates older films, in this case *Get Carter* (Mike Hodges), and displays a similar, cartoon-like disregard of squeamishness or political correctness. *Croupier*, also directed by Mike Hodges, presents London as part of the worldwide casino network. The central character, Jack (Clive Owen), an aspiring writer, is lured back into the croupier job he learned in South Africa. The London setting is hardly obtrusive, except for a prominent Underground sign in one of the exterior shots and dark streets that are reminiscent of a film noir aesthetic. The majority of the other sets are literally underground, in the basement flat Jack shares with his partner, and in the casino, an environment which re-acquaints him with a gambling world he despises. In spite of his professionalism, frequent insistence that he is not a gambler and the distancing effect of his voice-over narration which is the novel he is writing about the casino, he too becomes corrupted. The easy money, global language of gambling and proximity to criminal activity is depicted as compulsive but ultimately destructive of personal relationships and integrity.

Bullet Boy, set in Hackney, is about Ricky (Ashley Walters), a young black man who has just left prison, and the difficulties he has trying to extricate himself from gangland crime and a local culture of violence. His younger brother, Curtis (Luke Fraser), seems destined to follow the same pattern, particularly after he takes a gun that has been given to Ricky and accidentally shoots a friend. Ricky's involvement in revenge crimes ultimately leads to his own murder, an event that resolves Curtis to reject the

Plate 5.5 The urban pastoral. Ashley Walters in *Bullet Boy* (2004). (Courtesy of Shine Films /BBC Films / The Kobal Collection)

world of violence with a symbolic act at the end of the film of hurling the gun into the canal. In this film guns are not glamorised, except within the videogames we see Curtis watching in the high-rise flat he shares with his brother and mother, who despairs of the cycle of inevitable violence that has claimed her older son. A different, more hybridised sense of the 'urban pastoral' is suggested by the proximity of the flats to wasteland where Curtis plays and which invest the landscape with an ominous, borderland sensibility. The interior settings are also marked by this tension when on some occasions we see the flat decorated for a party or the site of a family meal, as a safe haven with a spectacular view, while on others this domesticity is disrupted by a rough police search and by the knowledge that the gun given to Ricky has been hidden there. As with *My Son the Fanatic* the differences explored in this film are not so much between communities but rather differences within them. Curtis's rejection of the culture that has doomed his brother is the film's utopian theme while at the same time it has drawn attention to the social deprivation and dead-end jobs that determine its persistence. As Charlotte Brunsdon has observed, *Bullet Boy* is representative of films that deal with 'local Londons', in this case Hackney, that contrasts with 'landmark London' which instead concentrates on an iconography of Big Ben, the Houses of Parliament, red buses or black taxis (Brunsdon, 2007: 21–88).

The films directed by Shane Meadows also reference place and identity as major themes, but this time from a non-metropolitan, local perspective. This is invariably Nottingham or, if not directly referenced, its environs in the Midlands in films such as *Once Upon a Time In the Midlands* (2002) and *Dead Man's Shoes* (2004). The council house milieu of working-class life is the main context for characters longing for direction, and who are usually vulnerable to influence by stronger, older characters, as in *A Room For Romeo Brass* (1999) and *This Is England* (2007). In both these films young boys become susceptible to being dominated by charismatic, unbalanced men. In *A Room For Romeo Brass* Romeo (Andrew Shim) falls under the spell of Morell (Paddy Considine) after being rescued by him when threatened by other boys. Morell is attracted to Romeo's sister but when she refuses his attentions Morell becomes increasingly violent towards Romeo and his friend. The film charts their confusion as Morell pitches one friend against the other, eventually rejecting both and in the process revealing how charisma is not always what it seems. Similarly, in *This Is England* Shim again stars as Milky, a black teenager who is caught between different varieties of skinhead in the early 1980s, a group who are not racist and one, led by Combo, who is a disturbed, demagogic National Front sympathiser (Stephen Graham). The film steers a shifting course through the dynamics of persuasion when Shaun (Thomas Turgoose), a young boy, seeks direction from Combo in trying to understand why his father died in the Falklands War. Initially a member of the non-racist gang of which Milky is a member, Shaun becomes increasingly drawn towards Combo's language of certainty and promise of identity as a skinhead, complete with the its uniform of shaved head, Ben Sherman shirt, red braces, jeans and heavy boots. After Shaun witnesses a violent situation towards the end of the film when Milky gets beaten very badly by Combo, the film however ends with Shaun, now wearing ordinary clothes, tossing his treasured St George Cross flag (a symbol of the National Front) into the sea in a symbolic gesture that indicates he has rejected the culture of racist violence into which he was welcomed by Combo. As with *Romeo Brass* the emotional seduction of a youngster by a charismatic older man has resulted in a traumatic learning experience whereby a promised stable identity is seen to crumble when the violent and racist realities on which it is based are exposed.

Among the other film-makers who have been similarly drawn to narratives about the spaces and places occupied by disaffected youth and 'the underclass' is Ken Loach. Ken Loach is a key figure in oppositional film-making culture and could equally have been discussed in Chapter 8, although he does not really belong to a tradition of experimental art cinema. As noted in Chapter 3, *Kes* was a seminal film in its demonstration of observational drama and the use of untrained actors for the creation of a realist aesthetic, first demonstrated so powerfully in the television documentary drama *Cathy Come Home* (BBC, 1966). Loach has worked in both film and television, the latter being suited for oppositional realism and where he worked productively with writers who shared similar political concerns, including Jim Allen. Allen wrote *Hidden Agenda* (1990), a devastating film about political corruption and the British Army's 'shoot to kill' policies in Northern Ireland, as well as two other notable collaborations with Loach, *Raining Stones* (1993, set in Manchester) and *Land and Freedom* (1995, set in the Spanish Civil War). Even though Loach's career has been far from consistent in terms of critical or popular success, there is a sense of artistic integrity evident in his preoccupation with naturalism and advancing the cause of political, polemical film-making within a range of distinctive locales. The most significant films in this respect include *Riff-Raff* (1991, set in London), *Raining Stones*, *Sweet Sixteen* (2002, set in a Scottish shipyard town with severe unemployment) and *The Wind That Shakes the Barley* (2006, set in 1920s during the Irish Civil War). Indeed, in this film and others Loach has frequently drawn on history to address current social themes and continues to be one of Britain's most respected film-makers, particularly on the film festival circuit (Leigh, 2002). He is attracted to international themes which reflect his concerns with struggles that are experienced worldwide, for example, the problems of American immigrant workers in *Bread and Roses* (2000), and *Carla's Song* (1996) which examines the plight of the Sandinistas in Nicaragua.

The Scottish location of *Sweet Sixteen* is indicative of much recent cinema that has been associated with 'New Scottish cinema' (Petrie, 2000). Agencies such as Scottish Screen have participated in the sponsorship of a range of films that address contemporary issues. After *Trainspotting* Scotland became more popular as a location for such films including *Orphans* (Peter Mullan 1999), *Ae Fond Kiss* (Ken Loach, 2004) and *Young Adam* (David Mackenzie, 2003). *Young Adam* is adapted from a Scottish novel by Alexander Trocchi who left Glasgow for France in the early 1950s and then moved to the USA where he was associated with the 'beat' culture generation of writers.

Young Adam was first published in 1954 as a pornographic novel which was revised later for re-publication in 1966 with some of the sex scenes cut but with the addition of a controversial scene of erotic sexual violence that also featured in the film. The book and film are about Joe (Ewan McGregor), a frustrated writer who works on a barge on the Union canal between Glasgow and Edinburgh with Les (Peter Mullan), his wife Ella (Tilda Swinton) and their young son. Both texts are inflected with the existential angst that was a feature of 1950s French literature. There is also an eroticised treatment of the different sexual relationships Joe experiences with Ella and, via a series of flashbacks, with his ex-girlfriend Cathie (Emily Morton), the latter being particularly disturbing for its violent nature in one particular scene. At the beginning of the film Joe and Les discover a partly clothed woman's body floating in the water. We later discover it is Cathie's body and that Joe knows how she died. This is revealed to the audience in

Plate 5.6 Les (Peter Mullan) and Joe (Ewan McGregor) on the Union Canal in *Young Adam* (2003). (Courtesy of Recorded Pictures Company / The Kobal Collection / Neil Davidson)

one of the flashback sequences about halfway through the film of a chance meeting between Cathie and Joe after they have parted. After talking in a café they walk to the quayside and have sex under a truck. Afterwards Cathie informs Joe she is pregnant and that she would like them to bring up the child together. Joe rules this out but says that he will send her money in the future. They quarrel and she accidentally falls into the water when trying to catch up with him as he walks briskly away from her. She does not surface and instead of informing the police Joe throws her bag and clothes into the water. Joe does not tell anyone that he knew her or of the circumstances of her death when he and Les later bring her drowned body ashore.

This event haunts the film which is otherwise preoccupied with Joe's sexual relationship with Ella. His intimate scenes with her are often the occasion for a flashback-memory scene with Cathie who we learn supported him in his failed attempt to be a writer. When Les eventually finds out about Joe's relationship with Ella he decides to leave since she owns the barge. Joe then shares the barge with Ella and her son but this does not result in a lasting relationship and Joe leaves. His lack of commitment to Ella is demonstrated when he has sex with her sister Gwen (Therese Bradley) when she visits them on the barge and Ella becomes distant. The cycle of transient, risky and uncommitted relationships begins again when Joe lodges with a friend and at the same time starts an affair with his wife. The film ends with the trial and conviction of Cathie's plumber boyfriend Daniel (Ewan Stewart) who has been accused of her murder. In an attempt to salve his troubled conscience, Joe writes an anonymous note confessing that he witnessed the accident, did not report it to the police and that Daniel is innocent. He leaves the note on a desk as he enters the court but in any case the plumber is sentenced to death. Joe looks set to move on in the final scene when he throws a mirror into the water at the place where Cathie fell to her death. The mirror, which we have seen him gaze into on many occasions, is a significant object since it was a gift from Cathie, engraved with the following message: 'Think of me when you look at yourself with undying love, C.' This obvious symbolism of him trying to forget her gains an ironic perspective when we know that he has been haunted by memories of their relationship, the implication in many of his contemplative interludes being that he did love her, but was unable to sustain commitment.

This representation of Joe as a transient person is similar to the central character in *Morvern Callar* (Lynne Ramsay, 2002, further discussed in Chapter 8), another film based on a novel and set in West Scotland. The latter centres on Morvern, a young woman (Samantha Morton) who finds her boyfriend has committed suicide in their flat. He has written a novel which she passes off as her own while not telling anyone that her boyfriend has died. The money he has left her enables her to leave Scotland with a friend, Lanna, on a trip to Spain which ends with Morvern leaving her friend, from whom she has become increasingly distanced, asleep on the roadside but with enough money for the return journey. Morvern stays in Spain for some time and then strikes a publication deal with 'her' novel which will make her rich and, for a while, independent. Spain haunts the narrative as an alternative space and place, the beginning of a journey into a new life and identity. Similarly, in *Young Adam*, when Joe leaves Cathie he tells her he is going to China, a trip that never materialises, casting him as a dreamer who cannot even complete the period of sustained writing which life with Cathie has permitted. In Lynne Ramsay's film the central character Morvern is also unable to settle since she too is haunted by a significant death that features at the beginnings of both films. The landscapes of *Morvern Callar* and *Young Adam* are also indicative of an anti-urban strand within New Scottish Cinema, rejecting the cityscapes of *Shallow Grave* (1994) and *Trainspotting* for pictorial, port and waterside locations that in themselves indicate points of possible departure. Both Joe's and Morvern's partners die. For Morvern the death is in some ways liberating, since it allows her to travel and experience a sense of freedom, while for Joe the death of his partner results in despair. Morvern's dead writer-boyfriend also links with Joe's intellectualism and authorial ambitions; in Morvern's case the novel she passes off as her own work serves as a catalyst for her escape while Joe's inability to write sends him off to seek experience on the canals, developing new relationships with people to whom he cannot ultimately commit. In a similar way Morvern's treatment of her friend Lanna has the same essence of transience. While they are clearly friends Morvern learns that she wants completely different things, not to stay and be 'safe' but to use her new-found life to seek independence and new experiences. Like Joe, the people she encounters never become permanent fixtures in her life and during the film she develops a purposefulness to move on that belies her at times eccentric demeanour. In *Young Adam* Joe drifts from place to place on the barge, yet at the same time he develops a similar desire to leave the past behind, letting go of the mirror given to him by Cathie much as Morvern's personal journey to independence is inspired by a tape of music ('Music for You') left to her by her boyfriend and which forms a sort of interiorised soundtrack for the character that becomes a key strand of the film's formal address. As explained further in Chapter 8, these devices, as well as the film's open-endedness and apparent existentialist sensibility, mark out Ramsay's work as inhabiting the territory of art cinema.

The characters Morvern and Joe could both be accused of demonstrating an amoral fecklessness. One review of *Morvern Callar* however argued that Morton's performance invested the character's deeds with 'a kind of honour . . . motivated by a kind of love' for the dead boyfriend (Brooks, 2002: 50). David Mackenzie, director of *Young Adam*, claimed that he wanted to 'bring out more of what's in the novel: dare I say it, the romance' (Mackenzie, 2003: 19). This softening of both characters is also supported by the decision to jettison the first-person narration of the novels. Rather than include voice-over narration both films are therefore more open to poetic sensibilities that link environment to character in a way that arguably absolves them from total responsibility for their actions. In Morvern's case her desire to escape is linked to the visual contrasts between Scotland and Spain, and Joe's character blends in with the canals which Mackenzie explained were 'decayed and often dangerous routes through cities' (2003: 19). In this way both characters are fundamentally linked to the landscapes they inhabit. *Chicago Sun-Times* reviewer Roger Ebert (2003; 2004) saw the class dimensions of both films as key to the presentation of convincing motivations behind the characters' actions. Reviews made much of the visible connections between Jean Vigo's celebrated poetic and elliptical depiction of a newly married young couple's life on a barge, *L'Atalante* (1934) and *Young Adam* (for example Ebert, 2004). While *Morvern Callar* did not invite so many direct comparisons with European cinema, the existentialist elements were commented upon and a review in *Variety* compared Morton's performance to that of Catherine Deneuve in Polanski's *Repulsion* (1965). In a similar desire to locate *Morvern Callar* within a European cinematic frame of reference Linda Ruth Williams compared Ramsay's film *Morvern Callar* to Antonioni's *The Passenger* (1975) for its similar themes and Spanish locations (2002: 24).

Contemporary British cinema therefore displays a wealth of images that explore a dynamic, if depressing, culture of difference on many levels, as these examples have shown. Many British films have been able to take advantage of the increasingly diverse market which includes release on DVD; television transmission including, as soon as Film Four became a freely available digital channel in 2006, a season of British films, as well as notoriety through the European film festival circuit. Funding packages that consist of a range of European and American financing and distribution can also have the effect of films gaining access to markets that have notoriously proved difficult for British films to penetrate. While it is far from the case that British cinema is a rival to Hollywood it nevertheless occupies an important space in trans-national cultural production, a space that in recent years has demonstrated considerable richness and diversity.

CONCLUSION

Since the Second World War British genres have developed in intriguing ways. One recurrent theme is their preoccupation with masculine problems and the male psyche, a theme which has been particularly noticeable in horror, war films and social-problem films. As we saw in Chapter 2, comedy is an especially British genre, and in the post-war years its concern with satirising bureaucratic structures ranged from Ealing to *Carry On*. In the 1970s, comedy went through a difficult period of adjustment to the relaxation of censorship, but Pythonesque satire transformed the genre to embrace an increasingly surreal style. One key characteristic has been the resurfacing of dominant aesthetic traits in different genres. The pleasures of costume, excess and escapism which made Gainsborough costume melodramas so successful are also evident in Hammer horror films and today's heritage cinema. Different genres, but similar pleasures, although the pleasures offered to the female spectator are arguably less in horror films than in melodramas.[1] The historical film re-emerged in the 1970s with Ken Russell's gothic biopics and then developed into the heritage genre with its sumptuous production values and highly visual pleasures. The reappearance of some genres, for example the musical, has been short-lived and arose from the desire to establish links with the popular music industry which fast expanded into the short pop-promo video market. While the 1970s saw the film industry attempt to come to terms with television, the 1980s inaugurated a more symbiotic relationship, particularly with the birth of Channel 4's *Film On Four* scheme to finance films for both the small screen and for theatrical release. The vicissitudes of film production continue to ensure that British cinema maintains an eclectic base. Repetition and difference have always been key features of film genres, but this dynamic process has been slowed down, particularly in recent years when most films are one-off productions without the security of a major studio's support. Companies come and go, and with them ideas and styles which, in a more stable economic environment, might have been developed in subsequent films. There is, however, an increasing international relationship between genres: Paul Anderson adapted the conventions of the American action movie in *Shopping* and in turn Scorsese employed heritage themes and stylistics in *The Age of Innocence* (1993). The popularity of French heritage films supports the idea that heritage is an increasingly pan-European phenomenon in film and television.[2] Since 2000 television continues to be of great importance to the funding of British films and although, as the above survey has shown, films have become increasingly subject to a mix of hybrid forms and identities, genre remains an important conceptual framework from which analysis can be undertaken. *Shaun of the Dead* (2004) and *Hot Fuzz* (2007), two films written by director Edgar Wright and actor Simon Pegg, for example, use genre in a broad comedic context. Both films are set in London and draw on the incongruity of this setting in comic dramas that, respectively, are immersed in references to American/Italian zombie films and to the US cop genre. With this in mind, Britishness becomes, perhaps, but one element in the increasing international, intertextual diversity of modern genre cinema. The fracturing of identities and the trans-national nature of much of British cinema since 2000 has also inflected the ways in which generic hybridity has dominated contemporary styles and themes.

Chapter 6

Acting and stars

STAGE TO SCREEN: DRAMA IN COLD STORAGE?

> The theatre has nothing to learn from its infant offshoot.... By comparison with the flesh and blood reality of a spoken play, it is drama in cold storage.
>
> (Albert Chevalier, 1910, quoted in Low, 1971: 261)

British cinema drew on a range of styles and traditions, particularly the London West End theatre and music hall.[1] The West End provided the first film actors and scripts, and music halls were the earliest public arenas for cinema exhibition, as well as bequeathing a stock of variety comedy acts. Ambivalent in their response to the new medium, with its ability to reach millions and its relative permanence, both theatre and music-hall were anxious to forge a symbiotic relationship with cinema. But as the above quotation shows, it was a relationship fraught with tension.

This tension has been reflected in critical discourse about what constitutes a good British film: one which consciously displays its literary/theatrical origins, or one which transforms them into the cinematic. British cinema critics often exuded profound reverence for theatre as a medium capable of conferring cultural prestige on film, the immature 'infant offshoot'. In nationalist terms, exploiting film's theatrical origins was considered to be an essential element in fostering a British cinema which could be identified by its specific cultural heritage. On the other hand, links between British cinema and the London stage have been blamed for the alleged uncinematic quality of many British films, as Norman Marshall lamented in 1931:

> This weakness of English directors for the pedestrian reproduction of stage plays on the screen is a symptom of their inability to realise that the film, even with the addition of sound, is essentially a visual art, and must express itself in movement.

Screenplays adapted from plays are still often condemned as verbose and unimaginative texts which ignore cinema's exciting visual possibilities.[2] The quest for cinematic realism is interpreted as an unfortunate legacy of nineteenth-century literature, as Jeanette Winterson has put it: 'the nineteenth century is a curious place for that vast battery of technical achievement to make its home' (Winterson, 1994: xi). The number of stage actors who have appeared in British films is extremely high, but it is often claimed that stage actors cannot transfer their skills easily to the close medium of film and – closer still – of television.[3] Julian Petley has identified a resulting 'problem of performance' in British film and television, with actors opting for awkward styles instead of developing performances which embody the essence of film acting: 'how to *look* without appearing to *act*' (Petley, 1985: 122).

This raises the crucial issue of adaptation: the *approach* is arguably more important than the source text for scriptwriters, directors and actors. While early film technology was basic there was only a degree of experimentation with the notion of moving performance. The majority of adaptations, particularly in the early silent period, were unimaginative, placing actors in front of static cameras accompanied by long explanatory inter-titles. Immobile cameras and few close-ups did not encourage a variety of approaches to a text. If the source was well known it was taken for granted that audiences would recognise characters and situations, making the work of the audience easier. But as the silent period progressed and technology became more sophisticated, many adaptations were not so literal and there was some exploration of different performance modes, particularly melodrama.[4] Many of these attempts appear awkward, but they nevertheless provide an insight into the impact of film on established acting techniques. As Burrows (2003) has demonstrated in his analysis of the intermedial exchange between stage stars and early cinema, the connections could often be highly productive. The high level of involvement of theatre actors in British films should not be seen as backward-looking and neglectful of developing 'the cinematic'. On the contrary, cinema provided actors with additional audiences they had already attracted in music-hall productions.

During the silent period there were hundreds of adaptations from stage plays and novels; Shakespeare provided film directors with a challenge and lured many established actors to the screen. Some directors managed to be creative with stage-based material, for example Hepworth and the Gaumont Company's 1913 version of *Hamlet*, featuring celebrated Shakespearean actor Sir Johnston Forbes-Robertson – an early example of a film being used as a star vehicle. W. G. Barker's 1913 production of the Victorian novel *East Lynne* 'was no stage production amateurishly filmed, but a major work of an experienced and enterprising firm unaffected by theatrical tradition' (Low, 1949: 229). Attention to the specificity of film was a gradual process, beginning with reviews of individual screen performances and critics' acknowledgement of the importance of screenplays (Low, 1950: 228–29). It was gradually recognised that the most successful adaptations had to offer something new in order to demonstrate the continuing technical development of cinema.

Hitchcock was one of the most creative innovators as far as adaptations from the stage were concerned in the 1920s. Geoff Brown has analysed *Easy Virtue* (1927), based on a Noël Coward play, in favourable terms:

> Hitchcock's treatment consistently breathes fresh life into the material. The script adaptation is radical . . . it is Hitchcock's early mastery of visual story-telling that impresses most: the use of symbolic objects and leit-motifs . . . the advancement of character and plot through natural, wordless human behaviour. . . . The film is also marked by subtle character groupings, eloquently conveying conflicting emotional viewpoints.
>
> (Brown, 1986: 151–52)

All of this exudes cinema, not filmed theatre, indicating how attention to *mise-en-scène* communicates detail and a restrained acting style conveys character development. Graham Cutts was similarly imaginative in his adaptation of melodramatic styles for the screen, particularly in *The Rat* (1925).[5] It was not so much a question of abandoning theatrical performance modes, but rather a move towards using cinema technology, particularly the close-up, to adapt gestures and melodramatic conventions to intensify the screen drama.

Despite the work of Hitchcock and Cutts, however, the arrival of the talkies in Britain placed the question of how to use cinema as a means of enhancing and developing acting styles low on the agenda. Dialogue-dominated scripts and less mobile cameras detracted from earlier experiments with gesture. In the 1930s Basil Dean, theatre and film producer (Associated Talking Pictures), made a few imaginative versions of stage plays, but the majority were literal and verbose. On the other hand, some developments with stage texts allowed for interesting and creative set designs, and for attention to *mise-en-scène* to be obtrusive. The 1930s was the decade when the theatre was however most suspicious of cinema, a fear which had been exacerbated by the arrival of the talkies: if plays could be filmed in their entirety, surely the death of theatre would soon follow. There was also an element of cultural snobbery about the particular theatrical traditions exploited by film. The majority of the top British box-office stars had been successful in music-hall and musical comedy rather than on the West End stage. Jack Hawkins, Michael Redgrave, Ralph Richardson and John Gielgud all considered their screen work as secondary to their professional theatre work in the 1930s (Richards, 1984: 163).

By contrast, the Second World War was an exciting period for creative adaptation when British film production was galvanised by its propaganda imperative. Britain's literary and theatrical heritage was an obvious source for scripts which communicated particular notions of nationhood: that which must be defended was articulated in high-cultural terms. Adaptations were not, however, filmed plays. It is hard to imagine a more cinematic production of *Henry V* than Olivier's 1945 version, and Noël Coward's *This Happy Breed* (1944) is another example of the transformation of stage techniques into Technicolor images, demonstrating a sense of mission, confidence and prestige which characterised wartime British cinema. Established theatre actors, directors and writers who contributed to the war effort on celluloid included Laurence Olivier, Ralph Richardson, Noël Coward, Basil Dean and Terence Rattigan. Apart from the fact that many theatres were closed during the war, film became more respected as a medium because it offered actors the promise of stardom in the name of patriotism.

After the war this trend soon evaporated and in subsequent years, apart from Joseph Losey's adaptations of Harold Pinter and Charles Wood's collaborations with Richard Lester, it is tempting to share Brown's pessimism about the uneasy partnership between stage and screen:

> It is hard to divine any imaginative forward thrust in the late 1960s upsurge of theatrical cinema. One senses, instead, signs of retreat, to the cinema as a transcription system for significant stage productions, to theatrical films as prestige cultural packages, precisely aimed at the British art house and selected foreign markets [particularly American].
>
> (Brown, 1986: 162)

As Brown acknowledges, theatrical adaptation continues to be a feature of film and television, generally confined to the niche film. In recent years, Kenneth Branagh's adaptations of Shakespeare have been popular in the international market, keeping alive a link with established theatre.

It could be argued that, paradoxically, television has been the main beneficiary of the link between the screen and the stage. As with cinema, television's claim for artistic respectability drew it towards older traditions in an attempt to corner the market for prestigious, exportable, quality broadcasting. Early television drama drew heavily on theatrical traditions and the emphasis on television as a writer's medium is a consequence of this link. While Petrie argues that this has tended to privilege dialogue and characterisation above *mise-en-scène* and montage, he does concede that writers such as Dennis Potter have challenged realist and theatrical conventions in fundamental ways (Petrie, 1991: 164). This can also occur when novels are adapted for the screen. When Jeanette Winterson adapted her novel *Oranges Are Not the Only Fruit* for the screen she knew she would have to make many changes:

The fairy tales and allegorical passages that weave themselves within the main story could be waved goodbye without any pain because their function could be taken over by the camera itself. . . . The power of the image means that you don't always have to spell it out.

(Winterson, 1994: 72)

The resulting television film, *Oranges Are Not the Only Fruit* (1990), was a popular and critical success which was admired for its imaginative use of dialogue and characterisation as well as for Beeban Kidron's direction, which was visually exciting, with impressionistic fairground sequences communicating the spirit of the novel's fairy tales and allegorical passages. The case of *Oranges* reiterates the point that while the narrative source of film or television drama is crucial, the most important factor is its adaptation, the approach taken to translating it into visual terms. The extent to which directors have grappled with the challenge of developing notions of screen performance has been, and continues to be, a key area of British film: drama in transition rather than in cold storage.

THE MUSIC-HALL AND BRITISH CINEMA

The other major influence on early British cinema was the music-hall, which provided the cinema with a distinct comic tradition of variety. Cinema, however, was quicker to exploit music-hall theatres than its stars, and in the late nineteenth century preferred to 'present anonymous, semi-professional actors in hackneyed situations and to trust to the novelty value of the medium' (Anthony, 1984: 34). The earliest films involving variety acts simply filmed popular performers – for example, the Warwick Trading Company filmed Will Evans in a series of films in 1899 and a top music-hall star, Dan Leno, had his dance and mime routines filmed at about the same time. The first music-hall star who is credited as adapting his variety acts for the screen and for integrating them into some sort of narrative is Fred Evans, renowned for the 'Pimple' series of devised films (1913–20) which satirised current events and parodied other films and plays in an exciting manner. Some comedians became film entrepreneurs, for example, in 1912 acrobat Will P. Kellino was a founder of the Ecko Film Company which churned out films made by some of music hall's most popular stars: Billy Merson, Lupino Lane, Seth and Albert Egbert.

The long-term influence of music hall is incontestable, as Andy Medhurst has observed: 'British popular culture would be unrecognisable without the diffused influences of music-hall modes' (Medhurst, 1986a: 185). Early short films lent themselves extremely well to silent mime-oriented gags, but it was when sound cinema was fully established in the 1930s that variety artists found their most important roles in feature films. Most of the top British stars in the period 1936–40, for example, came from music-hall backgrounds. Gracie Fields and George Formby found themselves starring in ninety-minute films where their variety acts were interspersed with often flimsy narratives. This was not always successful but, as with the West End theatrical tradition, it was during the Second World War that variety comedians came into their own: 'the central, crucial ideology of community which fuelled these films was the variety tradition's major contribution to wartime cinema' (ibid.: 181). The music-hall variety tradition can be identified in the later films of Norman Wisdom, and in early *Carry On* films, as examples of comedy based on innuendo, character actors, a British sense of humour and a regional appeal which the West End theatre could never capture. It is significant that variety-based films enjoyed enormous regional appeal, forming the basis of much British popular cinema. On the other hand, many British films have ignored geographical regions and traditions outside London, creating a metropolitan-centred impression of Britain, particularly to non-British audiences.

BRITISH STARS

It is commonly assumed that the star system functioned most fully in Hollywood and British stars have not received the degree of attention granted to their Hollywood counterparts. Dyer (1979; 1987) and Stacey (1993) have analysed Hollywood stars, suggesting useful theoretical models which enable us to appreciate the complex tripartite relationship between stars (their connection with industrial and social structures), audiences (the way audiences utilised star images in particular periods), and film texts (notions of performance). For a film industry which was formed so much in the shadow of Hollywood, home-grown stars provide a fascinating insight into the industry's self-perception in particular periods and reflect cultural assumptions about Britishness. Of course, most of the top box-office stars were American, but Britain was not without its film stars, and because of the British cinema's inferiority complex about Hollywood competition, home-grown stars were often invested with a patriotic imperative as bearers of British national culture. There has always been a tension between wanting British stars and resentment that, as a Hollywood invention, film stardom and all its trappings of gossip, fandom and scandal are somehow unseemly, *unBritish*. But there were British stars who performed interesting functions within the film industry and British society.

Most early film stars were already stars in the legitimate theatre and music-hall. Theatrical stardom is, of course, different from film stardom, and it is notable that many actors, preferring to stress the merits of a particular performance, claim that stardom does not exist in theatre. Individual talent is seen to be superior to the manufactured and industrial connotations of film stardom. But in the late nineteenth century theatrical stars were advertised, followed and exploited in a way that resembles the treatment of the first film stars. Indeed, building on an established West End or music-hall reputation guaranteed an actor who chose to work in film even greater exposure. By 1916 many film actors had to quote prior permission from their film companies when they appeared on the stage (Low, 1950: 229). After 1910 film companies began to realise the commercial value of star publicity campaigns, especially when the public was eager for news of stars' off-screen lives and bombarded the press with requests for photographs and biographical information. As Jon Burrows (2003) has shown, there was considerable two-way traffic between leading stars of the West End theatre and film production companies during the 1910s and later, producing an interesting convergence of acting styles that can be said to constitute 'inter-medial' (a productive combination) rather than parasitic (film merely borrowing from theatre) modes of performance. Stage actors' interest in film was not just as a means of cashing in on opportunities promised by the commercial exploitation of new technology, but presented them with new audiences they had already attracted in music-hall productions. Indeed, the link with commercial developments in music-hall entertainment was a key precedent that in many ways eased the path for actors who were willing to straddle careers on the stage and screen. While restraint and moderation had come to be appreciated as the dominant theatrical style at the turn of the century, the increasing popularity of film required actors to experiment with different methods of playing to the camera such as the gestural performance modes demonstrated by music-hall 'character actors' such as Will Evans.

In her volume on the 1920s, Rachael Low cites Violet Hopson as the first British actress to be groomed for stardom by a film company, Broadwest (Low, 1971: 263). But before her there had been lesser publicity campaigns in 1911 for actresses in Hepworth's stock company: Chrissie White, Alma Taylor and Gladys Sylvani, 'the first English film star to receive treatment similar to that given the Americans, was pasted on hoardings, hung in picture palace vestibules and subjected to the usual write-ups' (Low, 1949: 126). One reason for the relatively late appearance of British stars might be because the most important studios, particularly Hepworth, were opposed to the close-up, an essential technical device which provided audiences with a sense of intimacy with their favourite star. Rachael Low has written:

> It is hard to realize now the frequency and anger with which the close-up was attacked, and the passion with which people who regarded it as an odious fad hoped that it would soon disappear. The star system did substitute the promotion and glorification of personality for real advances in film technique, but it was never very highly developed in England.
>
> (ibid.: 266)

A history of British film style and technology has yet to be written and care must be taken when considering such an argument in relation to the development of film stardom in Britain.[6] The cultivation of stars is dependent on a highly organised economic infrastructure which Britain did not have and, in comparison with Hollywood stars, British film actors were paid very little. Of course, the industry was hardly in a healthy economic position later, but once the publicity methods of American companies advertised the drawing power of film stars, most British companies gradually accepted that stars were a crucial factor at the box office and no matter how bad things were they should at least try to promote home-grown actors as stars.

Declaring who was the first British star depends largely on how you define 'star', but most researchers use box-office polls from the trade press and fan magazines in conjunction with publicity material and commentary on the star's personality and private life. Together with film performances, these sources contribute to a star's overall 'incomplete and paradoxical' image (Ellis, 1982: 93). It would appear in this connection that serials were significant in impressing a star persona upon an audience. Gilbert Adair references Fred Evans, 'Pimple', the music-hall star of popular one-reel farces, and Alma Taylor, who topped the popularity polls, 1915–24. Taylor worked for Hepworth in the *Tilly* series with her co-star Chrissie White. Together they played a pair of daring heroines; in one film, *Tilly and the Fire Engines* (Lewin Fitzhamon, 1911), they steal a fire-engine and hose down a group of irate firemen who chase after them. Alma Taylor's leading man, Stewart Rome, was responsible for winning a legal case against Hepworth which established that his, and any other actor's professional name, did not belong to a production company (Adair, 1985: 16–17). This was, perhaps, more significant than the use of the close-up in encouraging actors to see themselves as *screen* stars, and audiences in turn to perceive them as professionals.

In the 1920s the most popular British stars were Ivor Novello and Betty Balfour. Ivor Novello was an established stage matinée idol and playwright who went on to work with Graham Cutts and Alfred Hitchcock. By the time he appeared in a film adaptation of his own play, *The Rat*, he had already made a few films in France, Hollywood and Britain, co-starring with Gladys Cooper in the British film *The Bohemian Girl* (Harley Knoles, 1922). As Williams (2003) has argued, Novello's popularity was based on his good looks but also on the relevance of his roles to the prevailing culture of post-war mourning. These frequently featured him as a tortured outcast, a suffering figure who endures rejection and hardship. Betty Balfour worked for George Pearson who established her as an international star in the *Squibs* series of films (1921–23) based on a music-hall sketch about a cockney flower-seller: 'she was able to register on the screen a charm and expression unequalled among the actresses in British films' (Low, 1971:

121). Unlike Novello, Balfour made her name on the screen rather than on the stage and she is important as an early example of a popular working-class heroine in a series of distinctive melodramas. Novello's appeal was more erotic, the silent screen highlighting his good looks as the British answer to Valentino. The ending of *The Lodger* (Alfred Hitchcock, 1926) could not show him as a murderer because of his popular reputation as a romantic hero – an interesting example of casting against type to intrigue the audience.

The economic problems of the British film industry in the 1920s made Hollywood an attractive place where many native actors tried their luck on the screen, including Ronald Colman, Walter Forde, Clive Brook and Percy Marmont. The exodus of many British stars to Hollywood continued in the 1930s: Errol Flynn, Herbert Marshall, Ian Hunter, Brian Aherne, George Sanders, Madeleine Carroll, Patric Knowles and John Loder. Even though they no longer made films in Britain their work for Hollywood studios nevertheless provided audiences with representations of Britishness in many top box-office films. Ronald Colman's image as the archetypical English gentleman was consolidated in many films, including *The Dark Angel* (1925), *Bulldog Drummond* (1929) and *The Prisoner of Zenda* (1937). Many of the stereotypes of British behaviour originated in these Hollywood roles, producing fascinating constructions of Britishness from an American point of view. It is likely that these stereotypes, for example the upper-class, laconic Englishman, influenced casting and characterisation in British films intended for the export market.

As already mentioned, in the 1930s the most popular British stars came from stage and variety backgrounds: Gracie Fields, George Formby, Jessie Matthews, Will Hay, Jack Hulbert and Jack Buchanan (although care must be taken to avoid taking polls from trade papers at face value, as demonstrated by Sedgwick's research [2000] on film stars' relative popularity during this period). Except for Anna Neagle, Robert Donat and Madeleine Carroll, 'Britain seemed almost incapable of creating and developing its own stars from scratch' (Richards, 1984: 172), an opinion that had been voiced in 1938 by Freda Bruce Lockhart who complained that British producers showed 'a lackadaisical neglect of the rudiments of a starring system' (*Film Weekly*, 9 April 1938, quoted in Petley, 1985: 112). But British stars who received attention were invested with special qualities. The fan magazines were full of stories of Hollywood stars and any account of British stardom should not neglect the fact that British stars were always seen in patriotic comparison with their Hollywood counterparts. As I will go on to show, Anna Neagle's image was exploited in this manner.

Dyer's insights on the social function of stars can easily be applied in the British context (Dyer, 1979). The stars of the 1930s, for example, form an interesting cultural backdrop to the politics of consensus, the dominant response to the Depression, appeasement and the relocation of industry.[7]

Plate 6.1 Ivor Novello, top British star in *The Lodger* (1926). (Courtesy of Rank Film Distributors)

Gracie Fields, in particular, has been interpreted as 'a symbol of the nation as a whole in the Thirties' (Richards, 1984: 172). She was working class, resilient and cheerful. As a representative of the working class her star biography embodied rags-to-riches aspirations. Born in Rochdale, Fields left the cotton mills behind and became a success in music-hall and as a recording star. Her first film, *Sally in Our Alley* (Maurice Elvey, 1931) exposed class conflict and made the working-class screen character 'Sally' synonymous with 'Owr Gracie', as Fields was affectionately known in the fan magazines. Richards sees her films, however, gradually blend into consensus mode by the end of the 1930s, an opinion corroborated by Tony Aldgate (Aldgate, 1983). But as Marcia Landy has pointed out, there are elements in Fields' films which defy narrative closure, allowing for complex and non-linear readings for a socially and culturally diverse audience cognisant with reading films in particular ways (Landy, 1991: 334–41). These observations demonstrate how hegemonic cultural structures operate as an overall context for a host of competing ideologies and groups. Thus, while there was clearly a dominant image of Gracie Fields, that image also contained malleable facets which audiences could adapt as they wished.[8]

The Second World War was extremely significant for the proliferation of British stars: James Mason, John Mills, Stewart Granger, Michael Rennie, Anna Neagle, Celia Johnson, Phyllis Calvert, Patricia Roc, Jean Kent and Margaret Lockwood all flourished during this period. The 1940s was the decade when female stars, many of whose images were associated with sexuality and assertiveness, dominated the screens (Thumim, 1992: 54). Lockwood in particular was extremely popular and much has been written about the significance of *The Wicked Lady* (Leslie Arliss, 1945) as the top box-office film of 1946, which the critics nevertheless despised. It is a costume melodrama telling the tale of bad, pleasure-seeking Barbara Skelton (Margaret Lockwood) who deceives her husband and becomes a highwaywoman. Although she dies for her sins at the end of the film, it offered audiences, particularly female, visual pleasures which invested her with excitement, strength, danger and thrills. She appealed to women who had tasted freedom and responsibility in the Second World War and the film can thus be read convincingly as expressive of optimism for the post-war world (see Harper, 1987 and Thumim, 1992). She forms an interesting contrast with Celia Johnson's image of middle-class respectability, restraint and self-sacrifice, most evident in *Brief Encounter* (David Lean, 1945), a film which won high critical praise but nevertheless did not fare as well at the box office as *The Wicked Lady*.[9]

As a case study of the interface between film stardom and national identity it would be useful to examine one British star, Anna Neagle, in detail since that study can stand metonymically for a particular construction of Britishness and femininity during the 1930s and 1940s. Janet Thumim has written:

The simple reference to the name of a popular star can summon up, evoke, a particular historical period: thus through their personae, stars come to stand as signifiers of the time in which they achieved their greatest popularity. Anna Neagle, for example, continued her career until the seventies but is forever associated with the late thirties and forties, the time in which, as a *Picturegoer* reviewer wrote in 1951, 'she [was] as much a part of Britain as Dover's white cliffs'.

(Thumim, 1992: 56)

That a film star could signify Britain and Britishness for such a long time is indeed worthy of analysis, and as with Gracie Fields, it is possible to assess culturally dominant values, and implicit challenges to them, by examining a star such as Neagle in context.

'Dover's white cliffs': Anna Neagle

Anna Neagle was a prominent star in British cinema, winning the *Picturegoer* Gold Medal award five times: 1938, 1947–49, 1951; British exhibitors polled by *Motion Picture Herald* voted her top international box-office actress, 1948–51 and top British actress 1941, 1947, 1952.[10] Films in which she starred regularly topped the domestic box-office. She was popular, but more so with the public than with contemporary critics who privileged quality-realist cinema. Although *The Courtneys of Curzon Street* (Herbert Wilcox, 1947) was one of the most successful films at the box office in 1947, critic Peter Noble wrote of it dismissively in *The British Film Yearbook* as a purely commercial film, poorly written and banal, displaying none of the 'artistic' qualities he praised in films such as *Great Expectations* (1946) or *Odd Man Out* (1947) (Noble, 1950: 18–19).

Nor has she fared well in recent scholarship. Despite the prominence given to the popular, Neagle's films and image have received scant attention, perhaps because of the stigma of her association with patriotic historical films under the firm control of her producer-husband, Herbert Wilcox, who directed her in 32 films. She starred in films which until relatively recently have not been a major focus of British generic analyses (historical biopics and musical comedies in particular).[11] As a genre, for example, British costume melodramas have been studied in some depth because their huge box-office success can be interpreted as evidence of the popular audience's desire to see what Sue Harper has termed 'spectacular and inaccurate histories which celebrated female pleasure and the aristocratic/proletarian alliance' (Harper, 1992: 110). But analysis of this particular trend has concentrated on British films of the 1930s, including *Nell Gwyn* (Herbert Wilcox, 1934), Neagle's costume melodrama, and the popular 1940s Gainsborough melodramas (see Aspinall and Murphy, 1983). In turn this has led to a privileging of the pleasures offered to audiences of *Nell Gwyn* over the more popular, but by comparison less melodramatic *Victoria the Great* (Herbert Wilcox, 1937) (ibid.: 110).

This critical tendency to concentrate on particular periods often neglects how a star displays an evolving screen persona at the same time as maintaining consistent elements of their total image, whatever the genre, and over long periods of time. Indeed, Neagle's popularity can be explored in terms of her star appeal, which operated across several generic categories: costume melodrama, the biopic, wartime melodrama, musical comedy and the social-problem film. Neagle's films and image over her entire career, 1930s–50s, are relevant in an attempt to explore some of the questions surrounding her image as a British icon and signifier of national identity. Christine Gledhill has described a film star as being 'an emblem of national celebrity' (Gledhill, 1991: xiii), and there is no doubt that Anna Neagle fits into this category. As we have already seen, a contemporary critic identified her with the White Cliffs of Dover, an image which was exported with her films to America and despite her appearance in a variety of genres persisted throughout her career. So why was Neagle successful and popular and what does this say about her articulation of Britishness?

The Wilcox factor

Accounts which detract from Neagle tend to highlight Herbert Wilcox's skill as an astute producer, an interpretation he encouraged. In his autobiography Wilcox claimed that 'as a box-office star-maker, my masterpiece was, of course, Anna Neagle' (Wilcox, 1967: 167). It was also a frequent assumption that Wilcox kept his finger firmly on the public pulse when choosing her projects, a fact which conveniently explained the successes but did not take into consideration the films which failed. Noel Langley wrote in *Close-Up*,

> What has put her in the front rank at the box office? Wilcox's shrewd, practical, old-time showmanship; catering solely and with experience to the public; keeping her at a consistent level; and presenting her as the public wants and expects her.

> (Langley: 1948)

Her status as public property comes up time and time again in the contemporary press, thus investing her with the status of a sort of monarch of the British cinema. *Picturegoer*, however, preferred to stress the interdependent aspects of the Wilcox–Neagle partnership: 'their set-up is unique in the film business' (*Picturegoer*, 27 March 1948); and, just before *Victoria the Great* was released, the fan magazine revealed how Anna Neagle had part-funded the film and had written much of the script (*Picturegoer*, 18 September 1937). Their working relationship was presented as unusual, in the sense that it did not appear to conflict with their marriage in 1943, implying that as a team they enjoyed a great degree of mutual respect. The words 'showmanship', 'professionalism', 'formula', were used again and again in reviews of the Wilcox–Neagle films, particularly at the height of their success at the end of the 1940s when the British film industry was providing competition for American films in a hitherto captive British market.

The Neagle persona

As with any other film star, intertextual information about Neagle gleaned from fan magazines and newspapers influenced the way she was perceived on screen. Unlike with many Hollywood stars, the public were never presented with information which conflicted with her highly respectable reputation on celluloid. Gossip columns rarely mentioned Neagle or discussed her in sexual terms, reassuring the public that good British girls were not 'like that'. Much was made in publicity of her modest personality and rags-to-riches story, her humble Forest Gate, London origins and rise to fame from the chorus. *Picturegoer*'s accounts of her early career stressed her ambition and determination to be on the stage and reminded readers many times how Herbert Wilcox cast her in *Goodnight, Vienna* (1932) after seeing her by chance in Jack Buchanan's stage show *Stand Up and Sing*: 'things are as they should be when a girl can by determination and hard work rise from the ranks of the chorus in a few years to international screen eminence in English films' (*Picturegoer*, 18 September 1937). Her screen roles also celebrated individual stoicism in the face of adversity as a means of communicating the overall liberal-conservative political ideology of the Wilcox–Neagle films. Neagle epitomised middle-class values of thrift, hard work, stoicism and feminine modesty. Just as the White Cliffs of Dover are associated with Britain's self-consciousness as an island, vulnerable to foreign invasion, Neagle also represented a resolutely British, non-European and white identity.

Contradictions?

The evolution of her image shows that while Anna Neagle had a distinct screen persona associated with pluckiness, politeness and poise, on several occasions she deviated from the norm to keep the public guessing. This was often presented to the press as a conscious Wilcox strategy, a pattern which had been established early on in her screen career. With its irreverent, passionate and witty heroine, *Nell Gwyn* was a very different film from its predecessor *Goodnight, Vienna*, Neagle's first major screen role. As Wilcox explained in his autobiography:

> In the film [*Goodnight, Vienna*] she had been hailed by the press as the typical English rose. That was good press up to a point, but it would be

fatal if she were to be labelled as such, or type-cast. So I decided her next picture must shock the critics into noticing the actress in her and also shock audiences out of the English rose image.

(Wilcox, 1967: 97–98)

Plate 6.2 The evolution of an image: Anna Neagle in the 1930s. Compare with Plate 6.3 (Courtesy of the British Film Institute)

It is ironic that the image which persisted throughout her career was precisely that of the English rose (English, of course, rather than British). In its turn, *Victoria the Great* was a very different kind of historical picture from *Nell Gwyn* and established one of the most enduring facets of the Neagle image: that of the regal heroine.[12] As a curious footnote to her regal

Plate 6.3 Anna Neagle in the 1940s. (Courtesy of the British Film Institute)

image, Neagle revealed in 1974 that she was a remote descendant of George III! (Neagle, 1974: 31). So despite this attempt to introduce variety into Neagle's screen persona, at core she remained the reliable national emblem who possessed rock-like qualities, and above all was nice in the same way that Laura Jesson was nice in *Brief Encounter* (1945) (Dyer, 1993b), although arguably Neagle displays less vulnerability. Neagle represented British national culture in similar terms to *Brief Encounter*. These terms were essentially narrow and class-specific, particularly in the London series of inward-looking society dramas which ignored unmetropolitan notions of Britishness and repressed questions of class conflict.

The most notorious case of manipulating Neagle's established image was with *Yellow Canary* (1943) when she played a Nazi sympathiser who, we are relieved to discover at the end of the film, has all along been a British intelligence agent. The film's trailer showed an enigmatic Anna Neagle confiding in her friends, the audience: 'I'm not apologising for playing Sally Maitland – as a matter of fact after all the good women I've played I found it rather exciting'. The stability of her upright persona was thus never really questioned. Other variations were the London series and her social-problem film of 1956, *My Teenage Daughter*, when she played a middle-class mother who is unable to comprehend her rebellious daughter (played by Sylvia Syms). The press book for this film commented: 'whoever thought to see Anna Neagle on the screen in dresses which can be bought "off the peg" by any of her feminine audience or fans!'. But, apart from costume, she remained the same familiar Anna Neagle: long-suffering, gracious, quaintly class-bound, a strong but unthreatening woman.

To encourage audience identification Neagle's films often displayed a visible self-consciousness about her star image, a tradition established early in her career. In a scene in *Nell Gwyn* we see her look directly at the camera, giving the audience an intimate look which operates on two levels: full comprehension depending on knowledge of her as Nell Gwyn but also as Anna Neagle, the girl who had also been a stage player and made it. In *Maytime In Mayfair* (Herbert Wilcox, 1949), there are references to the characters played by Neagle and Wilding, looking like the film stars Neagle and Wilding, and to the Michael Wilding fan club. *Spring In Park Lane* (Herbert Wilcox, 1948) also utilises the same kind of self-conscious intertextual referencing. Similar techniques are used by 1930s American screwball comedies which can also be compared with the British cycle in terms of their narrative concern with witty, charming, special couples who live in lavish, comfortable surroundings.

Feminine appeal

In retrospect it can be seen that the release of Neagle's films often coincided with conducive historical circumstances. Jeffrey Richards has observed that

Victoria the Great, a film which portrayed the monarchy as serving the needs of the nation, was released at a time when audiences sought relief from anxieties caused by the Abdication Crisis, fear of unemployment and social unrest (Richards, 1984: 264–65). Despite this essentially conservative image, I would argue that Neagle's films had a special appeal for women, particularly middle-class women.[13] To some degree her films could be considered progressive: she always played strong, professional women whose function in the narrative was never simply erotic interest. She was not marketed as a sex symbol like, for example, Diana Dors in the 1950s. A connection with the female audience was established early on in her career. *Nell Gwyn*, with its focus on a wicked lady, marshalled some of the melodramatic appeal Gainsborough films were later to harness in the 1940s.

Always the major protagonist, Neagle played monarchs, nurses, a secret service agent, a French resistance heroine, a Wren, a manageress of a large fashion house, a secretary in a publishing company. Marcia Landy has commented that *Victoria the Great* and *Sixty Glorious Years* (Herbert Wilcox, 1938) were not simply patriotic, rhetorical platforms because 'through spectacle they address viewers, particularly female viewers when the protagonist is female, with a vision of "the absolute power of monarchy" and hence of female power' (Landy, 1991: 70). In *Victoria the Great* she excludes Prince Albert from her work of being an important monarch and takes an active interest in politics. In *They Flew Alone* (Herbert Wilcox, 1942) she portrays aviator Amy Johnson, the 'girl from Yorkshire, born to be one of millions, she became one in a million'. Throughout the film she is determined, courageous and hardworking. All her flights are successful until she marries and flies to New York with her aviator husband, Jim Mollison; their marriage eventually breaks down and Amy disappears on a flight in 1941. In Neagle films, however, there are often competing discourses with those which might be construed as proto-feminist: the construction of her femininity is always tempered with modesty and decorum. In the context of the 1930s and 1940s, her image reveals contradictory messages about whether women should be traditional or progressive and their contribution to a sense of national identity.

Throughout *They Flew Alone* her success is placed in a context of British imperialism whereby her courageous behaviour is but one part of the collective national war effort. Despite her achievements she is always modest and selfless, above all, a lady. In a key reception speech after she has broken existing records by flying to Australia, Johnson speaks of her success purely in imperialist terms:

I want to try and do something for England so that out of my flight to Australia I can get the youth of our country to become air-minded. My message to youth is to abandon the slogan 'Safety First'. There are lots of things to come before safety – our country must come first. We must dream great dreams and see great visions. We've got to breed a race of airmen comparable to Drake's sea-dogs who will go out to the skyways of the air and help to bind still closer the British empire.

While she is making this speech she is watched by Mollison, whom she has just met and with whom a romantic involvement seems increasingly likely. He remarks to his companion that Amy's ambition is 'disturbing', in keeping with a series of remarks about her achievement being extraordinary because of her gender. Interestingly, such remarks are confined to male characters with, in this case, Amy remaining a diffident nationalist rather than an overt feminist, the meaning of her endeavours being articulated, and ultimately controlled, by men.

Other famous women played by Anna Neagle were Florence Nightingale, Nurse Edith Cavell and Odette Churchill. In *Elizabeth of Ladymead* (Herbert Wilcox, 1949) Anna Neagle played four women in different historical periods, awaiting their husbands' return from four respective wars (the Crimean, the Boer, the First World War and the Second World War). In *Odette* (Herbert Wilcox, 1950) she played an ordinary woman transformed into a heroine by wartime circumstances. In her own terms, Neagle thought that her roles were feminist. She made it very clear to the press that the women she played were not intended to be isolated cases of female heroism, but examples to all women to realise their own heroic potential, whatever their circumstances. When Neagle was interviewed by a *Picturegoer* reporter during the shooting of *The Lady With a Lamp* (Herbert Wilcox) in 1951, she proudly announced: 'I'm a complete feminist. There are big things for women to do, just as women like Florence Nightingale and Odette did big things. Bringing up children and being good housewives is not our only mission in life' (*Picturegoer*, 21 April 1951). This statement is particularly interesting and somewhat ironic in view of the period's concern to encourage women to stay in the home: on the one hand Neagle is the epitome of Britishness, while on the other she is an iconoclast of sorts.

Despite Neagle's optimism, the release of many of her famous women in history films around the war years and their association with nationalist concerns limited the extent to which they could be adopted as models for subsequent feminist advancement. The films appealed to female audiences who had gained freedoms in the Second World War and it is interesting that Neagle made no films of this nature in the 1950s when American films began to monopolise the market and when the dominant image of femininity was the dumb (or sometimes not-so-dumb) blonde: Marilyn Monroe, Judy Holliday, Diana Dors, Brigitte Bardot, etc. In the 1950s fewer women were top box-office stars compared with men, a downward trend which continued into the 1960s. Questions of audience response also have to be investigated in terms of the films' overall narrative trajectories and dominant cultural assumptions (see Thumim, 1992).

Plate 6.4 Amy Johnson (Anna Neagle) urges the Empire to become 'air-minded' in *They Flew Alone* (US title *Wings and the Woman*). (Copyright 1942 RKO Pictures Ltd. Used by permission of Turner Entertainment Co. All Rights Reserved)

Costumes and the 'London series'

On a different front, Neagle's feminine appeal was not confined to her roles in historical films or biopics. Her costumes were also a site of female pleasure, particularly in the London series of society melodramas/musical comedies, which were particularly successful at the box office. *Spring In Park Lane* (1948) and *Maytime In Mayfair* (1949), the latter in colour, had many dance sequences which showed off her glamorous gowns and introduced fantasy elements into their respective narratives. *Maytime In Mayfair* was set in a London fashion house and included a fantasy fashion sequence outside the main narrative which would have provided the audience with considerable pleasure. As the popularity of screwball comedies in 1930s America can be analysed in terms of the audience's desire to escape from the Depression, the success of the 'London series' in the late 1940s can also perhaps be explained by contextual social factors of postwar austerity and the attraction of bright fantasies set in the wealthiest parts of London, all without a hint of class conflict.

For a brief period at the end of the 1940s British films outstripped American at the box office and in political terms the films' conservative ideology may have reflected some of the middle-class disillusionment with the Labour Government by the 1950 election; while many middle-class voters had deserted back to the Tories, the working-class vote for the Labour Party increased. For all their frothy ebullience, the 'London series' nevertheless reflected fear of change and anxiety about the post-war world during the awkward transition period when the optimism of the 1940s evaporated into a cautious conservatism in the 1950s. As Brunsdon has noted in a study of London in the cinema, a film such as *Spring In Park Lane* presents the city as 'pleasant . . . partly make-believe, a post-war imagination of a 1930s Mayfair' (Brunsdon, 2007: 100). In support of analyses of the links between stardom and charismatic appeal it can therefore be argued that Neagle's popularity was effective during a period of doubt about the social order (cf. Dyer, 1979: 35–37). It is significant that Anna Neagle's last two successful films were *The Lady With a Lamp* (1951) and *Odette* (1950), again utilising her popular image as a national heroine but at a time when wartime unity was becoming established as an element of national nostalgia.

Anna Neagle and Britishness

Although Neagle worked in a variety of different genres she maintained an overall core image of Britishness, largely defined by class and patriotism, characteristics of the so-called national culture. The focus on London, as opposed to occasional regional products, in nearly all of her films is also indicative of the centralisation of cultural representations of Britishness. Neagle's role as a national emblem was also articulated by her portrayal of strong, Britannia-like women, a role which was frequently associated with the idea of ordinary women transformed into heroines by extraordinary wartime circumstances. Despite the pleasures offered to female audiences of seeing such women on screen as major protagonists, the potential feminist appeal of her films was qualified by their association with specific historical circumstances, by Wilcox's over-riding concern for nationalist rhetoric and by Neagle's image as the middle-class 'lady' who was hard-working and courageous but never radical. The films' narrative closures also constrained her heroines by leaving patriarchal structures unquestioned. Without a war on their hands, Neagle's plucky heroines found no scope for development and her attempt at the social-problem genre in 1956 *(My Teenage Daughter)* was clearly limited by her class-bound image (Hill, 1986: 104). The roles had perhaps become trapped by their star, the regal Neagle who nevertheless had served as a major cinematic signifier of the dominant articulation of Britishness for thirty years. Her films became symbols of a

blinkered national nostalgia, a comforting sense of Britishness, an idea associated with past certainties of class and national unity, material comfort,
stoic individualism, patriotism and, above all, those White Cliffs of Dover.

THE RANK CHARM SCHOOL AND BRITISH
STARS IN THE 1950s

The only institutional attempt from within the British film industry to
present a conscious strategy of stardom was the Rank Charm School, 1946–
50. Gainsborough Studios had tried to nurture a group of stars earlier in the
1940s, but not to the extent of the Charm School experiment which Geoffrey
Macnab has described as 'a sort of mixture between Lee Strasberg's Actors
Studio and a London finishing school' (Macnab, 1993: 141). Many British
would-be stars were involved in what amounted to a huge publicity campaign requiring them to *behave* like stars. They toured the country, attended
beauty contests, film premières and civic events and created an aura of
British stardom which was popular with the public. It is an interesting
comment on post-war austerity that the Rank Publicity Department was
bombarded with requests for photographs of stars and for guest appear-
ances, even when they were barely known on screen. The visibility of
stardom was clearly very much desired and by the 1940s stardom was deeply
embedded in popular cultural discourse (ibid.: 144–45).

Although in retrospect it is clear that Dirk Bogarde and Diana Dors were
two names associated with the School who justified genuine star billing,
they, and many others involved in the Charm School, resented not being
given screen roles which compensated them for being paraded for public
gratification. Diana Dors wrote an impassioned article which exposed the
frustrations of being a contract Rank starlet who had been cast as a 'bad
girl':

> It was not long before I realized that unless something drastic happened,
> or I could make something drastic happen, I was going to be Rank's stock
> 'bad girl'. . . . These appearances certainly got me on to the screen, but
> they didn't increase the range of my acting ability, and they certainly
> made picturegoers – and a good many people in the studios – think of me
> as a real-life edition of some of the girls I played in films.
>
> (Dors, 1950)

Macnab has written of the School's disbandment:

> With little chance of being cast in reasonable screen roles, and with every
> chance of having to fester, doing next to nothing, the artists' morale was
> liable to sink. The Charm School's exclusive preoccupation with leading
> men and women was possibly misguided. A smattering of character

actors would have introduced a little balance to the school, and reduced competition for the same roles There was something homogenized and bland about the crop of starlets, all uniformly good-looking, all wearing the same style of clothes, all photographed in identical light and poses.

(Macnab, 1993: 146)

Sue Aspinall has made the useful point that, in any case, many British female stars, particularly Margaret Lockwood and Phyllis Calvert, did not want to be associated with the razzmatazz of Hollywood-style publicity (Aspinall, 1983: 277).

The Rank Charm School must be seen in a context of increasing pressure to emulate the studio system. Ironically, in the 1950s the divorcement decrees forced the Hollywood studios to relinquish their exhibition interests and one consequence was that the dominant, vertically integrated monopolistic companies could no longer bind their stars to stringent contracts.[14] Despite frequent investigation by the Monopolies Commission (see Chapter 1), the Rank Organisation was not subject to similar legislation and the failure of the Charm School episode should perhaps be interpreted as indicative of the British film industry's perpetual double bind of neither having large companies to promote stars for sustained periods and *at the same time* give them adequate screen exposure, nor of possessing a diverse industrial base which could also sustain a large number of independent companies. Actors continued to receive low salaries and unlike the USA, there were no tax incentives to encourage them to initiate film projects.

One striking difference between the 1940s and 1950s is the gender imbalance between male and female stars. Whereas the 1940s was a decade when female stars dominated the screens, in the 1950s male stars were far more visible in terms of screen presence and box-office popularity. The most popular British male stars were Dirk Bogarde, Kenneth More, John Mills, Norman Wisdom, Richard Todd and Jack Hawkins. In terms of representation of male sexuality in this period, it would appear that the popular male stars continued to portray

> conflicts over identity, particularly concerning issues of competence, assimilation into the proper family and class position, and acceptance of institutional responsibility. While the films reveal underlying tensions in the characters' struggle to conform to social expectations, the overt emphasis is on the viability and necessity of that accommodation.
>
> (Landy, 1991: 40)

The exception to this general rule is Dirk Bogarde, who has been analysed in terms of his deviation from conventional norms of masculinity (Medhurst, 1986b; Landy, 1991; Dyer, 1993a). His films, particularly *The Blue Lamp*

(Basil Dearden, 1950), *Hunted* (Charles Crichton, 1952), *The Spanish Gardener* (Philip Leacock, 1957), *Libel* (Anthony Asquith, 1959), *The Singer Not the Song* (Roy Baker, 1961) and *Victim* (Basil Dearden, 1961), expose the problems of being male in the 1950s, most obtrusively with his portrayal of a homosexual in *Victim*.

There was no fiery 1950s equivalent to Margaret Lockwood; instead one thinks of Sylvia Syms, Phyllis Calvert, Yvonne Mitchell, Jean Kent and Googie Withers, who did not fare as well as the male stars at the box office. Syms most frequently appeared in supporting roles as a non-threatening, nice middle-class girl which earned her the title of starlet, as opposed to being identified as a fully-fledged star. She was not very sexual, an obligatory attribute in the 1950s when the dominant image of female sexuality consisted of a 'paradoxical coexistence of a desirable and glamorous physical appearance with vulnerable innocence', represented by actresses like Marilyn Monroe and Kim Novak (Thumim, 1992: 54). The closest any British star came to embodying this image was Diana Dors who, it can be seen in retrospect, transcended the sex-symbol label, or at least fully exploited its contradictory associations of 'knowingness and vulnerability' (Geraghty, 1986). Like Neagle, she rose to stardom from humble origins: the daughter of a Swindon railwayman, at thirteen she won third prize in a pin-up contest and had appeared in films by the time she was fifteen.

Far from being a dumb blonde, she combined natural wit and intelligence with threatening sexuality, as illustrated by a comment from *Films and Filming* in 1955: 'Dors, it is generally accepted, had her head screwed on; and her other attributes are equally well assembled. The first thing one studies on seeing her in the flesh is the floor. It seems the safest.' Newspaper reviews of her films reproduced stills of her in Monroe-like poses, particularly for *Passport To Shame* (Alvin Rakoff, 1959), a film about prostitution: 'there are no prizes for guessing the sort Dors plays in her latest film' (*News of the World*, 11 January 1959). She taunted the fan magazines with her frankness and her fascination with Hollywood which was revealed in her lively column in *Picturegoer*. Her image as a sullen but good-hearted sexpot in *Good Time Girl* (David Macdonald, 1948), and *Dance Hall* (Charles Crichton, 1950), changed dramatically when she starred in *Yield To the Night* (J. Lee Thompson, 1956). In this film she played Mary, an imprisoned woman awaiting a death sentence, which required Dors to appear unkempt and in a state of extreme emotional turmoil. The press were confused by this departure from her established image and produced endless comments about how strange it was to see a glamour girl who really could act: 'Dors sheds her mink and shows she can act.' But the reviews also drew attention to the parallels between Mary's story of goodtime girl turned contemplative victim of love and Dors' own transformation from sex symbol to serious actress.

Plate 6.5 Diana Dors – Charm School glamour queen. Compare with Plate 6.6.
(Courtesy of Lumière Pictures Limited)

Plate 6.6 Diana Dors after 'shedding her mink' to play Mary Hilton in *Yield To The Night* (1956). (Courtesy of Lumière Pictures Limited)

1960s STARDOM

For a long time it was assumed that the social-problem films of 1958–63 constituted Britain's New Wave of cinema: new in the sense that its directors, themes and stars were different and that the conventional star system (presuming that Britain had one) had been abandoned.[15] Revisionist histories, however, have stressed continuities between the angry young men films and earlier periods.[16] Although many of the stars who appeared in the films were new to screen acting, nearly all of them came from theatrical (particularly RADA or repertory) backgrounds, an established entrée into film. And the dawnings of auteur theories and comparisons made between the British New Wave and the practically simultaneous French *nouvelle vague* began to privilege directors above stars in critical film discourse.

If the immediate ethos of kitchen sink drama militated against the tinseltown connotations of stardom, the decade was certainly not without its British stars. As far as popular cinema was concerned, star names were still big box-office, and the kitchen sink dramas were by no means the most popular films.[17] Declining cinema attendances are, however, an important factor when examining stardom in the Sixties, and there is no doubt that aspects of conventional fandom and star culture were becoming more fragmented with the rise of pop music and television. *Picturegoer*, the major British fan magazine since the 1930s, folded in 1958 and its latter issues reveal how far pop culture was invading film fandom. Richard Lester's *A Hard Day's Night* (1964) is a fascinating film with four male stars, the Beatles, at the centre of its narrative and their new kind of celebrity is, indeed, the very core of the film. Both the narrative and publicity circulated an image of the Beatles as the embodiment of the meritocratic ideal and also worked to present them as individuals: collectively they were 'the boys' and individually were John (cheeky), Paul (pretty), George (quiet) and Ringo (gentle). The Beatles are a perfect example of the traditional attributes of film stardom being transferred and indeed elaborated at the onset of mass pop culture. Like other stars they were both ordinary and extraordinary, their very *un*attainability being a major focus of attraction for their girl fans (see Ehrenreich, Hess and Jacobs, 1992).

Robert Murphy has made the point that in the 1960s 'a wider range of acting talent came into the film industry and was allowed to flourish in a much less restricted way' (Murphy, 1992: 36). One only has to think of Albert Finney, Tom Courtenay, Rita Tushingham, Michael Caine, Sean Connery and Julie Christie to conjure up an instant image of the 1960s. Male characters continued to dominate as central protagonists and many of the themes of 1960s cinema were concerned with masculine problems, although there are examples of films which offer explorations of female experience, including *A Taste of Honey* (Tony Richardson, 1961), *The Pumpkin Eater* (Jack Clayton, 1964) and (lesser known) *The World Ten Times Over* (Wolf

Rilla, 1963).[18] And of course the decade was dominated by the phenomenal success of Julie Andrews in *The Sound of Music* (1965), a film which broke previous box-office records (see report in *Kinematograph Weekly*, 17 December 1966). Although the film was American, Andrews' Britishness continued the tradition of upper-middle-class respectability which Anna Neagle had represented in previous decades.

The proliferation of independent film companies and new directors gave chances to actors who would have found it impossible to make their way in the 1950s. Stars of the following decade, however, were more eclectic and transitory, far more tied to particular projects than actors had been in the 1940s and 1950s. From an early stage, stars and casting were of paramount importance for the new directors. For example, the casting of Richard Burton, with his established theatrical reputation and Hollywood credentials, as Jimmy Porter in *Look Back In Anger* (Tony Richardson, 1959), denied the film's central protagonist the gritty working-class centre the role clearly demanded. But it presented audiences with a familiar face in an unfamiliar style of film. After *Look Back In Anger* Burton returned to Hollywood and big-budget film-making to star in *Cleopatra* (1963). French actress Simone Signoret was chosen to play Alice in *Room at the Top* (Jack Clayton, 1959) to give the film international appeal (Walker, 1974: 47). Despite the profound tragedy represented by her character, Signoret nevertheless provided glamour, largely associated with her comforting and alluring French accent which contrasted with the harsh counties tones of Susan Brown and her mother. Indeed, one profoundly important result of the social-problem genre was the permission it gave actors to break free from BBC English and experiment with accents. In the case of *Room at the Top*, Signoret's voice beautifully complemented the occasional soft tones of co-star Laurence Harvey's (imitation) northern accent.

Laurence Harvey had tried for years to break into big-time film stardom, guided by James Woolf, but had to wait for the part of Joe Lampton to fully display his talents. When British films proved to be box-office successes the attitude to casting became more flexible. Julie Christie was cast to play Liz in *Billy Liar* (John Schlesinger, 1963) after Joseph Janni had seen her at the Central School of Speech and Drama. Many other new names were given chances – for example, Tony Richardson was responsible for introducing Rita Tushingham, Alan Bates and Albert Finney to the screen. Finney hated the trappings of stardom and deliberately tried to avoid type-casting and glamour. After his success in *Saturday Night and Sunday Morning* (1960) he refused to star in *Lawrence of Arabia* (David Lean, 1962), 'recognising how inevitably the star concept, to say nothing of the multiple picture contract, would tie him financially, restrict him imaginatively, consume him utterly' (ibid.: 87). Finney also refused to repeat his stage success as Billy for the screen version of *Billy Liar*. Audiences were still accustomed to stars maintaining their established personas, and one theory for the box-office flop of *Night Must Fall* (Karel Reisz, 1964) was that Finney had disappointed audiences by straying too far from the likeable rogue image he had cultivated to great effect in *Tom Jones* (Tony Richardson, 1963) (Murphy, 1992: 74).

The influx of American backing for British films in 1963–64 did not seem to have a negative influence as far as casting was concerned. When, for example, Albert R. ('Cubby') Broccoli and Harry Saltzman persuaded United Artists to back the James Bond series, they cast Sean Connery, a virtual unknown, as Bond.[19] Like Finney, Connery became one of the most popular male stars but, unlike the independent Finney, Connery was forever tainted with Bond 007 iconography: forever the laconic hero, Connery *is* Bond. United Artists took a risk with *A Hard Day's Night*, the Beatles' star vehicle: when it was being produced the group had not yet conquered America, but its huge success at the box office proved that such chances were often worth taking.[20] The film made an important contribution to the consolidation of Beatlemania in Britain and America in 1964.

The overall culture of expansion and experiment encouraged actors to become directors and producers: Bryan Forbes, Richard Attenborough and Jack Hawkins formed Allied Film Makers in 1959, a company which lasted until 1964, and Stanley Baker was involved in the establishment of a production company, Oakhurst. Albert Finney directed himself in *Charlie Bubbles* (1967) and formed Memorial Enterprises with actor Michael Medwin. This creative and exciting decade of film-making was curtailed when a large number of American-backed films failed at the box office towards the end of the 1960s and cinema admissions plummeted from 327 million in 1965 to 193 million in 1970. *Cinema TV Today* (7 January 1974) reported that in 1973 British output and investment had fallen by half in comparison with 1972, a trend which had serious implications for film stars.

British stars since the 1960s

After the American companies pulled out of financing British films in the 1970s, the industry faced an uphill struggle and few British stars could claim to be bankable. Since the exploitation of stars requires a fairly stable economic base, the fragmented nature of the British film industry since the 1960s has created difficulties for actors seeking to establish an image. Sean Connery as James Bond was a star partly because United Artists financed so many Bond pictures, creating a familiar body of work, knowledge of which audiences could bring with them when viewing each new Bond film. This fascination with repetition and difference is the foundation of genre cinema and consequently of stardom. Economic instability created a climate of uncertainty and, once again, Hollywood seemed to be the natural place for would-be stars. By the mid-1970s, Hollywood was recovering from the recession of the late 1960s and early 1970s, making it an attractive escape route for British actors whose opportunities in Britain were limited.

Despite patriotic declarations in support of British actors in British films, Michael Caine left Britain in 1978 and went on to international stardom. Sean Connery tried to jettison his Bond image and worked with a range of directors in Britain and Hollywood, while Albert Finney and Tom Courtenay returned to the theatre. John Walker has observed that in the 1970s some actors did not trust the screen or the onerous trappings of associated stardom, quoting Glenda Jackson on the alleged absence of such notions in the theatre: 'One marvellous thing about Britain is that you can do your work and go home afterwards with no pressure on you to live off-stage what you represent on it' (Walker, 1985: 111).

Julian Petley also identifies this anti-screen phobia and blames the weight of theatrical tradition for cinema's reluctance to exploit new talent evident in punk rock or pop music, citing critics' reservations about *Performance* (Donald Cammell and Nicolas Roeg, 1970) and *The Man Who Fell To Earth* (Nicolas Roeg, 1976) as evidence of cultural ossification and prejudice against '"Hollywoodian" explorations and invocations of star personae' (Petley, 1985: 115). For him, most British stars in the 1970s and 1980s were too stage-bound in technique and vision, the only real star being Jeremy Irons who exuded an upper-class representation of masculinity and Britishness:

> To date his success as a star is principally founded on his impersonation of a familiar English stereotype: a pre-World War Two English gentleman, slightly decadent, preferably with an ambiguous sexual identity. The fact that Rupert Everett has been so sensationally successful in just such a role in *Another Country* . . . suggests not so much the need for an English pin-up equivalent of Richard Gere but rather the potent appeal of this particular stereotype at the present moment, relating as it does to such familiar English vices as nostalgia for the Imperial past, an obsession with failure and humiliation and a highly ambiguous fascination with 'the mores (especially sexual) of the upper classes'.
>
> (ibid.: 118)

Described in this manner, Irons continues an established tradition of British actors, including David Niven, Michael Wilding, Kenneth More, James Fox, Michael York and other such upper-class English types, and looks forward to the aristocratic Hugh Grant with his very similar star persona in *Four Weddings and a Funeral* (Mike Newell, 1994). This particular representation has won consistent favour in America.

Julian Petley argued in 1985 that if you are looking for stars in the old Hollywood sense of the word, that is 'the creation of an immanent, readable, meaningful image' of someone who displays all the tensions of being both ordinary and extraordinary, like us and unlike us, you have increasingly to look outside the film and television industries (see Petley, 1985: 113; Dyer, 1979). The legacy of *A Hard Day's Night* (1964) was clearly a profound and lasting one. The star phenomenon is most prevalent in the music industry, complete with fanzines, high-key promotions, tours and all the trappings of major marketing strategies designed to create bankable images. Pop stars use videos and the internet to advertise themselves and, increasingly, hire established film directors to construct narratives for their songs, for example, the Pet Shop Boys' use of Derek Jarman as director of several of their pop promos. Many films use pop music as soundtrack in an attempt to appeal to a broad audience, as producer Steve Wolley commented on the theme for *Scandal* (Michael Caton Jones, 1989): 'if I can get The Pet Shop Boys audience, especially the older ones, to take the picture semi-seriously then I've got an enormous market there' (Wolley, 1988, quoted in Petrie, 1991: 129). A frequent pattern has been for successful pop stars to appear in films, including Cliff Richard in *The Young Ones* (1961) and *Summer Holiday* (1963); The Beatles in *Help!* (1965); Mick Jagger in *Performance* (1970); David Bowie in *The Man Who Fell To Earth* (1976); David Essex in *That'll Be the Day* (Claude Whatham, 1973); Roger Daltry in *Tommy* (Ken Russell, 1975) and *McVicar* (Tom Clegg, 1980); and Sting in *Quadrophenia* (Franc Roddam, 1979) and *Brimstone and Treacle* (Richard Loncraine, 1982). It is unusual, however, for famous pop stars to become better known for their film work.

It has been argued that Britain does not have a flourishing star system partly because of links with the theatre where, according to Glenda Jackson, the pressures to behave as a star do not exist off-stage in the same way that they do in film acting. If television produces personalities, not stars (Ellis, 1982: 107), can an actor be both a television personality and a film star if they work in both? Kenneth Branagh and many contemporary British actors work in theatre, film and television, a fact which poses interesting questions about the development of their star personae. As we have seen, the classic definition of a star requires them to be *both* ordinary and extraordinary. Alison Light has placed Branagh in the tradition of 'middle-brow ordinariness', associated with British stars like Robert Donat, John Mills and Richard Attenborough (Light, 1993). But does Branagh's ordinary image, his theatre and television work therefore disqualify him from being a true star?

I would argue that, on the contrary, his television work has not consisted of the personality variety which is primarily associated with series, soap operas and game-shows. *Fortunes of War* (James Cellan-Jones, 1987), for example, is a quality period drama with Branagh acting a similar role to that of Jeremy Irons' well-bred, educated English gentleman. And the extent of his ordinary image on and off screen is questionable. He has worked in

Hollywood and in a variety of genres and, while it lasted, his marriage to Emma Thompson placed him in a long tradition of film-star special couples who are constantly in the public gaze. But it is true to say that he is a different kind of star from the classical Hollywood type: he represents a sort of star eclecticism which is a feature of so many contemporary actors' careers. He has made a feature of that eclecticism: stars like Branagh become well known for a particular aspect of their work, for example television, and then branch out and elaborate on that initial image. Although subsequent film work might then conflict with a previously established reputation, the star's core image must adapt to accommodate any changes. By the time Branagh made *Frankenstein* he had, to some extent, strayed from his reputation as Olivier's successor by directing the Hitchcockian thriller homage, *Dead Again* (1991) and the contemporary comedy-drama, *Peter's Friends* (1992). Marketing *Frankenstein* therefore required Branagh to be high-profile, maintaining his star authenticity by emphasising his abilities to overcome the problems involved in adapting Mary Shelley's work, working within the Gothic horror genre and in competition with previous film versions of the Frankenstein story. When *Frankenstein* (1994) was released, Branagh appeared on television many times to advertise it, using his reputation in theatre and film to assist his claim that he had orchestrated the 'most authentic' adaptation of Mary Shelley's novel. His adaptations of Shakespeare further reinforce his persona as theatre director, from *Hamlet* (1996) to *Love's Labour's Lost* (2000). One of his films, *In the Bleak Midwinter* (1995), even uses the story of an amateur production of *Hamlet* as its theme.

It seems, however, that to win international fame British stars like Branagh still need assistance from Hollywood in the form of roles and the accolade of Academy Awards. Many successes, including Daniel Day-Lewis, Anthony Hopkins, Miranda Richardson, Gary Oldman, Emma Thompson and Alan Rickman, branched out from British film and television because

> the American machine chose to force these talented actors down the throats of the media – a kind of catapulting into the Hollywood star system – which via its global tentacles has promoted them to international fame. It is unthinkable that their names would be known across the world today if it had been left to the marketing forces of the British industry.
>
> (Finney, 1994: 23)

This quotation is typical of many critics' ambivalence towards the whole notion of stardom. As we have seen, discussions of British stardom have always been inflected with this patriotic ambivalence about slavishly aspiring to Hollywood models. Stardom is thus defined according to

Hollywood norms which require that successful film industries market actors as international stars. That this is somehow *unBritish* is a contradiction which has profoundly influenced the way British stars have been marketed. In the context of co-production and the increasing trans-national tendencies of many contemporary British films, we see a greater fluidity of personnel within the industry. This can result in actors resenting being involved in the international star machine, as demonstrated by Ewan McGregor's celebrated antipathy towards Hollywood even though he has appeared not only in Scottish, British but also Hollywood's *Star Wars* blockbusters. Another example is Daniel Craig whose first major role was on television in *Our Friends In the North* (BBC 2 1996). Like others from that series, including Christopher Eccleston and Gina McKee, Craig has gone on to develop a prominent screen acting career, appearing in British films including *The Mother* (Roger Mitchell, 2003) and *Enduring Love* (Roger Mitchell, 2004) to the mega-stardom of playing James Bond in *Casino Royale* (Martin Campbell, 2006). While Craig has not openly criticised the Hollywood machine along the lines of McGregor, he nevertheless appears to be uncomfortable with his role as sex-symbol in the James Bond role. In this, and other ways, the reservations expressed by British stars from earlier periods about inhabiting the publicity-intensive territory of major international stardom continue to be voiced.

CONCLUSION: BRITISH STARS, TRADITIONS AND CLASS

The question of British stardom brings us back to the theatrical legacy of a suspicious attitude towards the filmic, which originates in cinema's formative years. The British version of stardom was, therefore, profoundly determined and tempered by the example of Hollywood and a consistent reliance on actors from theatrical backgrounds. The resulting tension influenced the way stars were promoted and, in turn, their performances on screen. Actors and actresses with established theatrical credentials would be marketed accordingly: Yvonne Mitchell appeared in many British films, mostly playing neurotic characters which gave her the chance to demonstrate her acting abilities.[21] Yet she was rarely referred to as a star, a term which was more readily associated with glamour and a rags-to-riches personal biography than with impressive acting credentials. In publicity, her performance was commented on rather than her off-screen behaviour.

The class basis of many stars' images often militated against them being totally absorbed by publicity machines as seekers of fame and fortune.[22] A screen image based on class affected the self-promotional codes used by an actor or actress. Anna Neagle, for example, represented middle-class values which required her to be hardworking, humble and modest, factors which differentiated her from the stereotypical ambitious Hollywood star. On the other hand, Diana Dors was a working-class girl who became famous for her sex appeal and was well aware of how her image was being exploited as a British Marilyn Monroe. She sought out publicity, not vice versa, was outspoken about her career and wanted to defect to Hollywood. By contrast, interviews with Neagle give the impression that acting was a sort of hobby and patriotic duty which she performed selflessly, 'in the national interest'. Hugh Grant is an interesting example of an upper-class star whose career has been curiously assisted by his arrest in Los Angeles in 1995 with a prostitute. His persona is that of the well-bred Englishman whose off-screen behaviour merely confirms stereotypes about upper-class hypocrisy over sexual matters. Although international success has made him a star, he nevertheless comes across in interviews as a modest, stuttering, even bashful man. In turn, this behaviour has encouraged his fans to interpret 'the Divine incident' as an endearing schoolboy misdemeanour. The success of Keira Knightley is also inflected with connotations of class, an image ('the English rose') which is drawn upon in her Hollywood and British films, as well as in publicity. The persistence of heritage-inflected films and films based on royalty, for example, Helen Mirren's appearance in *The Queen* (2006), similarly reinforce these long-term developments in British stardom.

Stars function as essential components in terms of the unpredictable chemistry at work in the contract between a film and its audience. Stardom also raises questions of national cultures operating in a context of Hollywood domination but also within their own traditions and self-perceptions. The fact that for much of the last century the British film industry has been in poor economic health did not prevent British stars from being important cultural icons in particular decades – Gracie Fields in the 1930s, Anna Neagle and Margaret Lockwood in the 1940s, Kenneth More and Dirk Bogarde in the 1950s. Indeed, Hollywood competition invested British stars with inflections of Britishness, some stars resembling those in Hollywood while at the same time basing their appeal on a class image. This paradoxical position perhaps reveals something specific to British stardom: a tension between the democratic ideal that you do not need to be well bred or rich to become a star, and the British class system which would nevertheless keep you in your place.

Chapter 7

Borderlines I: modernism and British cinema

Although Truffaut argued that 'cinema' and 'British film' are a contradiction in terms, there is a considerable history of cultural debate about the artistic potential of British film and some evidence of practical application. Much of British cinema has been inflected with a realist/naturalist style, but there is also an aesthetic tradition which has explored film as a medium capable of conveying complex states of mind with a rich formal apparatus at its disposal, and as a means of political critique. Derek Jarman, Peter Greenaway and Sally Potter naturally spring to mind in connection with modernism/postmodernism and British cinema, but their work in the 1970s was not the first example of British interest in non-narrative experimental art cinema. As early as 1914, Duncan Grant created *Abstract Kinetic Painting With Collage*, a scroll painting which 'came to life' when viewed through a light-box at a particular speed to match the tempo of a piece by Bach. Grant is representative of early experimentation with film as 'visual music' and the majority of artists saw the creative development of the medium to lie in this direction rather than in story-telling/narrative structure (see Wollen, 1994: 5).

In general terms, cinematic modernism is concerned with interrogating linear modes of narration, exploring psychological traits and abandoning traditional forms of characterisation. It explores the visual rather than the verbal, form being obtrusive, and it is often presented as the product of an auteur which nevertheless places great stress on the audience's interpretation of the work (Bordwell, 1985: 206–33). As with other examples of modernist art, the question of representation is foregrounded, emphasising how images must be seen as versions of reality rather than reality itself. In terms of the institutional structures of the film industry, modernist film-making has posed questions about distribution and exhibition networks – indeed, criticising capitalist structures of film-making on a factory basis which appear to subordinate art to industry.

These characteristics are necessarily broad, and I would not wish to be confined to a rigid definition of the art film as opposed to the commercial feature which nevertheless might employ challenging techniques in terms of narrative structure or formal experiment. The question of film aesthetics is extremely relevant to ideas about national cinemas, national styles and the extent to which film-making must draw on a variety of methods and cultures to avoid becoming insular, yet at the same time preserve some sense of national identity. John Hill has argued that a 'nationally specific' cinema is one which represents diverse experiences of Britishness which in view of dominant representations can only be conveyed in all its complexities by challenging, 'oppositional' cinema (Hill, 1992).

Broadly speaking, there have been four major phases (each involving a certain degree of fluidity) of experimental activity in Britain, when particular themes and preoccupations dominated debate and practice. This chapter will deal with phases one and two and Chapter 8 with phases three and four.

The first phase was the inter-war period when early modernist films were seen and discussed by intellectuals who made films which aspired to explore cinematic properties outside the conventional narrative framework established by Hollywood. Modernist alternatives in Europe, Japan and Soviet Russia stimulated discussion of auteurs, stylistic and technical experimentation and the thinking audience. These assumptions were aligned with modernism's general disdain for popular culture and what was seen as the cultural debasement by Hollywood of a medium with great artistic potential. The arrival of sound disrupted many of the musical experiments of the 1920s, but there was some continuation of this approach in Britain by avant-garde members of the Documentary Film Movement. During this period there was also some attempt by workers' film groups to produce 'oppositional' films: oppositional in terms of their criticism of the National Government which was dominated by a political philosophy of consensus and because of their unorthodox distribution and exhibition strategies. The labour films (films produced by working-class groups and left-wing organisations) were not particularly oppositional in terms of aesthetic experiment, but are important as precursors of those produced by organisations with radical approaches towards form, and institutions which developed in the mid-1960s and 1970s.

It is important that this first phase should be seen in the context of Hollywood's rapid establishment of a hegemonic position in the world film market. In the early 1920s, Hollywood was quite prepared to learn from art cinema and many European directors, including F. W. Murnau, were lured to work there. By the end of the 1920s, however, the American cultural climate had become more confident about the classical narrative modes that were evolving in Hollywood, a trend which explains the confused response to Murnau's *Sunrise* (1927) which made use of both commercial Hollywood and European art film traditions (see Petrie, 1985: 25). This background of the growing ascendancy of classical narrative film was further strengthened by the arrival of sound. In the 1930s, film experiment in Britain was confined to institutions like the GPO Film Unit and, unlike in the 1920s, there was little evidence of modernist intervention within the commercial feature film.

The second phase or dominant area of activity concerns the extent of formal experiment in feature films, 1940–70. This recalled Hitchcock's silent films and developed, for example, some of the early ideas about the relationship between film and sound, most notably in the work of Powell and Pressburger. Their films are representative of deviant, non-realist British cinema which is also exemplified by the work of Losey, Anderson, Roeg and Antonioni. In the 1940s and 1950s, New American Cinema, the underground movement and Pop Art (Deren, Warhol, Brakhage, Anger), illustrated a shift of modernist activity away from Europe, to be reclaimed in 1958 by the *nouvelle vague* brigade who initiated what John Orr has termed 'the true moment of the modern in Western Cinema' (Orr, 1992: 2). The Hollywood studio system still dominated in the 1940s and early 1950s but was forced to retreat by 1960, allowing for the emergence of independent mainstream directors (Altman, Scorsese, Coppola, Penn, etc.) who incorporated modernist techniques and, increasingly, postmodern sensibilities into their films (see Kolker, 1988). Influenced by these wider developments, a shift to postmodern preoccupations can be seen to occur during this period: many films demonstrate postmodern attributes, for example Cammell and Roeg's *Performance* (1970) which focuses on questions of identity.

Phase three, 1966–80, concerns the modern independent cinema movement, initiated by the foundation of the London Film-Makers Co-Op in 1966. During this phase, practical experiment again coincided with debates about the nature and impact of popular cinema. In a more sustained and theoretical fashion than in the 1920s and 1930s, most of the films sought to question patterns of narration and formal expectations established by conventions such as genre and gender representation. The final phase, 1980 to the present, overlaps with phase three, but concerns the politicisation of art cinema under the impetus of opposition to a long period of Conservative government and particularly to Thatcherism, and into the twenty-first century. There appears to have been a fusion of most previous strands of experimental activity, producing some of the most exciting British cinema by Sally Potter, Peter Greenaway, Derek Jarman, Terence Davies, Bill Douglas and Lynne Ramsay. The last section will also examine black British films, animation and gay and lesbian films. Channel 4's establishment in 1982 has expanded the audience for art cinema considerably, and television in general is extremely tolerant of difficult and experimental material by writers like Dennis Potter. Importantly, the whole project of other cinemas has empowered many disadvantaged groups with access to image-making and provoked discussion about how to challenge the dominant forms of representation.

PHASE ONE: 1920s TO 1930s

CLOSE-UP TO *FILM ART*: THEORISTS, FILM-MAKERS, WORKERS AND DOCUMENTARISTS, 1925–39

Although there was considerable experimentation within early cinema, art cinema proper tends to be associated with the 1920s, coinciding with Eisenstein and Pudovkin's development of theories of montage, German Expressionism, French Impressionism and Surrealism. At the same time, Hollywood was, in retrospect, refining classical modes of narration which can be contrasted with these other non-classical cinematic forms. In terms of cultural debate, however, American cinema was seen as the enemy, a mass form which, it was argued, on the whole neglected the artistic possibilities of cinema in favour of attracting dollars at the box office. Concern to encourage a minority audience interested in intelligent cinema became the aim of several film periodicals in Britain in the inter-war years, representing a cultural attitude receptive to diverse film forms. The arguments for a European and British avant-garde were also connected with wider fears of American political and economic domination, the general response of cultural elites to mass culture and the eventual negotiation of cultural consensus (see LeMahieu, 1988).

The following quotation is typical of the attitude towards American cinema and its alleged mindlessness:

> When the film is not good enough to keep the brain working, the public sinks into a kind of hypnotic daze. The screen with its changing forms becomes something in the nature of a crystal, and the public in the nature of a crystal gazer. Mind in some way obliterates itself. The music, suave dusk and an amatory continuity with ardent close-ups is enough to work the charm, the public is under its spell, held drugged, entirely at rest.
>
> (Macpherson, 1927b)

Macpherson's dismissive comments on popular cinema in the 1920s are representative of a critical, modernist attitude which prevailed among the cultivated elites who were coming to terms with new media and technology. The artistic possibilities of film were celebrated and encouraged while Hollywood was consolidating its hold over the world's film markets with films which were considered, by these critics, to be inferior. Their writings are full of assumptions of European cultural superiority, as Macpherson argued in the same issue of *Close-Up*: 'American sentiment and American sob-stuff to the European mind is always, in its films, a damp and treacly rehash of 1880-ish yellow-back novelish eyewash. . . . We in Western Europe need a richer fare'. Macpherson was proved wrong when American modernism gained cultural ascendancy in the 1940s and 1950s and western culture became, essentially, US culture (Sinfield, 1989: 186–87). But in the 1920s it was assumed that Hollywood was not exploring the medium's creative potential.

In the inter-war years more people wrote about art cinema than made films. Dusinberre (1980: 48–49) listed fourteen people identified with the London avant-garde in the 1930s who made experimental films: Oswell Blakeston, Guy Branch, B. Vivian Braun, Francis Bruguière, Andrew Buchanan, Robert Fairthorne, Hilda Doolittle ('H. D.'), Brian Desmond Hurst, Len Lye, Norman McLaren, Kenneth Macpherson, Brian Montagu, Irene Nicholson and Brian Salt. Between them they produced over forty films, which were not widely distributed. Much of their work does not survive, but their writings in the two major art-film periodicals, *Close-Up* (1927–33) and *Film Art* (1933–37), give a good indication of the 'modernist attitude' in Britain which promoted such cinematic experiment. This attitude consisted of three main facets: an enthusiasm for Soviet, German and other non-Hollywood cinema; the development of regional film societies to show art films which were unavailable on commercial circuits; and the promotion of amateur 16mm film projects. The other main areas of experimental activity were in oppositional and political film, the Documentary Movement and in some mainstream films.

Close-Up and *Film Art* encouraged the screening of foreign films by film societies. The film society movement was a most important development in the appreciation of foreign and art films. Audiences were small, hard-core enthusiasts who, as members of societies all over Britain, inspired the modern independent exhibition circuit. In 1925 Ivor Montagu and actor Hugh Miller decided to form the Film Society to show imported art films and films which were not screened in London's commercial cinemas because of censorship which was conservative and restrictive, resulting in the banning of, for example, *Nosferatu* (Germany, F. W. Murnau, 1922), *The Battleship Potemkin* (Soviet Russia, Sergi Eisenstein, 1925) and *The New Babylon* (Soviet Russia, Grigori Kozintsev and Leonid Trauberg, 1929). Film societies flouted the law by exploiting a loophole which enabled films banned by the British Board of Film Censors to be shown on 16mm safety stock as long as local councils did not object, or to the membership of a private club (see Robertson, 1985; Mathews, 1994). Essentially a private club with a high membership fee, the Film Society's Sunday screenings therefore introduced British intellectuals to Eisenstein, Renoir, Vertov, Vigo and many others. Between 1925 and 1939 the Society screened about 500 films and the idea was taken up by regional societies all over the country (see Montagu, 1975; Samson, 1986). Its record, however, at showing British experimental work was poor: between 1925 and 1939 it showed only seven British avant-garde films (Dusinberre, 1980: 41–42). The high cost of joining the Film Society more or less excluded working-class enthusiasts, who formed their own societies.

As well as reporting on Film Society screenings, *Close-Up* featured articles by intellectual film enthusiasts, including the poet 'H. D.' who considered the intellectual duty-bound to rescue cinema from 'its hidebound convention'. To this end, she lamented Hollywood's conversion of Greta Garbo in the much admired *Joyless Street* (Germany, G. W. Pabst, 1925) into a star with a vampish image in *Torrent* (US, Monta Bell, 1925) (1927: 27). The editor, Kenneth Macpherson, elevated European cultural sensibilities above American cinema, which he tolerated as far as the occasional comedy. Early numbers of the periodical were much more anti-Hollywood than later in the 1930s when it was conceded that some American films were interesting and that independent American directors were similarly concerned with the development of film art. This more sympathetic attitude can also be attributed to the decision to distribute *Close-Up* in the USA and Canada from 1928. On the whole, however, much greater critical attention was paid to directors like Eisenstein, Pabst, Pudovkin and Dreyer and to the aesthetic challenges posed by the arrival of sound. This was a major blow to exponents of visual cinema – those who wished to see cinema progress in a way which exploited its specificity as a visual rather than an aural medium – whose fears that sound might encourage even greater dependence on theatre proved to be well-founded (see discussion of film and its relationship to theatre in Chapter 4). It is ironic that the experiments of Cavalcanti and others in the Documentary Film Movement in the 1930s were partly facilitated by the notoriously bad sound equipment available to the Film Unit. As a consequence, their films utilised unconventional soundtracks and a few were mainly silent except for musical accompaniment or intermittent voice-over commentary.

As far as the British industry's potential was concerned, the first number of *Close-Up* carried a pessimistic editorial by Kenneth Macpherson who wrote that 'the average attitude of England and the English to art is wholly nonchalant and clownish . . . it is quite useless to expect any art to indigenously flower there' (1927a: 8). Little interest was expressed in the debate on the 1927 Films Act, except a rejection of the idea that British films should include British stars (September 1927: 68). This concern with banishing prejudice against foreign stars is consistent with European modernism's general internationalism and cosmopolitanism. In opposition to mass culture anti-Americanism was condoned but, as far as the question of protection of the British film industry was concerned, the devotees of art cinema were ambivalent about how far protection *within* Europe was possible or desirable. This led to a confused response to British films: Robert Herring's review of Hitchcock's *The Ring* (1927), for example, dismissed the film as being full of flashy technique but a poor imitation of German films. There was no attempt to look beyond the known qualities of European modernist cinema, no attempt to see that Hitchcock was not merely borrowing another cinema's techniques but instead was producing a number of distinctive *British* films during this period which drew on a wide range of influences (see Ryall, 1986: 23–30). As we have seen in Chapter 2, British cinema of the late silent and early sound period displayed 'internationalist' sensibilities which drew from a variety of different film traditions.

Discussion of what a British film might look like was limited, relying on vague terms like 'restraint', 'reason', 'taste' and 'tradition' (*Close-Up*, January 1928: 33). In a later issue of *Close-Up*, Ernest Betts argued that to be distinctive British films should feature British cities (1928: 45). This point was made by other writers who fixated on location as a crucial indicator of national identity on film. In March 1929 Macpherson advocated a British film school so that technical backwardness could be rectified. It is ironic that the realist style of British film so applauded by later critics was here being advocated by the so-called champions of the avant-garde, although they did not specify exactly *how* British locations might be utilised.

When *Close-Up* folded in 1933, discussion of art cinema and the work of film societies continued in *Film Art*, edited by B. Vivian Braun until 1935 when Irene Nicholson and John C. Moore took over following an editorial dispute. Its general aims were similar, but it expanded on several of *Close-Up's* ideas, including film societies being more involved in production and film education. B. Vivian Braun's *Film Art* manifesto expresses the modernist attitude most clearly:

> To analyse the potentialities and solve the aesthetic problems of cinema art. To support any artistic film movement, society, group, club, cinema, or individual whose aims are similar to our own. To present the writings, theories, reviews, and opinions of both world-famous and unknown persons, and to present them exactly as stated however outspoken or revolutionary. To encourage the use of the cinema as a social reformer, as a means for international understanding and for general education.
>
> (1934: 9)

Despite its vanguard rhetoric, the periodical was primarily interested in aesthetic rather than political aspects of film. Avoiding too narrow a focus, *Film Art* could celebrate the work of isolated individuals at the same time as that of film-makers working for commercial sponsors (Dusinberre, 1980: 43). The periodicals also expanded the boundaries of British film criticism, which was never as lively or theoretical in subsequent years until *Sequence* (1947–52).

The writers in *Close-Up* and *Film Art* attempted to put their theories into practice, with limited results. Oswell Blakeson produced *I Do Like To Be Beside the Seaside* (*c.* 1927?), described by a contemporary critic as 'a brilliant and amusing commentary on the technical devices of many well-known producers of films, e.g. Dulac, Man Ray, Leni, Dreyer and Eisenstein' (ibid.: 37). Blakeston went on to collaborate with photographer Francis Bruguèire on a five-minute film, *Light Rhythms* (1930), an experiment with paper cut-outs and light, 'something so much more poetical than anything in the concrete cinema' (*Close-Up*, March 1930). Macpherson's *Borderline* (1930) was an experiment in 'overtonal montage' with the aim of representing characters' mental states, featuring Paul and Eslanda Robeson, 'H. D.' (Hilda Doolittle) and Bryher (Winifred Ellerman), who also edited the film. It was not particularly successful at the time in terms of screenings or critical comment but it is now regarded by some as 'the most outstanding British avant-garde film of the period' (Wollen, 1993: 39). Even though it was made by a small British production company, Pool Films, *Borderline* was shot in Switzerland and its subject matter was controversial: race. It was Paul Robeson's first screen role as a man who is discriminated against when he has an affair with a white woman. The film's form was experimental in its use of montage, but it also explored the use of light to convey racial tensions between the characters. Len Lye's *Rainbow Dance* (1936) was given an extremely favourable review in *Film Art*, intriguingly described as 'a ballet about a man who uses the Post Office Savings Bank. . . . This is one of the few films that have dealt as directly with the screen image as the painter with his canvas' (*Film Art*, no. 10, 1937).

Workers' film societies

As well as aesthetic modernism the trend of political modernism, based on the Soviet model, was influential in inter-war Britain, although champions of the avant-garde frequently ignored home-grown films about political struggle. Workers' film societies (less elitist than the Film Society) showed Russian classics, and despite a shortage of facilities and funding, oppositional films were made and distributed by groups like Atlas Films, Kino, the Progressive Film Institute, the Workers' Film and Photo League, the Workers' Film Association and the Socialist Film Council. Their content was mostly factual, including newsreels of contemporary events which provide an interesting working-class contrast with official newsreels which concentrated on the monarchy, military affairs and sport. An oppositional topical item entitled *Jubilee* juxtaposed coverage of the 1935 Royal Jubilee with shots of housing conditions and labour exchanges as ironic counterpoint. Indeed, the Left's record of film exhibition and production in the inter-war years is more distinguished than one would expect, especially when there were considerable obstacles: lack of funding, mass unemployment, censorship (the British Board of Film Censors objected to films which dealt with 'industrial unrest' or subjects which they thought gave 'a false impression of police forces in Britain') and the diversity of the various groups' political aims. Nevertheless, during the period 1927–39 the principal Labour film production agencies produced 112 films (see Ryan, 1983: 123). These groups were operating against the dominant newsreel culture which proposed a consensual view of British society, based on confidence in the National Government.

A major area of debate on the Left concerned the response to Hollywood and the notion of film as entertainment: the Communists were anti-Hollywood whereas the Labour Party saw no point in seeking to restrict the number of popular American films shown on British screens. These disputes prevented solidarity: initially the Labour Party refused to co-operate with the Communist-inspired distributor, Kino Films. But, by 1935, the United Front strategy encouraged greater collaboration between Labour and the Communist Party and permitted workers' film societies to screen opposi-tional *and* popular films (see Jones, 1987: 37–58). As a result, in the late 1930s Labour film-making and distribution reached its highest point of activity. The Second World War disrupted this and, after 1945 and the elec-tion of the Labour Government, the Labour movement felt less cause to make oppositional films.

There were some attempts to develop an oppositional film aesthetic. Avant-garde artist and film-maker Norman McLaren collaborated with sculptress and film-maker Helen Biggar to make *Hell Unltd.* (1936), a film which used experimental techniques to criticise profiteering from arma-ments. *Bread* (1934, produced by the London Production Group of Kino and members of the Workers' Theatre Movement), concerned a story about a man who is imprisoned for stealing after having been refused Means Test assistance. This is followed by footage of the hunger marches and the National Unemployed Workers' Movement, with the overall message of united-front labour organisation to combat poverty and discrimination. Such experiment was, however, limited because 'the financial poverty of the radical film movement made it impossible for the experiments of inter-weaving fictional and documentary materials in this film to be seriously developed into a school of film-making' (Harvey, 1986: 234).

It is easy to point to factors which explain the limited extent of modernist experiment in this period. These were: censorship which limited the themes which could be dealt with in the fiction film; artists who, by and large, turned their backs on film; the government's attitude; the ultimate conservatism of many of the art film periodicals and elitist film societies; and the overall popularity of the Hollywood film. Censorship in Britain was anti-modernist in that it banned most Soviet films and laid down distinct rules preventing the production of politically or morally contentious films. The British Board of Film Censors (BBFC) was established in 1913 by the film trade to recom-mend to local authorities whether a film should receive a licence for exhibi-tion (see Robertson, 1985). Although it was not a formal governmental body, its President had to be approved by the Home Office. It did not possess the official standing of the Lord Chamberlain who could authorise the showing of a film in London that the BBFC recommended should be banned. Exhibitors tended to comply with BBFC certificates and local authorities usually did not bother to disagree with its rulings. A loophole existed that, if a film was shown on 16mm safety stock, the rulings did not apply (because the legislation had grown out of fire regulations). Film societies were allowed to import and show films that the BBFC had banned, including *The Battleship Potemkin* (banned 1924–54). But, as we have seen, the societies were small and were often elitist, dominated by intellectuals.

In the 1930s the BBFC increased its powers by demanding that producers should submit film scripts to them before production commenced so that they could advise on changes or whether the film should be made at all. Films could be cut or banned on the basis of codified grounds divided into various categories: religion, politics, the military, social questions, sex, crime and cruelty. Each category had numerous subsections outlining specific topics. The political category included the following subsections: propaganda against the monarchy and attacks on royal dynasties; inflammatory subtitles and Bolshevist surroundings; equivocal situations between white girls and men of other races. The 'Questions of Sex' category included the following subsections: themes indicative of habitual provocative attitudes; female vamps; indecent wall decorations. There was much concern about the impact of horror films. In 1922 *Nosferatu* was banned and *The Cabinet of Dr Caligari* (Robert Weine, 1919) was only awarded a certificate in 1929, and even then with extensive cuts. Anything Soviet was taboo, such as *The New Babylon* (1929), along with *Potemkin* and *The Strike* (Sergi Eisenstein, 1925). A proposed adaptation of Walter Greenwood's novel *Love On the Dole* (John Baxter, 1941) suffered a scenario ban in the 1930s when mass unemployment was rife. Permission to produce a film version was not granted until 1940 when most people were employed in the war effort (Richards, 1984: 119).

As Dusinberre (1980) has pointed out, it is noticeable that no relatively established British artists worked with film. In Paris, by contrast, artists such as Leger, Duchamp and Man Ray elevated its status by being involved with some key avant-garde classics. The only consistent support in Britain came from artists who were rooted in literary culture and who promoted art film in elitist periodicals: Macpherson, Bryher, H. D., Robert Herring and Irene Nicolson. In any case, there was very little financial support for experimental films in this period and the government's attitude was determined by a desire to open up some of the market to British films but, at the same time, not disturb the import of American films (see Chapter 1). State financial support was out of the question and there was not even a quota for short films until 1938.

The Documentary Film Movement

Although the Documentary Film Movement (1927–39) has similarly been charged with aesthetic and political conservatism, it is important that it should be seen as a precursor of many of the aims of later attempts for independence: it received state and commercial sponsorship but was not state-controlled; it gathered together a group of diverse talents who produced both instructional and experimental work; and it operated outside the normal commercial distribution and exhibition circuits. The Movement should not be interpreted as an isolated grouping from the 1930s but as an important element of the independent movement which was developing into a tradition (see Kuhn, 1980). As a cinematic movement, documentary has been extremely influential, but it is important to remember that in the 1930s it was a movement inflected with different and often contradictory discourses, the two major ones being sociological and aesthetic.

Under the general guidance and philosophy of John Grierson, the Documentary Movement of state-funded films produced by the Empire Marketing Board Film Unit (1927–33) and the General Post Office Film Unit (1933–39), together with films which were commercially sponsored by corporate institutions such as Shell, the BBC and the British Gas and Coke Company, could be said to have had a modernist wing. One of the first films to be produced by the Empire Marketing Board's unit was Grierson's *Drifters* (1929), which drew inspiration from montage techniques used in Eisenstein's *The Battleship Potemkin*. In honour of this debt it shared a billing with *Potemkin* at the Film Society's showing of the banned Soviet classic. When the Empire Marketing Board was disbanded in 1933 Grierson continued the Film Unit's work at the General Post Office. Operating within an overall context of consensus politics, one of his main aims was to produce films with the social imperative of 'training for citizenship', including instructional films about housing or the mail service that were uncontroversial and uncritical of the government. Indeed, the common impression of the Documentary Movement is that instructional public-service material was placed above aesthetic boldness and political critique. But that did not prevent Grierson from employing people who were important in terms of experimental cinema in Britain in the inter-war years. Aitken has argued that Grierson's aesthetic was a modernist one and that he 'believed that the aesthetic and sociological functions of the documentary film went hand in hand, and that aesthetic experimentation was an important part of the work of the Film Unit' (Aitken, 1990: 143–44).

In support of this contention Grierson employed Len Lye, Humphrey Jennings, Norman McLaren and Alberto Cavalcanti. New Zealander Len Lye had already made an animation film, *Tusalava* (1929), which used Aboriginal symbols, for the Film Society and Publicity Pictures. One of his techniques was to paint directly onto sound-film stock, which he used in 1935 for *A Colour Box*, a film which Grierson saw and liked, added some slogans and produced as a GPO promotional film. Lye used this technique again for the GPO's *Rainbow Dance* (1936) and *Trade Tattoo* (1937), but this time he added abstract images and live action. Lye collaborated with Humphrey Jennings on an animation project, *The Birth of a Robot* (1936), for Shell-Mex and BP, and experimented with stop-frame in *N. or N.W.* (1937), a surrealist-influenced short film about the benefits of using the postal system! Lye moved to America in 1944 and became an American citizen before concentrating on painting and sculpture at the end of the 1950s.

Humphrey Jennings was influenced by 1930s surrealism and his work reflects his wide-ranging interests in theatre, poetry, art, science, literature and European cinema. He was one of the first members of the Cambridge Film Guild and after some time in Paris he became involved in the Documentary Film group through Stuart Legg. Jennings' *Spare Time* (1939) was mostly soundtrack, natural sound and a sparse commentary as background to images of working-class leisure activities pursued by workers in three different industries. Jennings went on to make distinctive and poetic Crown Film Unit documentaries including *Heart of Britain* (1941), *Words for Battle* (1941), *Listen To Britain* (1942), *Fires Were Started* (1943) and *A Diary for Timothy* (1944–45). *Listen To Britain* continued his fascination with sound and image, overlapping the two in order to create a sophisticated image of Britain at war (see Vaughan, 1983: 83–100).

Norman McLaren made his first films whilst a student at the Glasgow School of Art (1933–36). *Camera Makes Whoopee* (Glasgow School of Art, 1935), made jointly with Helen Biggar, focused on preparations for a costume party and utilised intricate cross-cutting designed to be accompanied by improvised music. Like Lye, McLaren was interested in animation work and painting directly onto film. The film he made for the GPO, *Love On the Wing* (1938), however, was not shown because of its erotic imagery. Another member of the Documentary group was Alberto Cavalcanti, a Brazilian who had been heavily influenced by the French avant-garde and by Surrealism. *Coalface* (1935) was an interesting experiment in the use of sound and image: how, as a discourse, sound can both counter and extend the visual sense. The commentary was written by W. H. Auden and the music by Benjamin Britten. Although the film is ostensibly about the coal industry, it is clear that the experimental facets interested Cavalcanti most – such as his use of image/music montage and his obvious debt to Soviet filmmakers in the photography of machinery. In 1937 Cavalcanti headed the GPO Film Unit after Grierson had left to establish Film Centre, an organisation for the promotion of non-governmental funding for documentary films. The unit became the Crown Film Unit in the Second World War when there was, to some extent, a fusion of the movement's style and philosophy with the commercial fiction film. Avant-garde experimental work was absorbed by a realist style of film-making and the baton of cinematic modernism passed to the maverick team of Powell and Pressburger.

Experiments in fiction

It would be a mistake to restrict analysis of the relationship between modernism and British cinema in this first phase to avant-garde and non-fiction film. In the silent period there was considerable room for innovation in fiction feature films, and later within the confines of sound genre cinema. The most celebrated auteur to have been heavily influenced by German Expressionism is Hitchcock, who worked in Germany for a time before directing *The Lodger* (1926), a film commonly assumed to draw inspiration from German techniques. When the viewer is first introduced to the lodger, played by Ivor Novello, we see him acting in an expressionist style, fore-boding and sinister, with close-ups rendering the matinée idol strange. When he has been taken to his room by Mrs Bunting, his landlady, he looks outside the window and in the next shot the camera frames his face from outside, imprisoned by the window, a shot which is reminiscent of the framing of the vampire in *Nosferatu* (Murnau, 1919). There are many expressionist shots of staircases, dark alleys and unmotivated close-ups. The Jack-the-Ripper theme was consistent with German cinema's preoccupa-tion with similar stories, most notably in *Waxworks* (Paul Leni, 1924) and later in *Pandora's Box* (G. W. Pabst, 1929). But, as Tom Ryall has pointed out, *The Lodger* 'is something more than striking lighting effects, unusual camera angles, staircase motifs and a terror theme' (Ryall, 1986: 24). This complex film also displays Hitchcock's interest in French Impressionism: the desire to probe emotional states and to convey the surreal – themes which characterised his later work in Hollywood. Ryall reminds us that the highly regarded shot of the lodger pacing anxiously on a clear glass floor above the Bunting family is reminiscent of a shot in René Clair's avantgarde film *Entr'Acte* (1924). Since Hitchcock was a member of the Film Society he would have been familiar with this film as well as with other European and Soviet classics. As well as having this interesting similarity, *The Lodger* is edited in a style which at times resembles Hollywood techniques but on other occasions Soviet montage, and the opening sequence is in a documen-tary style. Eisenstein-influenced Ivor Montagu was responsible for most of *The Lodger*'s editing, so it is not surprising that the film should employ Soviet editing patterns. Similarly, in *Blackmail* (1929), Hitchcock's cele-brated introduction of sound into a film conceived as silent, there is evidence of diverse influences: German silent cinema, D. W. Griffith, Eisenstein and documentary (ibid.: 24–30). This cinematic eclecticism carried on into the early sound period in, for example, *Number 17* (1932) which Charles Barr has described as 'a wildly inventive and surreal film' which included 'the creative use of manifestly unrealistic, dreamlike settings' (Barr, 1986: 22).

Other British film-makers in the 1920s who explored the formal boundaries of the silent feature film included Jack Cutts and Anthony Asquith. Cutts' most noted films are *The Rat* (1925), *The Triumph of the Rat* (1926), both starring Ivor Novello, *The Queen Was In the Parlour* (1927), *Confetti* (1927) and *God's Clay* (1929). Hitchcock's subsequent success in Britain and Hollywood has somewhat overshadowed the work of this interesting director who has nevertheless been described by Rachael Low as 'an uneven and unreliable film maker whose richness in imagination was not accompanied by discipline or control' (Low, 1971: 168). Anthony Asquith's *Shooting Stars* (1927), a drama about film stars and the film world, utilised rapid montage in two notable scenes: a stunt cyclist's fall off a cliff and a climactic sequence when a comedian is shot while swinging on a chandelier high above the studio floor. The lighting techniques were imaginative (by German lighting specialist Carl Fischer) and there are very few titles, leaving the story to be told as visually as possible. Asquith used Fisher's expertise again for *Underground* (1928), a thriller set in the London underground which, despite its obvious debt to German and Soviet cinema, was attacked by Harry Alan Potamkin in *Close-Up* for not being 'a document of the lives of the Underground people' (1929). Once again the art-film critics responded to British films in an ambivalent manner and had begun to advocate what was beginning to resemble realist criticism which dominated subsequent writing about British film. As has been noted in Chapter 2, British films of this period were generally subject to quite high degrees of European influence, not least because of the high number of émigré technicians working in the industry. German studios in particular were seen as models of technical and artistic achievement to which companies such as British International Pictures aspired. Films regarded as being mainstream, popular entertainment fare were also subject to an eclectic frame of reference, including films designed by Alfred Junge for Gaumont-British in the 1930s (Bergfelder, Harris and Street, 2007: 224–70).

At the end of the 1930s, therefore, it would appear that notions of 'independence', 'opposition', and 'modernist experiment' had been established as strands of critical and practical work in Britain. As we have seen, these existed alongside the mainstream industry and sometimes interacted with it. While film-makers wishing to promote filmic experiment did so at the risk of constant comparison with Eisenstein or Pabst, Britain was part of an international appreciation of cinema as an exciting medium waiting for someone to discover its full potential. To a great extent, this appreciative culture transcended national boundaries and the question of British cinema tended to confuse responses to new work. The fact, however, that these currents resurfaced in various forms at later points in the century (to be discussed in Chapter 8) is testimony to their relevance in an assessment of national cinematic practice.

PHASE TWO: 1940s–1970s

MAGICIANS OF CINEMA: MODERNISM AND THE FEATURE FILM

> . . . from this artistically broken-backed industry emerge groups of films which for all their imperfections, their dearly bought concessions either to art or to commerce, constitute a cinema which is a significant and valuable part of the culture they spring from.
>
> (Murphy, 1992: 101)

Powell and Pressburger

Film-makers who chose to experiment within the commercial feature industry often did so to their cost. Powell and Pressburger's *A Canterbury Tale* (1944), now regarded as one of their best films in a mystical tradition, suffered from studio cuts to render it more comprehensible in terms of narrative. Powell and Pressburger had enjoyed a fair degree of artistic freedom as The Archers, their production company which had been formed in 1943 and operated as an independent unit in the orbit of the Rank Organisation. But the Archers had to turn to Korda for future support after *The Red Shoes* (1948) exceeded its budget and had been unsympathetically received by Rank and his executive John Davis. Ironically, *The Red Shoes* was their most successful box-office film in Britain and America. Treading the line between art and commerce involved compromises on both sides, but the results were often exciting and significant contributions to the corpus of national cinema.

Ian Christie has argued that Powell and Pressburger's films were 'created out of no obvious cinematic tradition', citing Kipling and Chesterton as major influences (Christie, 1985: 20). It is clear, however, that their work should not be seen as an isolated exception to the realist rule but as an inheritor of the diverse traditions examined above. Raymond Durgnat, one of the first critics to broach a re-evaluation of Powell as a director, compared him to Méliès. Christie acknowledges the crucial significance of Pressburger's years in Germany at Ufa, particularly his experiments with screen time and real time in *Abschied* (1930), and the Germanic feel of *Contraband* (1940). Pressburger's fascination with time was further explored in *A Matter of Life and Death* (1946), an aesthetic experiment involving imaginative sets and innovative film techniques to represent a British pilot's hallucinations when he is on the verge of death. Erwin Hillier, the cinematographer on *I Know Where I'm Going* (1945), had worked with Fritz Lang and used excessive low-key lighting and deep-focus photography to create stunning shots of the Western Isles. Indeed, many of the technicians who worked on Powell and Pressburger's films were Continental.

The Red Shoes

Peter Wollen has related their work with the composed film (a film shot to a previously composed score, most evident in *Black Narcissus*, 1947, *The Red Shoes*, 1948 and *Tales of Hoffman*, 1951) back to debates about the affinities between film and music: early modernist attempts to align film with music rather than with literature (see Wollen, 1994). Music plays an extremely important role in *The Red Shoes*, a film which is very much a meditation on ballet, music, performance and cinema. *The Red Shoes* is about a ballet dancer, Vicky, and a composer, Julian, who fall under the tutelage of the great Lermontov and his famous ballet company. Both rise to fame with the specially composed ballet 'The Red Shoes' which is based on the Hans Christian Andersen fairytale about a girl who cannot stop dancing once she wears the red shoes. Vicky's story in the main narrative parallels the fairytale. The ballet company is run along strict, patriarchal lines by Boris Lermontov, who is enraged when he learns that Vicky has been having an affair with Julian, the composer of the ballet's score. On the pretext of disliking a new score Julian has written, Lermontov dismisses him and Vicky follows in protest. Vicky more or less retires from public performance but Julian continues composing and they marry. Lermontov eventually tempts Vicky into performing 'The Red Shoes' ballet once more but when she is about to go on stage she hears on the radio that Julian has not turned up to conduct his new opera which opens on the same night. Instead, he arrives at the theatre and forces Vicky to choose between dancing for Lermontov and her marriage. Wearing the red shoes, she runs out in an anguished state and jumps into the path of an oncoming train; as she is dying she asks Julian to remove the red shoes. When Lermontov hears of the tragedy he decides to put on the ballet of 'The Red Shoes' in her honour with a spotlight illuminating the empty space on the stage which would have been occupied by Vicky.

As a meditation on the arts, the film asserts its revelational properties as a medium capable of exposing the myths surrounding fairytales, the world of classical ballet and cinema. The myth that fairytales all have happy endings is challenged. Instead, with their interweaving of Andersen's tale with the ballet story, Powell and Pressburger expose the horror that is often latent if not (as in Andersen) explicit in fairytales. The first half of the film leads us to believe that Vicky and Julian will live happily ever after, but the second half frustrates that outcome. In the fairytale a young girl, like Vicky, wishes to wear the red shoes. Once she has acquired them a soldier touches them and from then onwards she cannot stop herself dancing. When she can bear the situation no longer she pleads with an executioner to chop off the shoes. This is done – she is released from the power of the red shoes but it is only after further suffering that she is redeemed. The fairytale is rich in sexual metaphor – the colour red, for example, so often used in fairytales to

Plate 7.1 Vicky (Moira Shearer), caught between two male egos, Julian (Marius Goring) and Lermontov (Anton Walbrook), in *The Red Shoes* (1948). (Courtesy of Rank Film Distributors)

signify sexual awakening, is present: by willingly donning the red shoes the girl is compliant with her own sexual downfall, and suffers a horrific punishment. The appeal of 'The Red Shoes' fairytale therefore relies very much on the combination of beauty and horror: the girl is beautiful, especially when she is dancing in her red shoes. The act of severance, however, also holds a twisted appeal in that it leads to her redemption – but it is nevertheless suggested as a suitable punishment for being tempted to dance in the first place.

In fairytale and main narrative alike, patriarchy emerges as an unforgiving, repressive regime whereby the Law of the Father wins against the transgressive female (see Young: 1994). At the end of the film Vicky has been truly punished for her ambition and for seeking to combine it with love. The Ballet Lermontov is an example of a patriarchal community. Lermontov dominates the company and all the key artistic roles (costume, choreography, musical direction) belong to men. Vicky is only accepted as a full member of the company when Lermontov demonstrates his faith in her by choosing her for the principal role in 'The Red Shoes'. The world of the company is represented as a family, a sort of corporate allegiance which must over-rule personal commitments. As a father-figure, Lermontov is an interesting character: his power is such that he creates Vicky and also takes part in her destruction. He is capable of dominating Vicky more than he is capable of dominating Julian. Once Julian has found his place in the ballet company he constantly asserts that his music is the most important element. Whereas Vicky's life is dependent on the ballet his is not and he can take his talent elsewhere. And, in turn, Julian's insistence that Vicky must choose between the Lermontov ballet and himself forces her into an impossible position.

The Red Shoes exhibits a playful tension between realism and spectacle and in many ways undermines its own enterprise. On an intertextual level, Julian's insistence that 'it's the music that matters' encourages us to privilege musical sensation and by implication, visual images which can be equated with music in their dual reference to opulence, feeling and emotion. The film exposes the problems of the dance world, but in so doing aims to assert its superiority as a revelational medium. Our pleasure in the sequence of the ballet within the film depends on our knowledge of events in the film's main narrative: the dynamics between Vicky, Lermontov and Julian. Within the ballet there are many moments which do not function purely as representations of theatrical performance. By employing camera tricks, superimpositions, matte techniques and swooping camera, Powell and Pressburger take the viewer beyond a mere presentation of a ballet. Art emerges as a destructive neurosis which punishes, takes advantage of people and ultimately destroys. At the same time it is depicted as a fatal attraction whereby all its lures and excitements, promises of fame and egotistical satisfactions are understandable but nevertheless presented as being in conflict with ultimate personal well-being and fulfilment. Cinema is presented as a superior medium: able to show the audience the often cruel reality behind the exquisite façade of the world of the ballet But cinema itself is an art form and subject to similar conflicts. The production history of *The Red Shoes* was fraught with difficulties: it went well over budget and alienated its backers; it involved creating an entire ballet from scratch and many of the dancers, including Moira Shearer, were unused to the interruptions involved in filming. The core of the film is the nature and value of art and the sacrifices it entails. As Michael Powell wrote in his autobiography: 'The world is hungry for art. *The Red Shoes* is an insolent, haunting picture, in the way it takes for granted that nothing matters but art, and that art is something worth dying for' (Powell, 1986: 660).

Indeed, much of Powell and Pressburger's work displays a tendency to relish *all* the visual and aural properties of cinema, including rich dialogue. Against the realist grain, Powell and Pressburger used fantastical situations, dream sequences, bold colour and disjointed narratives. Ian Christie has referred to *I Know Where I'm Going* as 'the nearest thing to a dream while being awake' (*I Know Where I'm Going* fiftieth anniversary celebration, BBC2, 1994). Documentary influences can be detected in many of their films, for example the opening sequence of *I Know Where I'm Going*, when a documentary-style voice-over introduces us to brief scenes from the early life of Joan Webster (Wendy Hiller) and these are intercut with the film's titles which appear on objects which are part of the *mise-en-scène*. But this use of documentary is later subverted by lapses into fantasy and dream-like states: when Wendy Hiller is on the train to Scotland to marry her rich fiancé she fantasises about her future, which is conveyed by an ironic documentary-style montage of the industrial capital she is to 'marry'. Her wedding dress wrapped in cellophane is superimposed on a shot of a vicar saying, 'Do you, Joan Webster, take Consolidated Chemical Industries to be your lawful wedded husband?', which is superimposed on a third layer of visual material: documentary shots of industrial machinery. This is followed by a barrage of insistent overlapping voices ('everything's arranged, everything's arranged') which give a brief, but succinct sketch of the world of order, wealth and discipline which the film challenges and which Joan eventually rejects. As I have commented elsewhere, *Black Narcissus* similarly experiments with film forms and aesthetics. In particular the sets, designed by Alfred Junge, created the Himalayas in Pinewood Studios, suggesting an atmosphere that was entirely fitting for the location: an exotic, unfamiliar environment which causes the nuns, who have gone there to set up a school and dispensary, considerable emotional disturbance. Jack Cardiff's cinematography was also remarkable, using techniques that manipulated light to create expressionist tones within the Technicolor palette of the film (Street, 2005).

Critical reappraisal of Powell and Pressburger's work since the mid-1960s has placed them near, if not at the top, of the list of misunderstood British film-makers who drew on a wide range of traditions and genres: fantasy, realism, lyricism, Romanticism, Gothic, melodrama, the war film, the thriller and the musical. Many of their films subvert conventional film genres and explore geographical areas as peripheral in their relation to London as their cinema is to the dominant realist aesthetic. *Close-Up*'s observations on the importance of British films using British locations in a creative way were certainly evident in Powell and Pressburger's films: *A Canterbury Tale* is very much a meditation on the English countryside and *The Edge of the World* (1937) is set in the Shetlands. *I Know Where I'm Going* extends the fascination with landscape that was so evident in *A Canterbury Tale*. It pointed to a geographical and imaginary world which is placed in direct contrast to the city and its values, its metropolitan version of Britishness. A sense of difference *within* Britain was highlighted by the subordination of wealth and class to Scottish traditions and non-materialist values, individuated in the film by Wendy Hiller's rich fiancé (whom we never see) and the Scottish laird (Roger Livesey) with whom she falls in love. Caught between two worlds, she rejects the certainty of Consolidated Chemical Industries for her laird and the romantic sense of timelessness he represents.

Losey, Antonioni, Anderson, Roeg and others

It is significant that Pressburger, a Hungarian, wrote films which probed the limitations of a static conception of Britishness. The same outsider insight has been attributed to Joseph Losey, who worked in Britain after being blacklisted by the House Committee on UnAmerican Activities in the 1950s. From his fascinated perspective, his films were oppositional in the sense that they illuminated some of the worst features of the British class society, most forcefully in *Blind Date* (1959) which, according to Robert Murphy is 'a textbook example of how a director at the height of his powers can make a great film despite an unremarkable story and limited financial resources' (Murphy, 1992: 204). The film's hero is Dutch and the *femme fatale* is French which, according to Losey, allowed him even more freedom 'in presenting my own, still foreign, observations about England' (Losey in Ciment, 1985: 178).

Bearing in mind Murphy's reservations about separating art cinema from commercial cinema, it is possible to identify more films which were oppositional in aesthetic style and/or political content whether they examined the individual psyche, sexual politics or the class system. In his detailed examination of the period, Murphy (1992: 70–101) has grouped these films by thematic concerns like madness and psychologically disturbed major protagonists which includes films such as *Peeping Tom* (1960), *Night Must Fall* (Karel Reisz, 1964), *Repulsion* (Roman Polanski, 1965) and *Morgan: A Suitable Case for Treatment* (Karel Reisz, 1966). Another category is films dealing with women's problems, including *The L-Shaped Room* (Bryan Forbes, 1962), *The World Ten Times Over* (Wolf Rilla, 1963) and *The Pumpkin Eater* (Jack Clayton, 1964). While some of these films have long been recognised for their unusual qualities, Murphy's revisionist work has drawn attention to, for example, interesting films by Alexander Mackendrick (*Sammy Going South*, 1965 and *A High Wind In Jamaica*, 1965), a director more commonly associated with his work at Ealing in the 1950s. The 1960s was clearly a period when the film industry was full of variety and experiment and the realms of the art film intersected with the mainstream commercial industry to a greater extent than in previous or subsequent decades. Under the influence of the *nouvelle vague*, Lindsay Anderson's *This Sporting Life* (1963) heralded a more sustained attempt by British film-makers in the 1960s to make art films with modernist leanings, including the well-known examples of Michelangelo Antonioni's *Blow-Up* (1967), Lindsey Anderson's *If . . .* (1968) and Nicolas Roeg and Donald Cammell's *Performance* (1970). From their different perspectives, through bold thematics, challenging narratives and experimental form, these films raise important questions about the relationship between social environment, individuality and collective action.

Blow-Up refuses the spectator conventional character identification and the narrative is elliptical, revolving around the sequence where a fashion photographer (David Hemmings) blows up shots he has taken in a park and in the process discovers that he has photographed a murder. But we never discover the full story behind the murder or, indeed, whether despite its apparent significance it actually *is* the most important strand of the film's narrative. Importantly, *Blow-Up* provides a critical image of 1960s London, sketching an amoral empty world which, like its photographer protagonist, attempts to control reality by making phoney images of it. The film points to the modernist project exactly: the revelation that representations are not reality but particular *versions* of it. An altogether more light-hearted vision of swinging London was Richard Lester's *The Knack* (1965) which is notable for its bold technical style (jump-cuts, slow-motion and play-back).

Anderson employed fantasy and surreal images in *If . . .*, his film about rebellion in a public school which is used as a microcosm of British society, urging direct action in the face of repression. By using this device, the world of hierarchy, bullying, intense patriotism and an overwhelming sense of harshness is contrasted with the rebel schoolboys' gradual discovery of the power of insurrection. The boys break free, first in a spiritual manner (through music, the motorcycle ride and through sex) and then more literally by violence at the Founder's Day shoot-out. Whereas the boys in *If . . .* learn to find their identities as well as a spirit of collective action by rebelling against the military-style regime of the public school, Roeg and Cammel's *Performance* is an exploration of the gradual erosion of and interchangeability between the individual identities of two men, a gangster, Chas (James Fox) and an ex-pop star, Turner (Mick Jagger). Chas is on the run from the Flowers gang and hides out in Turner's house, pretending to be a juggler who needs to rent a room. Both are initially presented as very different characters: Chas is a 'hard man', a tough, macho, homophobic working-class gangster, whereas Turner is an effeminate, drug-taking hippy who talks in riddles about Persian culture. The film explores the extent to which they gradually become similar, both visually and psychologically, as Chas succumbs to Turner's bohemian household and its norms. In turn, Turner becomes more controlling and even implicated in Chas' gangster world in a hallucinatory sequence. Heavily influenced by Jorge Luis Borges, the Argentinian writer of dream-like, labyrinthine stories, *Performance* demands much of its audience and can be read as a postmodern film which blurs identities, posing questions rather than suggesting answers for characters and audience alike.

Like other postmodern works, *Performance* pays homage to high art and popular culture: allusions to Borges are accompanied by references to pop art, popular music and underground films by Kenneth Anger and Bruce Conner. The sense of one clear meaning is frustrated, as Turner says at one point: 'Nothing is true – everything is permitted'. This undermines modernism's utopian project of a 'grand narrative of emancipation' in a welter of heterogeneous discourses competing with each other in an ever-changing arena of contested meanings. Indeed, the first half of the film, which presents Chas in his brutal gangster milieu, has a more or less linear narrative but once Chas enters Turner's world it becomes fragmented and confusing. The film is highly intertextual, full of parody and allusion as it invites us to read Turner as Turner *and* as Mick Jagger. Rather like *Blow-Up* the film ends in an ambiguous manner with the nature of coherent individualism rendered entirely questionable. The idea of the unified subject is questioned from very early on in the film when characters relate to each other in purely *performative* ways. When Turner first meets Chas he chooses not to question him about his career as a gangster, even though it seems unlikely that Turner has not guessed. Instead, he buys the story of Chas as a juggler, an interesting choice which privileges fantasy above reality. Both Chas and Turner's 'performance' of gender roles and sexuality are ambiguous, a theme which is reinforced by the presence of two bisexual women who live with Turner. When Chas finally emerges from the house, a car is waiting for him; as it drives away he looks back, and we see that he has become Turner. In these ways *Performance* can be seen as a key film which firmly placed the uncertainties of postmodern society firmly on the agenda of British cinema.

Chapter 8

Borderlines II: counter-cinema and independence

The last chapter examined the links between modernism and British cinema until 1970. Since then there have been considerable developments in avant-garde, experimental mainstream and art cinema, encouraged by new structures of funding and distribution and by the convergence of film practice and theoretical concepts including structuralism, feminism and postmodernism. In relation to these developments this chapter will examine the final phases of experimental activity briefly outlined in the previous chapter, beginning with oppositional 'counter-cinema' and going on to deal with subsequent independent film-makers. The central idea underpinning many of these narratives was formal experimentation. But there was also a concern to present a range of oppositional narratives that could be said to question dominant images of the nation. As observed by Homi Bhabha, these work to 'continually evoke and erase its totalising boundaries – both actual and conceptual' (Bhabha, 1990: 330).

PHASE THREE: 1966–80

OPPOSITION, STRUCTURALISM AND INDEPENDENCE

During this period the locus of experimental cinema moved away from the mainstream. *Herostratus* (1967), a film directed by Don Levy, has been cited by Murphy as 'a startling precursor of the avant-garde cinema which sprang up in Britain in the late 60s' (Murphy, 1992: 87). It concerned a narrative about an unsuccessful poet who offers an advertising agency the chance to make a stunt out of his suicide. After he falls in love he changes his mind about killing himself but accidentally pushes another man to his death. The actors used improvisation and the film included a distinctive series of fractured images which Levy called 'an emotional abstract'. But the most important development in the organisation of an oppositional cinema was the foundation of the London Film-Makers Co-Op in 1966 which aimed to produce films which challenged the commercial industry in terms of industrial organisation and aesthetics. In its first year it concentrated on establishing a film library and then a few films were produced, including acclaimed work by John Latham and Steve Dwoskin. Perhaps symbolically, Anthony Scott made *The Longest Most Meaningless Movie In the World* (n.d.) from discarded footage discovered in Wardour Street dustbins.

Key influences were the New American Cinema and its radical film cooperatives which had sprung up in the USA and the European avant-garde, but some commentators were keen to stress the unique characteristics of the British avant-garde in this period, claiming the 'structural' film as primarily British (see Dusinberre, 1976). The primary features of the style were formal obtrusiveness, expanded cinema (that is, containing events which stressed the role of projection as an aspect of cinema technology) and the landscape film (which revealed natural and formal determinants of the cinematic experience). There was a preoccupation with image-production rather than image-content, as explained by Dusinberre:

> The ascetic structural films do this on the level of the material nature of the image itself, projection cinema engages it at the level of the role of projection processes in the formation of the image, and the landscape films on the level of the visual illusions of movement, space, and change through the mechanical recording of an image which has a direct referent in 'reality'.
>
> (Dusinberre, 1976: 46)

The availability of funding from Regional Arts Associations was crucial for the establishment and survival of the collectives which aimed to destroy middle-men distributors who held such power over the composition of the film market. The political unrest which exploded in 1968 promoted the formation of more radical and oppositional groups in the 1970s including the Berwick Street Collective, and the formation of the Association of Independent Film Makers in 1974 was an extremely important development (Dickinson, 1999).

Claire Johnston and Jan Dawson described the variety of independent film-makers' aims in 1970:

> Some of them aspire to professionalism in the established sense but find themselves frustrated by the limited opportunities that a closed industry can offer them. For some, the dissatisfaction has a wider and more ideological basis, and they have no desire either to work within an industry whose structure reflects the values of a capitalist society they despise or to produce pictures acceptable as entertainment to the audiences already conditioned by that industry and that society. Others are simply

fascinated by the unexplored physical possibilities of film itself and are experimenting with it much the same way that printers experiment with paints or a poet with words.

(Johnston and Dawson, 1969/70: 29)

Sylvia Harvey has argued that, although the radical film groups appeared to revive the independent tradition which had been established by the workers' film societies and oppositional production groups of the 1930s (Harvey, 1986), the dominant emphasis, however, was on formal experiment and the deconstruction of popular cinematic codes and conventions. The structural film stressed the devices of image production, urging the spectator to take an active role in making meaning from images. Although the films were inspired by the spirit of the New Left, their political thrust was weak and their content often difficult or even unintelligible. Johnston and Dawson's desire for links between political activism, formal experiment and a cultural climate which would promote a dialogue between critics, film-makers and audiences proved to be a little over-optimistic.

Johnston and Dawson's writings in *Sight and Sound* (a periodical not normally interested in covering the avant-garde) and film festival reviews give further indication of the optimism surrounding British independent activity in this period. They covered groups such as the Tattooists, film-makers who were preoccupied with making direct links with the audience by explicitly addressing them from the screen. Other film-makers who received critical acclaim included Malcolm LeGrice whose phenomenological cinema made great use of multiple screens, home movie footage and various printing processes. Phenomenological cinema is defined as 'cinema that has its locus *only* in the direct experience of the film projection situation – in the interaction of audience, light, sound, space, time, performers' (Ryans, 1973/74: 18). *Little Dog for Roger* (LeGrice, 1967–68) used home movie footage which had been transferred from 9.5mm to 16mm. To draw attention to the film's materiality LeGrice exaggerated all the elements usually classed as mistakes: scratches, frame slips, dirt, fingermarks and splicing marks. Several expanded cinema events were held, including LeGrice's *Horror Film I* (1971) which involved him performing in front of projected images. Other film-makers held similar events which drew on performance art traditions, particularly Tony Hill (*Point Source*, 1974) and Annabel Nicholson (*Reel Time*, 1973).

Stephen Dwoskin was noted for his interesting technique of characters applying layers of mask-like make-up to their faces, particularly in *Chinese Checkers* (1964) and *Take Me* (1968). When Tony Ryans reviewed the Fifth International Experimental Film Competition in the Spring 1975 issue of *Sight and Sound*, he praised the 'inventive and witty' work of British film-makers, including Anna Ambrose's *Noodlespinner* which took some basic documentary footage of a Chinese noodle spinner and then looped, split, reduced and staggered it to present a series of multiple-image collages in motion: in an inventive way the film's form thus resembled the process it was seeking to represent. Mike Dunford's *Still Life With a Pear* (1974) showed a camera obeying prerecorded instructions as to which path to follow around a room and its subsequent confusion when forced to negotiate a series of obstacles randomly placed in its path.

The landscape film sought to 'assert the illusionism of cinema through the sensuality of landscape imagery and simultaneously assert the material nature of the representational process which sustains the illusionism' (Dusinberre, 1976). An example of this technique is Chris Welsby's *Park Film* (1972), which involved a camera being set up for three days in Kensington Gardens; its shutter was released each time a passer-by entered the frame. The result was a seven-minute film whose shots were determined by random interaction between the passers-by and the camera (the number of passers-by being influenced by the weather). Welsby made other films in this tradition, including *Windmill II* (1973) and *Seven Days* (1974). *Windmill II* used a windmill's blades as a sort of second shutter for a camera set up in a park facing a windmill. The blades were covered with melanex to give them a mirror-sheen effect and when they were moved by the wind at different speeds they created entirely different light patterns within the frame, as explained by Dusinberre:

At a moderate speed, they [the blades] act as an extra shutter which fragments 'normal' motion, emphasising movement within the deeper plane and critiquing the notion of 'normality' in cinematic motion. When moving quite fast, the blades act as abstract images superimposed on the landscape image and flattening the two planes into one. And when the blades are stopped (or almost so) a completely new space is created – not only does the new (reflected) deep space contain subjects in foreground and background to affirm its depth, but these objects are seen in anamorphosis (due to the irregular surface of the melanex) which effectively re-flattens them; the variations in the mirror surface create distortions which violate (or at least call attention to) the normal function of the lens of the camera.

(Dusinberre, 1976: 45)

Seven Days was a twenty-minute time-lapse film shot in Wales over seven days, one frame shot every ten seconds throughout the film by a camera which was mounted on an Equatorial Stand which selected an image according to the amount of sunlight.

In the late 1970s, most of independent film-making was influenced by theoretical questions raised in academic film journals (particularly *Screen* and *Afterimage*) concerning formal opposition to the workings of popular cinema, particularly the (as it was then perceived) masculine positioning of female spectators (see Mulvey, 1975). Mulvey argued that there are three 'looks' in the cinema, all three profoundly controlled by a masculine gaze: male characters who gaze at female characters; the gaze of the camera and the gaze of the audience which in this positioning is forced to identify with the male gaze. At this time also, psychoanalysis and the Oedipal nature of many film narratives was influencing theories of subjectivity, equating, for example, Lacan's[1] 'mirror phase' with the act of watching a film, producing 'split' subjectivity, especially for female spectators who saw their 'lack' replicated on the screen. These ideas influenced a few key experimental films of the period. Peter Wollen and Laura Mulvey collaborated on *Riddles of the Sphinx* (1977), a film which demonstrated the dynamic potential of narrative forms. *Amy!* (Laura Mulvey and Peter Wollen, 1980) sought to reveal how heroic women, in this case, aviator Amy Johnson, have been represented by the media as isolated cases of pluckiness. Johnson's exploits were individualised so as to render them safe for patriarchy. Mulvey and Wollen's film juxtaposes the popular imagery of Amy's historic flight to Australia with contemplative inserts which concentrate on her engineering skills and the mechanics of aviation science; her long, tedious flight – a sense of which is evoked by a long, tracking shot of a map showing all the countries she flew over, accompanied by a voice-over commentary signalling the news headlines; a meditation on notions of 'femininity'; and some schoolgirls talking about female heroism in 1980.

In her examination of films by Richard Woolley, Phil Mulloy, Frank Abbott, Sally Potter, Joanna Davis, Sue Clayton, Jonathan Curling and Jan Worth, Harvey has noted several common themes: fragmentary structures, formal obtrusiveness and a refusal to provide the spectator with conventional character identification. Harvey concludes:

> At worst, these films offered themselves as product within a radicalised middle-class enclave; at best, they presented a challenge to the existing state of things, contributing to the creation of a cinema space in which society is represented and interpreted so that it can also be improved.
>
> (Harvey, 1986: 243)

One particular film, *The Song of the Shirt* (Sue Clayton and Jonathan Curling, 1979), is a visual meditation on the history of sewing women in the mid-nineteenth century. Unlike feminist documentaries which had employed realist conventions to promote consciousness-raising, *The Song of the Shirt* interrogated the means of representation and left it to the audience to construct its possible meaning. It employs self-reflexive devices, not only in terms of filmic artifice but also as a means of questioning the status of various sources used by historians to interpret the past. This film, and many others from the late 1970s, drew inspiration from new feminism and traditions of art cinema.

Many of these films also operated according to a strategy known as counter-cinema, named after Peter Wollen's essay 'Counter-Cinema: Vent D'Est' in *Afterimage*, no. 4, Autumn 1972. Wollen argued that avant-garde films differed from classical in seven important ways: their narratives were more complex and fractured, avoiding 'closure'; their multi-faceted characters often eschewed empathetic identification with the audience; their form was obtrusive; their diegesis was multiple, conveying different worlds and experiences within a single film; they were awash with intertextuality; they often made the spectator feel uncomfortable; and they sought to convey the truth of life's improbabilities and inconsistencies. The concern with the erosion of boundaries, intertextuality and heterogeneous discourses was also a feature of postmodern ideas which can be applied as a reading strategy for many post-1970s films.

PHASE FOUR: 1980s–2000s

Potter, Greenaway, Jarman, Davies, Douglas and Ramsay

As we have seen in Chapter 4, social and political events induced a fascinating cultural response from film-makers who in their different ways articulated anxieties about Thatcherism and its aftermath. Art cinema expressed the cultural backlash most acutely, particularly the films of Derek Jarman which engaged with their immediate social and political context with perceptive analysis and profound sadness. From different perspectives, the following film-makers also introduced levels of formal and thematic experimentation which had been lacking in the two previous decades.

Sally Potter

Sally Potter, Peter Greenaway, Derek Jarman, Terence Davies and Bill Douglas were all making films in the 1970s. Potter's early work reflects her experience as a dance choreographer. In *Hors D'Oeuvres* she experimented with projecting 8mm dance footage, filming it on 16mm and finally editing the result with some 8mm close-ups from the original film. She went on to establish the Limited Dance Company with Jacky Lansley and spent two years touring Britain and the USA. From 1976–78 Potter worked in solo shows and collaborated with various theatres and galleries. In 1978 she joined the Feminist Improvising Group (a musical group) and spent two years touring Europe. She also made *Thriller* in 1979, funded by a grant from the Arts Council of £1,000, and at the time of its release she was still heavily involved in dance.

Thriller is based on Puccini's opera *La Bohème* (1895), a love story about a poet and a young seamstress who dies of consumption. The opera's narrative is from the poet's point of view and the woman, Mimi, is positioned as a tragic figure who must be sacrificed so that the poet can be free. Her death is almost inevitable, her sole purpose apparently being to invest the male characters with a tragic, admirable sensibility. What Sally Potter does is to have the two narratives in play at the same time: one is the observations of Mimi I, a woman who questions the narrative of Mimi II (the figure in the opera).[2] Mimi I's investigation therefore is into why Mimi II had to die and why her role is so predictable. *Thriller* is an example of the 'deconstructive' text which 'foregrounds the means of its construction, refuses stable points of identification, puts the subject "into the process" and invites the spectator into a play with language, form and identity' (Gledhill in Pribram, 1988: 66). Whereas Mimi II is a passive, static figure ('frozen in arabesque') who has no choice but to comply with the dictates of the patriarchal narrative, Mimi I is granted an investigatory discourse which is completely at odds with that of Mimi II. As the film progresses Mimi I gets more and more active, at one stage simulating boxing with one of the male characters. Mimi I's voice-over is a key device which positions us with her as participants in the quest as she tells us the story of the opera and then asks, 'Did I die? Was I murdered? If so, who killed me and why?', before proceeding through, and eventually subverting, the Lacanian mirror phase, privileging a series of shots which link her identity with the Mimi of the opera and the sleuthing scenes which follow. The result is a devastating deconstruction of classical cinema, the opera text standing in for a wider comment on the representation of women in art and the media.

The film draws on the thriller genre in a parodic fashion. Hitchcock's *Psycho* (1960) is referenced as Mimi I starts to question the official version of events. The musical reference to *Psycho* conjures up the image of Marion Crane's murder in the shower, the montage sequence of shots of parts of her dying body are linked in the viewer's mind with Potter's own fragmented images of a murdered woman on the attic floor. Like Mimi II, the doomed Marion Crane of *Psycho* is punished,[3] a fate to which *Thriller* does not consign *its* heroine, Mimi I, the transgressive, questioning woman who achieves insight and life by the end of the film. Other intertexts are referenced, including a historic one where we see shots of a very different representation of the life of a seamstress than the one the opera offers us: Mimi II's costume reflects her role as an opera heroine rather than that of a working woman. The realities of the latter experience are suggested to us by use of photographs of a nineteenth-century seamstress and her sewing equipment. Mimi I's own plain costume and androgynous look suggest a link between the bare facts of the historic Mimi II and a contrast with her patriarchally-constructed operatic counterpart who displays all the familiar trappings of femininity: ankle-length, full skirts, a pale face, fragile appearance and long, flowing hair. The psychoanalytic intertext has already been mentioned, a discourse which Potter by no means subscribes to wholeheartedly. As Mimi I gets deeper into her investigation, she turns to Marxist texts and Freud for clues. Her subsequent hysterical laughter is ambiguous in its address, and we are unsure whether the joke is on the theorists, herself or on us, the audience.

Potter's next film, *The Gold Diggers* (1983), is preoccupied with similar themes: the deconstruction of classical narrative and representations of women. But this time they are pushed even further into the realms of political and aesthetic critique. In *The Gold Diggers*, Ruby (Julie Christie) is a character who is presented at the beginning very much as a construction of filmic imagery and the film concerns the desire of Celeste (Colette Laffont) to know her and learn everything she can about her past and her hopes for the future. We are invited to align ourselves with Celeste and her investigation, as well as with Ruby and her own quest to understand her past. The casting of Julie Christie, not normally associated with experimental cinema, adds a further layer of intertextual significance since many of the scenes which examine Ruby's construction as a screen heroine recall Christie's own film career. The film's title refers to the Busby Berkeley musical *Gold Diggers of 1933*, another example of Potter's reworking of classic film genres. 'We're In the Money', a key number in the musical, suggests the power of capitalist currency as responsible for both economic booms and crippling recessions. The women in the number are dressed in coin-costumes, suggesting an equation between gold currency and the notion of women as commodities, and it is also suggestive of the idea that film stars (particularly women) are commodities, commodities which are vulnerable to all the uncertainties and vagaries of the Hollywood system. In Sally Potter's film she takes this analogy further by suggesting that capitalism encourages the commodification of women and the dual worship of a constructed, unthreatening femininity and the accumulation of capital as the cornerstones of capitalism and imperialism. One scene shows Ruby being carried on a sedan chair; we later see the men carrying blocks of gold bullion to the same destination. This political and feminist critique unites the film's main theme, the relationship between 'gold, money and women' (Potter quoted in Mellencamp, 1990: 163). By the end of the film this has been probed by Celeste and Ruby, who emerge enlightened and united by their recognition of the mechanics of oppression. The final scene is optimistic when we see the two women swimming towards an image of a feminist cinematic heroine, Rosie the Riveter, who gives them a knowing look which is suggestive of continuity between women's struggles for independence during the Second World War and the present.

After *The Gold Diggers* Sally Potter made *The London Story* (1987), a short dance film which alluded to the spy thriller in a comic manner, and she also worked in television. Her next film, *Orlando* (1993), had a long gestation, mostly because she found it difficult to get financial backing (the film was an international co-production), and was very much conceived as a project designed to appeal to a wider market than *Thriller* and *The Gold*

Plate 8.1 'Gold, Money, Women'. Ruby (Julie Christie) being carried on a sedan chair in *The Gold Diggers* (1983). (Courtesy of the British Film Institute)

Diggers. During their first screenings, when many people were confused by their complex narratives and exacting demands on the spectator, Potter became disillusioned with the avant-garde as a filmic mode for political and/ or feminist goals, and with *Orlando* aimed at a more comprehensible narrative and a less binarist conception of gender. Woolf's novel gave her the perfect text with which to explore the notion of an 'essential self which is beyond gender' (Potter, quoted in Glaessner, 1992: 14). Potter was concerned to highlight the theme of class struggle (which she felt the novel rather neglected) and its dependence on patrimony and land: once Orlando is discovered to be female she is forced (unless she has a son) to relinquish her inheritance. This is consistent with Potter's earlier films' critiques of capitalism and its links with patriarchy. The extent to which she is successful in eroding binary notions of gender is debatable. At the end of both *Thriller* and *The Gold Diggers* the women go off together, united in the recognition of male oppression and there is even a hint that they will be sexual partners.[4] These themes are not ignored in *Orlando* which, it should not be forgotten, was a novel inspired by Woolf's relationship with Vita Sackville-West. In

Potter's film it is hard, for example, to accept that Orlando is male when we know Tilda Swinton is playing the role. In the Love section, the affair with Sasha does not come across as heterosexual. All this is suggestive of continuities between Potter's earlier films and more recent work, continuities with the avant-garde tradition which a film-maker seeking to acquire a niche in the commercial art film market would probably rather de-emphasise.

Peter Greenaway

Peter Greenaway's work connects with many traditions of experimental cinema. One of the most striking is his link with the modernists of the Documentary Movement in his subversion of classic documentary traditions. His films question the notion of truth in the cinema and present the viewer with the pleasures and difficulties of the counter-cinematic possibilities offered by pluralist narratives and complex visual structures. Greenaway came from a documentary background, working for the Central Office of Information (an inheritor of Grierson's GPO Film Unit) as an editor in the 1960s before he became a film director. This is interesting in terms of his delight in parodying official-sounding voice-overs and the place of speech and sound in his films generally. Often the bureaucratic nature of the voice-overs is inflected with an ironic tone which underlines the absurdity of much information-speak and the whole fallacy of there being a voice of truth. In conjunction with images which bombard the viewer with multiple layers of meaning, this approach to sound (and his use of Michael Nyman's music) is reminiscent of Cavalcanti's experiments in the 1930s.

Greenaway's experimental short films *Dear Phone* (1976), *Water Wrackets* (1978) and *A Walk Through H* (1978) make particular use of the documentary voice. In *Dear Phone*, different shots of telephone boxes are interspersed with shots of scribbled anecdotes from telephone users with the initials H. C., at first messily handwritten and then typed, gradually becoming more legible. The anecdotes are read out by a documentary-style voice-over throughout, its delivery inflected with harsh, unemotional and unrelenting tones. The viewer is frustrated and challenged by the difficulties of reading *Dear Phone*. As Peter Wollen has pointed out, the operations of 'counter cinema' are at work – in that classic narrative and conventional viewing expectations are frustrated: familiar codes of address and representation are made strange, destroying the traditional relationship between signifier and signified (see Wollen, 1972). The telephone usually signifies an uncomplicated public amenity, readily available and somehow comforting. Yet in *Dear Phone* it is invested with complicated associations, misinformation, confusion and mistrust. There is a high degree of self-reflexivity present in that both sound and image comment on their production and staging: the modernist aesthetic is pitted against a realist mode which is revealed to be equally unreliable in communicating the truth. The telephone boxes signify communication, but the accompanying information supplied by the voice-over does not build up to produce a satisfying whole. Instead, it consists of discrete elements which are punctuated by shots of telephone boxes in different landscape settings. By the end of the film the text has become more legible and the last paragraph tells us that in terms of the habitual telephone caller, form has become more important than content to such an extent that he rings people up and simply reads out 'Dear Phone'. This is perhaps Greenaway's statement that his film is ultimately dependent on film form and that by the end the viewer will have acquired means of deconstructing it which depend more on images than on verbal information. Greenaway's making the familiar strange by the act of filming also connects with other structural film-makers of the 1970s who similarly made the spectator aware of the impact of the mechanics of film-making.

Greenaway was influenced by the structural film-makers who worked in Britain and the USA in the 1970s, particularly Michael Snow and Hollis Frampton (USA). Both Greenaway and Frampton were concerned with riddles and logical exercises. *Zorn's Lemma* (Hollis Frampton, 1970) was a complex, three-part, hour-long film. Its second section, lasting 45 minutes, consisted of a silent series of images of New York signs, each one beginning with a different letter of the alphabet. Each sign was held on screen for exactly one second (24 frames) and Frampton used the Roman alphabet so that the number of letters and frames was almost identical. The film goes on to create a new alphabet of visual imagery by associating images with a particular letter which do not relate to it in the conventional way. Similarly, Greenaway's films are all concerned with classification systems and playing with conventional relations between signifier and signified. In this sense the spectator is being invited to work at decoding unfamiliar associations in relation to the narratives and to intertextual overspill.

This counter-cinematic strategy is also at work in *Water Wrackets*. Here, beautiful landscape imagery is pitted against a harsh, military-style voice-over which tells the story of the 'wracket army' and its strategy to conquer an uncharted area of natural beauty. What we see and what we hear is at odds: the device of using image and voice-over in stark counterpoint invests the landscape imagery with a natural resistance which (ironically) has been created by the act of selective filming. The montage of shots which suggests the infinite flow of water in contrasting still and lively locations shows how film can capture a moment in time of the private world of nature. Greenaway exposes the artifice of film-making in the basic conflict he constructs between the timeless properties of the subject matter in *Water Wrackets* and the carefully engineered shots that are provided as evidence of the secret life of waterscapes.

In *A Walk Through H*, Greenaway constructs a landscape out of abstract drawings which are filmed in extreme close-up and are then imbued with the same sense of authenticity that we attribute to a conventional map by a voice-over which narrates the story connected with specific marks. Any sense of stasis or unity is, however, disturbed by the ebb and flow of camera movements: small details being singled out, small movements directing the spectator's eye followed by wider shots, the film beginning and ending with the total context of the art gallery. The spectator is made conscious of the flight of fantasy which has been constructed out of filmic artifice, offering a meditation on the relationship between fine art and film. In *A Walk Through H* Greenaway uses music beyond its familiar filmic context in classical narrative cinema. Greenaway's fascination with systems of categorisation and methods of random procedure aligns him with the concerns of modernist musicians like Michael Nyman and John Cage, who apply modular and serial structures to their compositions to discover a content in the accidents and coincidences which occur. *A Walk Through H* is one of Greenaway's earliest collaborations with Nyman and this piece corresponds with the overall exhaustive narrative structure in its tendency towards repetition, emphasis and punctuation.

Most of Greenaway's films can be described as 'animated paintings' and often use particular sequences of colours, for example in *The Cook, the Thief, His Wife and Her Lover* (1989). His films are often dotted with references to art history and pay homage to particular artists' work, as with Bruegel paintings in *The Draughtsman's Contract* (1982) and Hals in *The Cook, the Thief, His Wife and Her Lover*. Peter Wollen argues that Greenaway's penchant for enigmatic objects and fanciful detail can be compared to the fine-art work of R. B. Kitaj, an American painter who worked in Britain, who invites intertextual readings connected with the mythical aesthetics attached to engravings, emblems, maps and incunabula (Wollen, 1993: 44–45). Similarly, the images in *A Walk Through H* have a vivid collage quality which is created through the interplay of variations of texture, colour, motifs and markings. In this sense his concern with bricolage and textual overspill invests his work with postmodernist qualities.

Greenaway's short films are important as aesthetic precursors of his feature films. They display a similar preoccupation with categorisation; complex narratives; unusual juxtapositions of sound and image; landscape; an abundance of intertextual references; and continual experimentation with film form and its relationship to content. *The Draughtsman's Contract* (1982) develops these themes considerably, making use of the challenges posed by feature film narrative and more conventional characterisation. The Herbert estate appears to be excessively man-made with its carefully designed gardens and regimented trees. Yet there is a suggestion that this regimentation is a temporary phase in the garden's life and that man's desire to impose order on it is ultimately doomed. At the end of the film the draughtsman Neville is found drowned, engulfed by the lake after his murder. Nature has defeated him on another count: his careful drawings,

Plate 8.2 Mr Neville (Anthony Higgins) attempting to create a rational, ordered world in *The Draughtsman's Contract* (1982). (Courtesy of Artificial Eye Film Company Ltd)

which represented the garden as regimented, tidy, without obstacles or people to spoil his balanced compositions, were used against him as evidence of his guilt of the murder of Mr Herbert. Neville has thus been framed by the aristocrats he thought he could control, his activity being similar to that of the artist who, according to Greenaway, also endeavours to impose structures and controls over his or her work.

Derek Jarman

Derek Jarman's work was characterised by an irreverent attitude towards the film industry and its structures and by experimentation with the conventions of narrative cinema. These basic areas of opposition influenced all his films, resulting in a body of work which, along with the work of Peter Greenaway, revived the art film tradition in Britain and continues to be influential since his death in 1994. Jarman insisted that huge budgets and expensive equipment were not necessary to produce work of creative distinction. He opposed technical elitism in the industry, particularly the whole question of broadcast quality which instituted rigorous technical and aesthetic hierarchies. Jarman's most lavish, sumptuously designed film, *Caravaggio* (1986), cost £475,000, a low-budget film. Although it was made on 35mm stock, Jarman generally preferred to experiment with lower-budget technology, particularly Super-8 and video. *The Last of England* (1987) used a variety of formats, including home-movie footage shot by his grandfather and father between the 1920s and 1940s, investing the film with a virtuoso quality which works to celebrate the basic properties of film, taking Jarman and the spectator directly back to 'the pleasure of seeing language put through the magic lantern' (Jarman quoted in Hacker and Price, 1991: 237).

Jarman's painterly approach to film and its textures affected work at the shooting stage and during post-production. Images were often first shot on film at a fast speed of 3–6 frames per second (fps), projected at a slow speed and then refilmed on video at normal (24 fps) speed. A degrading of the image occurred, producing a textured, dream-like quality which communicated the bleak thematics of *The Last of England's* blitz imagery extremely effectively. Jarman often used filters on lenses and manipulated film at the processing stage by means of tinting. His rebellion against the industry and its structures also affected his approach to crewing: most of his films were collaborations with friends, many working for nothing. Much of the creative

Plate 8.3 The present dreaming the past future? Refugees on the quayside in *The Last of England* (1987). (Courtesy of The Sales Company)

process took place on set, actors contributing lines as they went along and Jarman insisting on a community sense about all his projects. He defended this approach by insisting that an improvisational production context fostered the best ideas. Many of his films had little or no script, another fundamental challenge to the commercial industry's cardinal rules of process: scripting, finance, shooting, post-production.

Like the work of Greenaway, Jarman's films are permeated with intertextuality, a key reading-strategy for his work which endeavours to make the familiar strange. There are many references to paintings, for example at the beginning of *The Last of England*, Spring is trampling on a Caravaggio painting, 'Profane Love', the irony being that an oppositional character is destroying an oppositional work of art. Jarman draws upon punk (a subculture which clearly both fascinated and repelled him) by means of characters and iconography in *Jubilee* (1977) and to a lesser extent in *The Last of England*. In these works he could be said to communicate both the conservative and progressive elements of subcultural style, referred to by cultural studies theorist Dick Hebdige in his study of the ways in which subcultural style relates to the hegemonic process (1979). Homoerotic imagery and the suffering of the male body is present in all Jarman's films as well as a usage of camp and gay subculture which is either presented in the spirit of Kenneth Anger or Andy Warhol, or with more lyrical inflections, as in *Angelic Conversation* (1985). Some references are quite traditional: Shakespeare, Benjamin Britten, Wilfred Owen, Renaissance painting, classical art, neo-romanticism and blitz culture.

Other intertextual references are less specific, drawing on shared memories, including home movies, communicating a sophisticated, multi-layered sense of the past. *The Last of England* refers to Ford Madox Brown's painting of emigrants leaving for the New World, a theme which connects with the film's imagery of what Annette Kuhn has called 'the *memory* of England which lies in a future' (Kuhn, 1995: 109). The emigrants are leaving a country about which they share certain memories: these memories will be carried with them to the New World, forever shifting as memory becomes myth. The connection with the painting came *after* the film had been completed when Jarman was searching for a title. His memory of the painting was triggered by the scenes of the refugees at the quayside, which bear a certain visual similarity (Jarman, 1987: 190–93).

In many senses, Jarman's films can be called *histories*: they revel in presenting history as a complex process which interweaves past and present. In *Jubilee* Ariel conjures up the image of punk Britain for Elizabeth I. One of the punks, Amyl Nitrate, has a hobby of writing history in a manipulative sense, seeking to destroy the idea of shared memory in favour of dictatorship. By contrast, *The Last of England* is a dialogue between the 1940s and the present, an attempt to reveal the poverty of the values Jarman's father fought for in the Second World War. Annette Kuhn has usefully compared

Jarman's film to Jennings' *Listen To Britain* (1942) in its use of music and shared national imagery, but for quite different ends: 'While the overall tone of *Listen To Britain* is one of synthesis, that of *The Last of England* is of disintegration' (Kuhn, 1995: 120). In many ways *The Last of England* accords with Paul Willemen's schema for 'an avant-garde for the 90s' which interests itself in history and context:

> The avant-garde narrative no longer solely appeals to an interest in the way stories are constructed and told. Instead, it seeks to address an audience's knowledge and experience of history. As such, it is no longer a theory of discourse or of representation that is at stake, but instead an understanding of history, of social change.
>
> (Willemen, 1994: 155)

The Last of England does, however, pose interesting questions about narrative in the art film. Its images are in constant flux, ephemeral fragments of possible narratives about a junkie; about two young men; about someone who gets shot; about a family in the 1940s; about a marriage; about a woman who cuts up her wedding dress and runs defiantly along the seashore; about some refugees; about Thatcher's Britain and the 'imagined community' of somewhere called England.[5] By use of montage, the repetition of certain images, colours and shapes, the film invites the viewer to contemplate a 'queer' perspective on the iconography of nationalism, a subversion of dominant myths which is structured as a 'dream allegory' where 'the present dreams the past future' (Jarman, 1987: 188).

Terence Davies

The autobiographical films of Terence Davies deal with similar themes to those present in Derek Jarman's films. Funded by the British Film Institute Production Board, Davies' 16mm trilogy, *Children* (1976), *Madonna and Child* (1980) and *Death and Transfiguration* (1983), and his 35mm features, *Distant Voices, Still Lives* (1988) and *The Long Day Closes* (1992) all deal with questions of history, gender and sexuality. Thematically, the stories are about growing up in a stifling and at times cruel working-class family environment in 1950s Liverpool. The potential and actual conflict between awakening homosexuality and the strict and dictatorial Law of the Father is ever present in Davies' earliest films.

Davies' style is far more minimalist than Jarman's, less 'overtly painterly or florid', as he explained in an interview (Dixon, 1994: 255). Davies' compositions are precise and pictorial, making frequent use of static poses and, particularly in *Distant Voices, Still Lives*, an almost sepia-like, still-photograph look. In *The Long Day Closes*, the camera is more mobile in a slow, tracking, observant manner, creating transitions from realistic to fantasy sequences and the impression of fluid memories. In this film the young boy, Bud, grows up in a safe, cosy environment, looked after by his mother and brothers after the oppressive father has died. Davies uses popular and traditional music to evoke the working-class community his films celebrate, albeit in a sentimental way. Long tracking shots create a sense of gentle flow between one situation and another, frequently settling on Bud looking out of the window, his perspective being that of a spectator at the pictures and in the world he will enter once he has left the safe haven of his home.

As a film about working-class experience, *The Long Day Closes* has been accused of aestheticising the past at the risk of losing authenticity. As John Caughie has argued, this involves a reliance on certain visual myths in the representation of working-class life:

> the values of community, resilience, having a good time, virility (verging on brutality) and the enduring 'mam' map out the real, which holds its natural shape behind the simulations of an acquired culture, and legitimates the nostalgia of the left for a past it may never have had. Terence Davies has the virtue of having been there, on the inside, in the know. This gives him a complicated relation to the past, marked in the films by an aesthetic formalism which struggles to keep its distance from sentimental nostalgia even while it is celebrating sentimentality. The problem is how to remember the class, now from outside it, other than in the images which the myth provides, memorialising a loss which can only be registered in moving pictures and still lives. Despite the distance of its former brilliance, *The Long Day Closes* seems to me still to linger lovingly on the old images of passivity and endurance which can only celebrate happiness by celebrating stasis, a fantasy of the past in which memory holds things in place.
>
> (1992: 13)

It is difficult to judge how far this might be a consistent feature of Davies' work, located as it is in a particular experience of being a working-class Liverpudlian male. There has been no autobiographical sequel to *The Long Day Closes*; Davies' film *The Neon Bible* (1995) is set in Georgia in the American South just after the Second World War and relates to his previous films in terms of its thematic (a lonely childhood) and formal preoccupations. *The House of Mirth* (2000), a British–French–German–American co-production, adapted Edith Wharton's novel set in America at the beginning of the twentieth century, and starred Gillian Anderson as the heroine Lily Bart who suffers from the crushing hypocrisy of the period. This particular film can be related to the heritage genre, but it certainly neither celebrates the time in which it is set, nor its values. After experiencing difficulty obtaining funding for Davies' most recent project, *Mad About the Boy* (in production 2007), this comedic film has been co-sponsored by the UK Film Council. A previous proposal, for an adaptation of the novel *The Sunset Song*, was however turned down by the UKFC. In many ways Davies represents the vulnerability of many directors who do not operate firmly within the mainstream. Even though *The House of Mirth* won considerable critical praise funding subsequent work has by no means been easy, a tortuous path also trodden by Lynne Ramsay.

Bill Douglas

Bill Douglas' major work was similarly autobiographical: he made three short films, *My Childhood* (16mm, 1972), *My Ain Folk* (35mm, 1973) and *My Way Home* (35mm, 1978), and he also completed a long feature *Comrades* (1987), which was about the Tolpuddle Martyrs.[6] Douglas was Scottish and, like Davies, his Trilogy was loosely based on the brutalities and insecurities of his working-class childhood and adolescence. Douglas's films, however, have a much harsher edge, following a boy's early life from 1945 with anything but aestheticised nostalgia. *My Childhood* opens with the sound of an air raid siren and then immerses us in his milieu: growing up in a Scottish mining village where German prisoners of war worked the fields. After being parcelled out amongst various family members, the boy lives in a children's home before going to Egypt to complete his National Service. The third film *My Way Home* deals with the transition from Scotland to Egypt and the boy's friendship, or possible future relationship, with another soldier who offers to share his home at the end of the film.

In an assessment of the Douglas Trilogy John Caughie has written:

> Douglas's work seems to be one of the key indicators of a possible British or Scottish art cinema equipped with a hard enough edge to cut through the bland cinema of nationalist nostalgias and clearer ironies, or the 'made for television' cinema of production values and quality quotas.
>
> (Dick, Noble and Petrie, 1993: 204)

Caughie argues that in the 1970s Douglas's films did not get the institutional and academic support they deserved because, although the British Film Institute funded the Trilogy, it became more and more critical of Douglas's working methods and conflicted with him over editing decisions. On top of that, Douglas's films seemed 'too individualistic to point to film as a social practice, and too realistic to open the way to the avant-garde' (ibid.: 197–98). He was thus a victim of the limited and increasingly exclusive support structure for art films in the 1970s and of the academy's rather narrow theoretical orthodoxies.

In retrospect, Douglas's films are highly interesting as examples of a British/Scottish cinema influenced by Soviet montage and by European art cinema. Douglas's style depended on the contemplative effect induced by the static image, its ability to convey lyrical imagery with a stark simplicity of composition. Many of the actors used by Douglas were unprofessional, yet he succeeded in drawing performances from them which relied on gestural condensation: understated actions and subtle facial expressions which were nevertheless capable of conveying a complex emotional spectrum. We do not always know where a scene will lead, whether it will end in violence or tenderness. In *My Childhood* the boy throws some dead flowers which are in a cup onto the floor, fills the cup with hot water from the kettle, spilling it over the table and floor as he does, empties the cup and then takes it to his grandmother who is hunched up, sitting by the fire. The child gently wraps her freezing hands around the warm cup, and in a brief moment of physical tenderness, his own fingers over hers. Also in the Trilogy the boy frequently stares at adults – his father, his grandmother, the German POWs – watching them out of curiosity, occasional affection but mostly fear.

Interiors are shot with a static camera, conveying a harsh, cold life where the children seem to have no place. By contrast, exterior shots take the camera high, following the boy running through fields, kite-flying and watching trains; images which are full of the promise of escape. Within the broad trajectory of childhood to adolescence, the fragmented narratives encourage the audience to make meaning from their multiple scenes and static frames. The stark black and white cinematography is perfect for the bleak childhood scenes, becoming more bleached-out for the location shots of Egypt where the friendship between the two young men offers hope. The Trilogy is punctuated with several references to cinema: at the beginning of *My Ain Folk* we see an extract from *Lassie*. Its rich Technicolour comes as a shock after the sparse, grainy, black and white images of *My Childhood*, conveying something of Douglas's own fascination with cinema from an early age. In Egypt the young man tells his friend that he wants to be a painter or a film director, an unusual path or 'way home' for a boy who is expected to keep his place – down the pit.

Comrades used similar stylistics to the Trilogy but departed from it in several important ways which illustrate how Douglas's film-making was developing. It is a much longer film and used professional actors throughout, dwelling on relations between characters rather than story events. Duncan Petrie has observed that 'at the heart of *Comrades* lies a reconciliation of two opposing philosophies of cinema: a realist Bazinian philosophy of the medium as a "window on to the world", and a self-reflexive acknowledgement of its artificiality' (ibid.: 196). Self-reflexivity is achieved through the device of a magic lanternist who appears throughout the film to make visual comment on the Tolpuddle Martyrs' story, making us aware of the different versions of their history made possible by the magic lantern and, by implication, its successor, cinema.

In many ways, Douglas's own experience of film-making was as difficult as that of the early pioneers. Throughout his career he struggled to get funding for his films and, just before his death in 1991, was refused backing for a project he had worked on for twelve years – an adaptation of James Hogg's *Confessions of a Justified Sinner*. He was supported by the British Film Institute for his Trilogy, but all three films had tortuous production histories and, apart from being successful at film festivals, were not widely distributed. Nor was *Comrades*, which received most of its funding from Channel 4.[7]

Lynne Ramsay

Another key director to work within the art cinema tradition exemplified by the film-makers discussed above is Scottish director Lynne Ramsay. With a background in photography and a National Film School background, her first success was with short films, most notably *Small Deaths*, which won the Prix du Jury at Cannes in 1996; *Kill the Day* (1997) and *Gasman* (1997) also won numerous awards. These critical successes enabled her to obtain finance for her first feature film, *Ratcatcher* (1999), which was won considerable critical acclaim, most notably on the film festival circuit. Associated with 'New Scottish Cinema' (the spate of films made by Scottish directors and/or films with Scottish themes following the success of *Trainspotting*), Ramsay has been heralded as a gifted auteur who makes films with elliptical narratives and striking imagery which bears all the hallmarks of a photographer's sensibility for the potential of the framed image (her films often include shots that contain frames within frames). The aesthetic strategies developed in her films are sensitive explorations of film texture – sight, sound and mood.

Ratcatcher is set in the 1970s, during a rubbish strike in Glasgow. It centres on twelve-year-old James, a sensitive boy who is distanced from his family. After witnessing the accidental drowning of a boy while playing beside a river, James forms a friendship with a young girl. The film captures James's experiences of poverty on the council estate where he lives, of his encounters with others, of his impressions and dreams of escape to a new local housing development that is being built. The theme of utopianism is a key element of the film. In particular, James's dreams of change are fixated on the development which functions as a dual register of both optimism and disillusionment. As Murray (2005: 222–23) has pointed out, while the character sees in it a possibility of hope, of a brighter, more comfortable future, with hindsight the audience recognises the development as the site of post-war urban deprivation, the world which is explored in such graphic detail in films such as *Trainspotting*. In terms of film form, the images are resonant with experimentation, pictorial lyricism and intense visual beauty.

Ramsay's second feature, *Morvern Callar* (2002, see also discussion in Chapter 5) is based on a cult Scottish novel by Alan Warner. The book and film focus on a central character who is preoccupied with dreams of escape. But instead of this remaining at the level of dreaming, as in *Ratcatcher*, Morvern Callar (Samantha Morton) is eventually able to leave Scotland for Spain, but only because of a financial windfall that has been gained by unusual means. Morvern Callar is a supermarket worker who lives in a port town in the West of Scotland (Oban, where Warner grew up) with her boyfriend. The film opens with a striking scene of a dark room with a view through a doorway to a brighter kitchen area in the centre of the frame (another frame within a frame). In many ways this shot serves as an emblematic taster for the main theme of the film: a character seeking to escape, to adjust to disturbing events and eventually re-locate. The narrative proceeds with no dialogue as we understand that Morvern's boyfriend has killed himself. We see him lying on the floor in the darkened room, the only light source being a Christmas tree with pulsating, coloured lights flashing on and off. At first it is not clear that he is dead but the gradual revelation of his blood-stained wrists indicate suicide. This is confirmed when Morvern reads a message on the computer (signalled by a screen prompting 'Read Me') which is his suicide note to her.

In subsequent scenes in a pub and then a club Morvern does not tell her friends that her boyfriend is dead but that he has 'left'. At home she covers him up with a sheet and then cuts up his body in the bath before burying it in the mountains. She invites her friend Lanna (Kathleen McDermott) on a holiday to Spain, paid for by money left by the boyfriend that was intended as payment for his funeral expenses. This is the first 'escape mechanism' in the plot, the second being the boyfriend's novel which is also on the computer for her to find ('I wrote it for you') and which Morvern sends to a publisher in her own name. Lanna and Morvern go to Spain to a resort designed for British holidaymakers. Morvern grows tired of it and drags Lanna away so that they can see 'real' Spain. The discomfort of walking in the mountains and of not having a place to stay does not suit Lanna who Morvern leaves asleep on the roadside with some money. She hitches a lift to a town where she arranges to meet a couple from a publishing firm who are so interested in the novel that they fly to Spain to see her. To Morvern's surprise they are prepared to pay her an advance of £100,000 for the novel. The film ends with her back in Scotland, leaving the flat she shared with her boyfriend and after picking up the cheque she suggests once again to Lanna that they go away together. Lanna prefers to stay: 'There's nothing wrong here – it's the same crap everywhere, so stop dreaming', she says. But Morvern does leave, the final shots are of her walking down a dark street, case in hand, and then waiting for a train on a deserted railway platform. This is followed by a final, emblematic series of shots of her dancing in a club, strobe lights punctuating the scene (a striking formal resonance to the opening shots of the intermittently flashing Christmas tree lights) as we hear the Mamas and Papas on the soundtrack singing 'Dedicated to the One I

Love'. Diegetic music is a striking feature of the film in the form of a tape cassette labelled 'Music For You' that Morvern's boyfriend left for her. The songs on the tape are pertinent and symbolic registers of her mood in several key scenes throughout the film. This last scene is somewhat out of time – we are not sure whether it is a flashback to one of the earlier clubbing scenes, or sometime in the future.

Ramsay's work clearly resonates with the preoccupations of counter-cinema. Her narratives are rarely linear and the visual imagery dominates at the expense of dialogue or tightly constructed plot. She uses colour in particularly interesting ways, for example the contrasts between scenes in Scotland which are conveyed with predominantly blue and grey hues and the bright, warm colours of Spain. The scenes when Morvern and Lanna go to Spain are representative of Ramsay's ability to suggest multiple registers of experience that range from the regimented holiday complex which is filled with British tourists who are isolated from the 'real' Spain, to the mountains and small villages. As with *Ratcatcher* the search for a utopian homeland is elusive, as the film ends with the clubbing scene that is ambiguous both in its temporal placement in the narrative, as well as its significance as an emblematic image suggesting Morvern's possible future. In this way, Ramsay's films are striking for their elliptical nature, confirming her place in the canon of much-heralded auteurs of the art cinema market.

Black British film

A key area of recent British film has been the black British renaissance which began in the mid-1980s. Black film-makers sought to challenge dominant representations and there was some intersection between theory and practice, particularly concerning wider debates around the concept of Third Cinema. The term was used in the late 1960s as a banner for Latin American cinema and became a central reference point throughout post-1970s debates about the relationship between politics and film culture, particularly the connections between film and ethnicity. In broad terms, Third Cinema referred to the possibility of an international cinematic tradition which addressed itself to questions of ethnicity, standing outside Hollywood and Euro-centred national cinemas. In many ways, it drew on and extended the concept of counter-cinema with its anti-capitalist ethos, aligning itself with traditions of low-budget film-making with some elements of state subsidy. In the 1980s the creative emphasis tended to shift away from the director and instead insisted on the importance of collective work. In recent years, with the decline of the workshop movement, the attention has reverted somewhat back to the director.

Exponents of Third Cinema argued that cinema should not be blatantly crude/propagandistic, although increasing social understanding was a goal whereby experiences of otherness were explored, particularly the experience of being black and British. As Paul Willemen has put it, those who worked towards notions of Third Cinema aimed at 'summing up and reformulating the encounter of diverse cultural traditions into new, politically as well as cinematically illuminating types of filmic discourse, critical of, yet firmly anchored in, their respective social–historical situations' (Pines and Willemen, 1989: 4). This involved a degree of formal experimentation but also an engagement with popular cinema. As Reece Auguistel of the Black Audio Film Collective argued, 'Black film practitioners in Britain occupy a specific historical space, and it is one that has been forged by our particular experiences of race, politics and cinema aesthetics in Britain' (Auguistel in Pines and Willemen, 1989: 215–16).

The black British renaissance was most evident during the years 1985–91. It was encouraged by grants which sponsored minority art in the aftermath of race riots in the 1970s. The renaissance films emerged out of a growing critique of the few opportunities open to black artists who had little or no access to the dominant media organisations. The Greater London Council and Channel 4 responded to these criticisms by setting aside funds for training and encouraging the growth of black film collectives. The films produced by these groups, particularly by Sankofa, Black Audio and Ceddo, included elements of black experience not probed by earlier film-makers. A key director who emerged from this tradition was Isaac Julien, who focused on questions of masculinity, desire and sexuality. Julien was co-founder of Sankofa in 1983, a group which made the experimental documentary *Territories* (1984) and *Passion of Remembrance* (1986). Many directors have been influenced by the Sankofa tradition, most recently Gurinder Chadha's *Bhaji On the Beach* (1993), an attempt to document the Asian experience in contemporary Britain. Chadha's *Bride and Prejudice* (2004) updates Jane Austen as inspiration for a comedic romp in the form of a Bollywood musical that satirises tensions between generations.

Sankofa derives from the African Akan language, meaning 'returning to your roots, recuperating what you've lost and moving forward'. A major theme in the work of renaissance film-makers was the diasporic narrative which revolved around the idea of introducing ideas and themes from other cultures to address and empower the contemporary one. Manthia Diawara cites *My Beautiful Launderette* (1985) as an example of such a narrative where 'an Asian and the English presence are combined to produce a third space, which is occupied not only by the youth of Asian descent, but also by the white youth of the punk generation' (Diawara in Friedman, 1993: 157). Another example of the diasporic narrative is Julien's stylish *Looking for Langston* (1989), about black American poet Langston Hughes (1902–67). A connection is made between the historical context in which he wrote, the Harlem renaissance of the 1920s, and contemporary issues concerning homosexuality, inter-racial sex, ethnicity and power relations in general. Julien's concentration on representations of black homosexuality were informed by a desire to challenge the dominant construction of black masculinity as strong and uncomplicated.

In terms of overt political content, many films of the black British renaissance highlight the issue of policing and how black people have frequently been represented as being on the other side of the law, a concept which is invoked to protect a white, exclusive and discriminatory conception of Britishness. *Territories* has a distinctive image, a single shot of multiple superimpositions of people and the police, suggesting an uneasy co-existence. John Akomfrah's *Handsworth Songs* (1986) documented race riots in a poetic, experimental manner, while the Black Audio Film Collective's *Mysteries of July* (1991) dealt with the controversial issue of deaths in police custody. Isaac Julien's first feature film, *Young Soul Rebels* (1991), has a classic interrogation scene when one of the central characters, Chris, is accused of murder. Although this film adhered more to classical stylistic norms than Julien's previous films, its loose narrative structure encompassed generic conventions of thriller and romance, as well as several contrasting storylines. And the subject matter was new. Co-funded by the British Film Institute Production Board, it was set in 1977, the year of the Queen's Silver Jubilee, and was concerned to depict black soul subculture, which co-existed with Punk. It also dealt with homosexuality and similar questions about representations of black masculinity which Julien had addressed in *Looking for Langston*.

In the 1990s black and Asian film-makers continued to find it difficult to gain a niche in the market, as Malik observed, they 'find themselves marginalized and restricted within a British film culture that is currently engaged, on many different fronts, in the struggle to make itself known and coveted on the ever-expanding global stage' (2002: 90). Funding for the workshops virtually ceased after 1990 and experimental work was not given priority by financiers. After *Young Soul Rebels* Julien retreated increasingly into the arena of multi-screen art and video installation work, a position within which he has assumed a key position but to the neglect of film-making. The culture of retrenchment led to a decline of the workshop movement and funding from television, particularly Channel 4, decreased, even though some key South Asian films such as *Bandit Queen* (1994) were aired on television while their commercial distribution in cinemas was limited. Recent Black and Asian films produced for the mainstream (such as *East is East*, *Bullet Boy* and *My Son the Fanatic*) are described in Chapter 5 and do offer some fascinating perspectives, but suffice it to say here that despite the UK Film Council's commitment to diversity of cultural representation it is difficult not to agree with Malik's judgement that on the whole 'Black British film remains undercapitalized, poorly distributed, selectively exhibited and widely unknown. The new commercialism has not successfully assimilated or encouraged Black-produced work as part of British national cinema' (2002: 100).

Animation

Oppositional work in animation has been a relatively expanding area, especially by women animators since the 1980s.[8] In general, animation is particularly appropriate for experimental work because of its anti-realist
associations and connection with art-school traditions since the late 1960s.
Animation allows considerable opportunity for an artist's intervention by
painting directly onto a film frame, a technique favoured by many early
animators, and by planning shots to the minutest detail. Fine artwork is of
direct relevance and many styles and techniques are used to create a sense
of movement, structure and form: models are sometimes used, strange
designs can be counterpointed and live action interwoven into a primarily
animated film. Animation is relatively cheap, the major cost being the time
it takes to produce a short film which will have little chance of distribution
unless it is shown at a festival, on Channel 4 or on BBC2.

Since the late 1970s women have produced a large and impressive body
of animated films. As Jeanette Winterson (1992) has explained: 'For women
the combination of absolute control over their material and the financial
capacity to make their project has resulted not in complacency but in experiment'. There are many similarities between the work of Sally Potter and
animator Vera Neubauer, a Czechoslovak who moved to Britain in 1968.
Neubauer's films interrogate conventional narrative structures and patriarchal society. Her influential film *The Decision* (1981) deconstructs classical
narrative by reworking a fairytale about a princess who has to decide which
prince she should marry. The voice-over communicates a soothing aural
discourse which is undermined by animated and live-action sequences
which punctuate the story with ironic counterpoint. Romantic fantasies,
many of which are created by films, are juxtaposed with harsh images
detailing women's more realistic experience of heterosexual relationships
and motherhood. The experience of fantasy from a male point of view is
explored in Joanna Woodward's film *The Brooch Pin and the Sinful Clasp*
(1989). It tells the story of a man's desire for an elusive female figure who
dances and shines above a tower block. He climbs the block in pursuit of
this vision, witnessing on the way a variety of people and situations which
contrast greatly with the beautiful, shimmering ballerina. When he has
nearly reached the top, a giant woman (filmed in live action) captures him
and he ends up being baked in one of her pies as a punishment for seeking
to satisfy his heart's desire. This act of violence was prefigured when he was
climbing the tower: he did not notice the words 'Femme Futile' scrawled on
the wall as a warning. Like *The Decision*, the film thus stresses the futility of
pursuing voyeuristic and male-centred images of femininity.

Some animators made overtly political films, including Gillian Lacey,
one of the founder members of the Leeds Animation Workshop in 1976.
During her time at the Workshop and subsequently, Lacey has been
involved in films dealing with issues including education, domestic violence

and local government. *Murders Most Foul* (1988) concerns women and the law. It takes the form of a melodrama, passing satiric comment on how leniently a man is treated for murdering his wife (he is acquitted) who appears to have 'neglected' her wifely duties by eventually becoming a lesbian. The film shows how her various 'faults' become exaggerated during the legal process: taking tranquillisers brands her as a drug addict and having a drink as an alcoholic. In the end, the court-room performance is over and the jury applauds the man's acquittal. But Lacey has the last word when she shows the judge eating the words which have condemned the woman, not the man, during the trial. Films such as these revived animation's traditional links with nineteenth-century satirical cartoons. That tradition was also evident in the early work of Bristol-based Aardman Animations, who also animated pop videos and created the popular Wallace and Gromit series. Channel 4 had a significant influence in broadcasting animated shorts, thus introducing them to a wide range of audiences and encouraging many to enrol on animation courses that have proliferated since the worldwide success of Aardman.

The satirical cartoon was evoked effectively in Joanna Quinn's *Britannia* (1993), a short animated film in which a British bulldog keeps guard over a map of Britain. The dog is disturbed by the sounds of Scottish bagpipes, Irish folk music and Welsh choirs which are stifled at the instruction of the shrill voice of Britannia (Queen Victoria/Margaret Thatcher?). In a direct reference to British imperialism, the dog plunders the globe, swallowing it in a grotesque fashion, before transforming itself into a crude and terrifying cartoon of Queen Victoria. She wears a necklace made up of subject peoples who escape when she falls asleep, exhausted by her conquests. In the end the dog is put back on the British map, becoming a woman's pet lap dog kept on a tight leash, while Indian women walk freely by, laughing and looking happy. The film is thus a wry comment on British imperial history with a defiantly optimistic ending.

British animation has a worldwide reputation, thanks in large part to Aardman Animations and their commercially successful, Academy Award-winning films. Yet the market is a very competitive one, and many graduates from colleges and film schools that teach animation find it difficult to obtain work. Film festivals, short film competitions and television companies (particularly S4C and the BBC) are highly influential in gaining exposure for animated films. As with other brands of non-mainstream film-making, animators can also take advantage of the opportunities provided by websites such as YouTube which bypass conventional forms of distribution while at the same time creating awareness of a wide range of products.

Gay and lesbian film

As far as British cinema is concerned, gay and lesbian subject matter has not been central. Homosexual characters did feature in social-problem films of the 1960s, most explicitly in *Victim* (1961), starring Dirk Bogarde as a lawyer, Melville Farr, who is blackmailed by a criminal gang who photographed him with a young man. When the young man is arrested and commits suicide, Farr begins his own investigation but finds it particularly difficult to enlist the support of those in high places who are desperate to conceal their own homosexuality. Farr's marriage suffers and his wife cannot understand his predicament: women's demands and the malfunctioning of the family are presented as possible causes of homosexuality. Like many of the social-problem films, *Victim* is awash with contradictory messages, as Landy has pointed out:

> In certain ways *Victim* is not a radical ideological departure from earlier British cinema that sought to legitimate the primacy of law, the role of the family, male relationships, female subordination, and social institutions. Where this film differs is in its surfacing, though not resolving, the contradictory nature of these institutions. In the final analysis, the 'realism' deconstructs itself. Rather than offering a transparent 'slice of life', the film calls attention to the difficulty of trying to resolve the problem it sets out to investigate.
>
> (Landy, 1991: 481)

The 'heritage' genre of costume dramas featured homosexual characters, particularly *Another Country* (1984) and *Maurice* (1987). In these films, homosexuality is located as an upper-class problem where the establishment seeks to conceal its vulnerability with a range of hypocritical double standards.

Lesbianism has not featured as subject matter in many British films. *The Rainbow* (1988), Ken Russell's adaptation of the D. H. Lawrence novel, deployed heritage stylistics of soft-focus, high production values and exquisite costumes but could hardly be described as British cinema's coming out on the subject. A lesser-known film, *Wild Flowers* (Robert Smith, 1989), is a sensitive story about a young girl's growing awareness of her sexuality when she falls in love with her boyfriend's mother on a visit to Scotland. From an altogether different perspective, *Butterfly Kiss* (Michael Winterbottom, 1994) placed two lesbians in the road-movie genre, but made them so violent and psychologically disturbed that many audiences were alienated. One of the most effective films to deal with aspects of lesbianism is a comedy short, *Came Out, It Rained, Went Back In Again* (Betsan Evans, 1991) which features a northern learner-lesbian, played by Jane Horrocks, who travels to London in search of what it might be all about. The witty script places her in hilarious situations which nevertheless bring out issues not probed in more serious films: political correctness; class; the tyrannies of fashion; age; the agonies of the club scene; and finding a partner.

In the 1970s, identity politics sought to encourage positive stereotypes to counter dominant representations of gay men as camp and effete and of lesbians as butch predators. The disadvantages of this position were that diversity was repressed in the search for the exclusively positive role model who could not be dismissed by wider society. The arrival of queer politics and 'new queer cinema' in the 1990s has had an altogether different impact on representations of gays and lesbians. Parody, performance and subversion form the basis of queer cinema, as B. Ruby Rich has explained:

> The new queer films and videos aren't all the same and don't share a single aesthetic vocabulary or strategy or concern. Yet they are nonetheless united by a common style. . . . There are traces in all of them of appropriation and pastiche, irony, as well as a reworking of history with social constructivism very much in mind. Definitely breaking with older humanist approaches and the films and tapes that accompanied identity politics, these works are irreverent, energetic, alternately minimalist and excessive. Above all, they're full of pleasure.
>
> (1992: 32)

More specifically, many queer films share the following characteristics which I will illustrate: the subversion of dominant film forms; intertextuality; and the notion of gender performance.

Isaac Julien's *Looking for Langston* (1989) takes the dominant form of documentary and makes it strange by integrating it with evocative imagery and anti-realist strategies. This film involves unconventional dialogue (voice-over, poetry) and an immersion in style which seeks to integrate past and present. The Harlem Renaissance is evoked but we are made aware of its connections with present-day struggles. The film's final sequence is particularly interesting in this respect. It begins with a scene in a gay bar, frequently shot from above, where the clients are at ease listening to jazz. Two angels, one of whom is gay pop star Jimmy Somerville, watch from above, providing a sort of ironic, omniscient presence which is carried over into subsequent scenes. The mobile camera suggests a sense of fluidity and freedom within the confined space of the bar, but we are alerted to co-existing contradictions and problems when we hear the poetic voice-over speaking in ambivalent terms about inter-racial gay relationships and questions of power. The sequence then proceeds according to a different formal strategy: we see static images of a dark alley, followed by a torch and then by a gang, clearly intent on storming the bar. We hear contemporary disco music which effects a transition to the present, although the men in the bar are the same as before. These shots are juxtaposed: danger and pleasure, until we finally see the men dancing to disco music. But when the gang finally storm the bar the men have vanished: the gang and the audience are deprived of the anticipated queer-bashing climax; the audience is made painfully aware of its investment in generic conventions. To make a final political point, Julien ends the film with documentary footage of a jazz television programme featuring Hughes, reverting to the genre of documentary as a means of emphasising Julien's overall theme of how the black contribution to art has been kept firmly in its place over the years. For a moment, the music is the thing, and Hughes comments, 'Sun's a' risin'. This is gonna be my song'. But Julien's film has shown us much, much more about Langston's 'song', milieu and his relevance today.

Intertextuality is a major feature of both queer and postmodern film. Richard Kwietniowski's short film *Flames of Passion* (1989) is a homage to *Brief Encounter* (1945), Noël Coward's classic story of the emotional turmoil wrought by the prospect of an extra-marital affair between Laura, an ordinary middle-class housewife, and Alec, a doctor she meets on a railway platform in the late 1930s. The film has long been a gay classic, even though its protagonists are heterosexual, because of its suitability for queer readings which easily translate Laura's predicament to a gay context, particularly the way she is torn between her safe homelife and the lure of romance and how she has to keep her meetings with Alec secret. The secrecy, danger and sense of shame expressed in *Brief Encounter* strike particular chords of recognition for gays and lesbians. *Flames of Passion*, named after the film Laura and Alec walk out of on one of their Thursday meetings, updates the story and makes the leading protagonists male. The cinematography pays direct homage to *Brief Encounter*: the use of black and white, canted camera angles and images reflected in windows. The sense of danger and emotional turmoil is not so great and the couple end up together. Interestingly, *Flames of Passion* is silent, with a distinctive soundtrack of contemporary music, a decision which comments indirectly on the role of language in *Brief Encounter* which often comes across as limiting, class-bound and unable to express emotion as adequately as the evocative Rachmaninov concerto chosen by David Lean for *Brief Encounter*.

As well as intertextuality, the notion of gender performance and its subversion, labelled 'genderfuck' by June Reich, pervades new queer cinema.[9] Dangerous To Know's 1994 film about British lesbian photographer Tessa Boffin is a good example. One segment deals with her set of photographs entitled 'The Knight's Move'. It begins with a mystery established by the title:

Somewhere in a cemetery
Down a dark pathway
I stumble across your photographs.
Where is my knight
My knave
My angel
My casanova
My lady-in-waiting?

I could hardly find you
In my history books
But now in this scene
You all come together.

The photographs take familiar images of knights, classical male and female poses and make them strange by introducing androgynous figures, two of whom are holding placards featuring the names of famous lesbians in history. At the end they gather together, united in their desire to shatter previous codes of patriarchal representation.[10]

Plate 8.4 Intertextual borrowings. Laura (Celia Johnson) in *Brief Encounter* (1945). Compare with Plate 8.5. (Courtesy of Rank Film Distributors)

Plate 8.5 Johnson (Richard Seymour) in *Flames of Passion* (1989). (Courtesy of the British Film Institute)

Conclusion

This image is a fitting one on which to end a survey of independent and experimental art cinema. Many British film-makers have made familiar images strange, encouraging audiences to participate in the production of their meaning. The notion of 'Queer Cinema' has continued, even though commentators in recent years note its incorporation into much of mainstream production (Stacey and Street, 2007: 6). Yet these films do not always problematise stereotypical images of queer sexuality, nor do they seek to generate the formal experimentation that has been associated with New Queer Cinema. An example of this would be *Notes On a Scandal* (Richard Eyre, 2006), a film which pathologises the attraction of an older school teacher (played by Judi Dench) for a younger colleague (played by Cate Blanchett). The 'mainstreaming' of queer work has arguably had the effect of reducing the impact of queer festival work, or of work that is produced outside conventional structures. As we have seen, of crucial importance is funding for such films. The extent and degree of counter-cinematic work has depended in good part on funding available to film-makers who seek to operate outside the structures of the mainstream industry. Against these odds, their work has produced formal and thematic precedents which suggest the contours of a cinema which is diverse, experimental, profoundly intertextual and political: not to be stumbled across but given a prominent place in British cinema history books.

Conclusion

The British film industry has produced a rich and varied corpus of films throughout the twentieth century and continues to do so into the twenty-first. But the 'last machine' was not always as efficient as many would have liked, its problems being as notorious as its cinematic milestones. In conclusion, I would like to isolate five particular themes which have had a profound influence on British cinema, explaining some of its peculiarities, the specifics of a cinema which can be described as British. These themes are: Hollywood's economic and aesthetic prominence; Britain's weak production base; the stylistic and thematic variety of British cinema; the importance of class and gender; and, finally, film culture.

The extent of American influence has been mentioned many times in this book and it is more or less impossible to think of British cinema without reference to its relationship with Hollywood. At different times this has varied from being mutually supportive to antagonistic, with the government taking a consistently ambivalent attitude towards the extent to which Anglo-American collaboration is necessary for the encouragement of the British industry. As we have seen from Chapter 1, economic domination was established from an early stage, the world marvelling at how well the vertically integrated structure of the American film industry minimised the risks involved in film production. Britain's industry consolidated in the late 1920s, fifteen years or so behind Hollywood, a time lag which had significant consequences. The impact on production was profound. The exhibition sector was capitalised to a far higher degree than production, which lurched from boom to crisis without a stable infrastructure. This affected budgets, market projection, stars and even popularity. The charge that British films were shoddy and unprofessional provides ample evidence of prevailing standards of quality being identified primarily with Hollywood. It was considered to be an important goal for a production company to own cinemas, as Rank's example demonstrates, but even then it was extremely difficult to finance British films when for most of the century the market was dominated by American films. Nevertheless, Rank and independent producers succeeded in gaining a small foothold which has been more secure in some decades, for example, the 1940s and the 1960s, than during others. And as Chapter 6, on stardom, demonstrates, British films and stars have been popular at the box office on many occasions.

In aesthetic terms, American genre cinema exercised a profound influence over British film style, particularly as far as films for the export market were concerned. But even domestically oriented films like *Sing As We Go* (1934), which diverges from classical Hollywood cinema in significant ways, nevertheless displays some affinities. Hollywood's international style and approach ranged from narrative and continuity principles to the centrality of the studio system and its stars. It also served as an oppositional focus for British directors who worked in the counter-cinematic tradition. As well as Hollywood, the importance of European and Soviet influences on British cinema should not be underestimated.[1] The success of many British films which did not look as if they were American, or cost as much, indicates that Hollywood did not entirely call the shots. Except for a few notorious big-budget British films, including *The Private Life of Henry VIII* (1933), *Henry V* (1944), *Caesar and Cleopatra* (1945), *Raise the Titanic* (1980) and *Revolution* (1986), the budgets of British films were lower than their Hollywood counterparts. *Trainspotting* (1996) cost its backers, Channel 4, only £1.7 million, a figure soon exceeded in pre-sales. *Four Weddings and a Funeral* (1994) cost only £2 million but was the top film at the British box office in 1994, earning £27,762,648 (*BFI Handbook*, 1996: 37).

The chapters on genre and art cinema have illustrated the great variety of British film-making. Although there have been discernible trends, it would appear that there is no such thing as a typical British film. The range of representations has been diverse, particularly as far as Britishness is concerned, although in particular periods certain representations have been more striking than in others. During the Second World War, the dominant articulation was of a united community at war against fascism. In other periods, however, there has been a multitude of styles, genres and representations competing for the audience's attention, for example the simultaneous existence of *Carry On . . .*, Hammer horror films and social-problem films in the 1950s. Similarly in the 1980s, the cinematic backdrop to Thatcherism was punctuated by films which dealt with extremely different versions of Britishness: *The Ploughman's Lunch* (1983), *Local Hero* (1983), *My Beautiful Launderette* (1985), *Maurice* (1987), *Withnail and I* (1988) and *High Hopes* (1989), to name a few striking examples. The issue of national identity can pervade a film which is not even set in Britain: Roeg's *The Man Who Fell To Earth* (1976) uses David Bowie's British star persona as a way of critiquing American capitalism, even though he plays an alien who has landed in America and who happens to speak with a London accent. Not all British films are therefore overtly concerned with questions of national identity, the expression of which will be evident according to readings which choose to privilege Britishness.

Class and gender have had a significant impact on British films. Raymond Durgnat studied the years 1945–58 as 'a climax period of a middle-class cinema with its intimations of controversy and its premonitions of decline' (1970: 1). Such an analysis can also be applied to the years before 1945 and after 1958. The operation of the class system has preoccupied many film-makers, a fascination which extends from *Squibs* to Losey and on to heritage films. As we have seen, however, the class issues which pervade many British films do so in different and conflicting ways. A film may well be made by a middle-class team and be seen to reflect their beliefs – for example Ealing comedies or the 1960s New Wave films – but, as with national identity, readings which concentrate on class can detect contradictions, unspoken assumptions and, by implication, exclusions which contribute to a cultural critique of class. That for much of the century there was a social distinction between audiences (primarily working class) and film-makers (primarily middle class), lends credence to the possibility of readings against the grain which are not purely the province of film scholars.

There have been very few women directors in Britain, a gender bias which has exercised an undoubted influence on British cinema. The exceptions are Muriel and Betty Box, Jill Craigie, Kay Mander, Wendy Toye, Sally Potter and Lynne Ramsay.[2] There is no doubt that the majority of cinematic representations of the feminine have been articulated from a textual standpoint of masculinist anxiety, through which feminine spectators must chart their course. Of course, input from women does not necessarily mean that the female point of view will predominate, or that feminist issues will be foregrounded, but as we have seen from the example of Gainsborough's historical costume films, women's contribution to scripts and costume design were often key ingredients in securing their popularity with female audiences. In their different ways, particular stars have also contributed to a more complex characterisation of gender issues, including Jessie Matthews, Anna Neagle and particularly Diana Dors. Sally Potter's early films grappled directly with the idea of dominant cinema as a masculine construct and began to explore what an alternative, feminist cinema might look like. The tendency in many recent films to collapse gender boundaries altogether is perhaps a development towards the depoliticisation of gender. As Harper shows, the history of women both on screen and in the studios is a fascinating story of exclusion, containment and, at times, downright discrimination. Michael Balcon, for example, claimed that women could not direct, a view plainly contradicted by the evidence of the careers of Muriel Box, Wendy Toye, Sally Potter and Lynne Ramsay. Women have also made significant contributions to screenwriting, art direction and costume design (Harper, 2000).

The last area I want to touch on is film culture: the power of film criticism which has elaborated particular myths which have become entrenched, influencing both scholarly and, to a more limited extent, popular conceptions about British cinema. Charles Barr (1986) has described how for many years Britain was marginalised from film history and criticism, thereby giving tacit approval to the opinion, also held by respected film-makers like François Truffaut and Satyajit Ray, that apart from a few isolated exceptions British films were not particularly interesting or worthy of study. In the 1980s and 1990s this situation has been in most part rectified, with journals like *Screen* and *Sight and Sound* giving serious attention to questions of British cinema. The *Journal of British Cinema and Television* (and its precursor the *Journal of Popular British Cinema*) is also an important academic initiative since the late 1990s as the first journal devoted specifically to the subject of British cinema and television. In the past twenty-five years or so, some key books and articles have been written, particularly those which challenge long-held notions of British cinema being solely about 'quality' and 'realism' rather than *cinema* (see especially Barr, ibid.; Landy, 1991; Murphy, 1989 and 1992; Higson, 1995 and 2003; Sargeant, 2005 among others).

The centenary of cinema was celebrated by a plethora of conferences, exhibitions, screenings and publications. It was easy to bask in their inevitable retro qualities, laced with nostalgia for our favourite films and fascinated about the moment when mass cinematic consciousness was born. But, like the pioneers of cinema, we are now into a new century, new technologies, new media, new imaginings. Cinema may well have been the 'last machine' of Victorian invention, but its scope and usage have far exceeded the limits of that description. Cinema is now only one screen format among many which will continue to communicate images which contribute to our understanding of the complex and diverse experience of being British.

Notes

1 THE FISCAL POLITICS OF FILM

1 American experimental film-maker Hollis Frampton wrote in 1971 of cinema as 'The Last Machine', a title used by Ian Christie for his 1995 BBC series on early cinema.

2 The 'institutional mode of representation' is Noël Burch's description of early films based on editing principles determined by continuity, an unobtrusive camera style, linear narratives with a clear sense of closure at the end and featuring goal-oriented characters who operate within a fictional world governed by regimes of verisimilitude: 'a stable system with its own inherent logic and durability' (Burch, 1990: 220). This was the basis for Bordwell, Staiger and Thompson's concept of 'classical Hollywood cinema' (1985).

3 Although this did not entirely replace the open market system: in 1914 400 films were released via exclusive contracts as opposed to 6,648 which were available on the open market (this figure is high because it includes serials, topicals and shorts whereas most films available via exclusive contracts were longer features). Gradually the exclusive system dominated: 'for commercial reasons it was obvious that the distributors of the films had to adopt the "exclusive" system and with it the hierarchy of first and subsequent run cinemas, for this system was more profitable' (PEP, 1952: 28).

4 The Lend-Lease Act had been passed by the US Congress in March 1941, authorising the President to lease or lend equipment to any nation 'whose defense the President deems vital to the defense of the United States'. The second Anglo-American Film Agreement and the decision to release blocked funds was, therefore, inextricably bound up with the need to maintain Lend-Lease support.

5 Entertainments Tax was paid by exhibitors. It was abolished in 1960 after many campaigns organised by the Cinematograph Exhibitors' Association, who had vigorously opposed the tax from its inception in 1916.

6 An independent producer was one who had no direct financial link with the combines. Michael Balcon had founded Gainsborough Pictures in 1928 and went on to work for Gaumont-British in 1931 and MGM-British in 1936. His concern for the independent producer and for distinctively 'British' films developed after he headed Ealing Studios from 1937. In the 1950s Balcon advised the NFFC and in 1964 became Chairman of British Lion. He published an autobiography in 1969.

7 The divorcement decrees of 1948, arising from an anti-trust suit against Paramount, required the US majors to separate their exhibition holdings from

production and distribution. In Britain there were many reports after Palache: the Plant Committee, 1949, *Distribution and Exhibition of Cinematograph Films*, Cmd. 7839; the *Report on the Supply of Films for Exhibition in Cinemas* (Monopolies Commission), HC, 206, 1966–67; and the Monopolies Commission reports of 1983, 1993 and 1995 – all these continued to present evidence about the power of the combines, but very few of their recommendations were enacted.

8   A comment made by Robert Boothby during a speech in the House of Commons, 6 November 1945, on the dollar problem: 'If I am compelled to choose between Bogart and bacon I am bound to choose bacon at the present time.'

9   The value of the commodity (film) for the calculation of the duty was one quarter of its gross value. The duty was then set at three times its dutiable value.

10 Several Rank films were doing well in 1947. The American trade paper *Variety* reported on 23 April that 'J. Arthur Rank is rapidly winning the Anglo-American sweepstakes for foreign theatres, and the results to date have Yank film execs fretting and worried'.

11 The Marshall Plan was a $17,000 million aid programme to assist European post-war economic recovery. It was administered from 1948 by the Organisation for European Economic Cooperation.

12 British Lion was incorporated as a production company in 1927, branching out into distribution in 1930 which was its main activity until 1946 when Korda's London Film Productions acquired a controlling interest in British Lion and British Lion Studios, owner of Shepperton Studios. Filippo del Guidice was an Italian banker and lawyer who had co-founded Two Cities Films in 1937. Two Cities produced several of the most prestigious British films in the 1940s, including *In Which We Serve*, *This Happy Breed*, *The Way Ahead*, *Henry V*, *Blithe Spirit* and *Odd Man Out*. When the NFFC was being planned in 1948, del Guidice was in dispute with Rank which had financed some of the films produced by Two Cities. He went on to form a new independent production company, Pilgrim, which soon ran into trouble with Korda and British Lion. For fuller details on the evolution of the NFFC see Dickinson and Street, 1985: 211–19.

13 These were 'alignment' and 'minimum exhibition periods'. The abolition of alignment meant that in the same location MGM Cinemas and Odeon could offer films to *both* circuits, not just to their aligned circuit. To free some screen-time for independent films the Committee recommended the reduction of minimum exhibition periods of new releases.

14 In 1969 the BFI Production Board was the successor organisation to the Experimental Film Fund established by Michael Balcon in 1952. It has part-funded several significant low-budget features including *Distant Voices, Still Lives* (1988).

15 Goldcrest was established as a film development company in 1976 by banker Jake Eberts. The company expanded, with a capital base of £26 million in 1983, but ran into financial difficulties in the late 1980s. Handmade was established in 1978 by George Harrison and Euroatlantic to make Monty Python films. Palace started out as a video retail outlet in 1980 and then ventured into film distribution and, to a lesser extent, production. The record company, Virgin, began financing films in the early 1980s. By the end of the decade their involvement declined dramatically and by 1996 it had completely ceased. Working Title produced pop promos before entering the film world.

16 According to this deal BSkyB provided 8 per cent of the budget for each film invested in by British Screen and the European Co-production Fund in exchange for UK pay-television rights.

17 The Fourth Circuit was another major cinema circuit in addition to Odeon, Gaumont-British and ABC. For details on it see the PEP report, 1952: 154–56. In 1950 Lord Reith proposed a scheme whereby the NFFC would extend its functions and operate in conjunction with a distribution company and state-owned studios. The Board of Trade was not impressed. R. G. Somervell wrote a memorandum to Harold Wilson on 8 March 1950: 'To my mind Lord Reith's proposals would involve the nationalisation of the industry. I think that this would be fatal to the future of British films' (BT 64/4519).

2 STUDIOS, DIRECTORS AND GENRES

1 Steve Neale (1980) has theorised genre, arguing that successful genre films depend on a dynamic process which draws on recognisable generic conventions (repetition) and more novel elements (difference). Marketing techniques will exploit both familiar associations and newer characteristics in a process known as intertextual relay, encouraging audiences to appreciate a film as a multi-referenced text. Hybrid films are those in which the conventions of several genres appear to be in operation.

2 Rank's production centre was Pinewood Studios, opened in 1936, and ABPC operated from British National Studios at Elstree.

3 The central-producer system involved creating specialised departments and a separation of the function of director and producer. The producer exercised a great degree of management control as described by Bordwell, Staiger and Thompson, 1985: 134–37. It is important to note that the British studios are only approximate variations on the Hollywood model. More research is needed on the working practices of individual British studios.

4 The work of Powell and Pressburger is discussed in Chapter 5. John and Roy Boulting were involved in independent film-making as producers and directors from 1937. Their most notable films were *Fame is the Spur* (1946), *Brighton Rock* (1947) and *I'm All Right Jack* (1959). In 1942 Frank Launder and Sidney Gilliat founded a production company, Individual Pictures. They were either both, or individually, involved in many key British films including *Millions Like Us* (1943), *Green For Danger* (1946), *The Happiest Days of Your Life* (1950) and the popular St Trinian's series.

5 Georges Méliès was an early French film-maker who specialised in fantasy and trick films.

6 Consensus politics involve a defence of the status quo, a desire to put up with social and economic inequalities in pursuit of a middle way. In the 1930s, Britain was governed by a National Government, a Conservative-dominated coalition.

7 'Excess' refers to elements of narrative which cannot be contained by a 'preferred reading'. For example, although the narrative thrust of a film might indicate closure, the elements previously introduced, or discourses which can be derived from *mise-en-scène* analyses (e.g. costume) might nevertheless contradict the finality of that closure.

8 The Abdication Crisis of December 1936 was when King Edward VIII was forced to abdicate his position as King because he wanted to marry Wallis Simpson, an American divorcee. Prime Minister Stanley Baldwin and his Cabinet believed that marriage to a divorced woman was inconsistent with the King's role as Supreme Governor of the Church of England. Rather than give Mrs Simpson up, Edward VIII chose to abdicate, marry her and live in exile in France. He was subsequently created Duke of Windsor by his successor, George VI.

9 In 1918 the vote was given to women aged over thirty and in 1928 the minimum age was lowered to twenty-one.

10 *First a Girl* was a remake of the German film *Viktor und Viktoria* (1934).

11 'Potteresque' refers to the style of television drama utilised by British writer Dennis Potter who explored the boundaries of genre in films like *The Singing Detective* (1987). Many of his films included music, flashbacks, fragmented narratives and disturbing content.

12 Fields married Monty Banks, an Italian comedian and director and lived in America in the early war years. She returned to Britain in 1941, but never regained her former popularity.

13 See my comments earlier in this chapter on 'preferred' versus 'resistant' readings which draw on notions of 'textual excess'.

3 GENRES FROM AUSTERITY TO AFFLUENCE

1 The Suez crisis was instigated by the nationalisation of the Suez Canal Company by President Nasser of Egypt in July 1956. This move was fiercely opposed by the British and French who had shares in the canal, which was of acute strategic importance. At the same time, military conflict between Israel and Egypt was brewing and when Nasser rejected an Anglo-French ultimatum to halt military operations, the British and French attacked Egyptian bases. Many thought this was extremely heavy-handed and the combination of diplomatic and economic pressure from America led to the withdrawal of British and French troops. The crisis highlighted the decline of British and French influence in international politics. The Cold War refers to post-war conflict between the Western Powers, led by America, and the Eastern European bloc.

2 The term Teddy Boys is derived from the Edwardian style of the clothes they wore.

3 John Hill (1986: 13) discusses the 'moral panic' about teenagers in the 1950s, particularly the links between concern about youth, race and violence.

4 Spivs were people who illegally procured and sold at a profit goods which were scarce in the years of post-war austerity and rationing; they were also referred to as people who ran the black market or simply as racketeers. The subgenre of spiv movies will be discussed below.

5 This feature is discussed, largely in relation to the Hollywood melodrama, by Steve Neale in his article 'Melodrama and Tears' (1986).

6 The Campaign for Nuclear Disarmament, led by philosopher Bertrand Russell and Canon L. John Collins, called for nuclear weapons to be abandoned and for a reduction in British defence spending. The CND drew many supporters, particularly during the years 1958–64.

7 Harold Wilson's electoral success in 1964 ended a long period of Conservative government. He won the election by presenting himself and the Labour Party as efficient and forward-thinking promoters of technology.

8 Harold Wilson (1916–95) was from Huddersfield and went to Oxford University. He was President of the Board of Trade from 1947 to 1951 where he was involved in shaping film policy (see Chapter 1). He first became a Member of Parliament in 1945 and was Prime Minister 1964–70 and 1974–76.

9 See Arthur Marwick (1996: 165) who charts these confused and often contradictary features of the 1960s.

10 Terry Lovell (1990) has discussed how the centrality of female characters in *A Taste of Honey* and its maternal discourses were rare among New Wave films.

11 See also a consideration of *Blow-Up* and *Performance* in Chapter 7.

12 The Profumo affair concerned the relationship between War Minister John Profumo and a call-girl, Christine Keeler, who was allegedly also involved with a Soviet naval attaché. In March 1963 Profumo denied the allegations, but later admitted he had 'misled' the House of Commons and resigned. Although it was later proved that national security had not been endangered, the affair was a blow to the image of the Conservative government.

13 See further discussion of Terence Davies in Chapter 7.

4 GENRES IN TRANSITION, 1970s TO 1990s

1 'The Troubles' refers to the historic conflict in Northern Ireland (which is part of the United Kingdom) between Ulster Unionists (Protestants) who wish to remain part of the UK and the Irish Republican Army and their supporters (Catholics) who want a united Ireland. Bombings and violence between the two factions resulted in British troops being sent to Northern Ireland in 1969, a move which exacerbated the situation considerably.

2 Germaine Greer's *The Female Eunuch* had been published in 1970, announcing itself as an aspect of the second feminist wave, the first being the suffragette campaigns of the early twentieth century.

3 Thatcherism refers to the policies which were put into operation under Margaret Thatcher's period as Prime Minister, 1979–90. Broadly summarised, these involved a doctrinaire assertion of the market economy; the contraction of the public sector; fiercely nationalistic policies; opposition to links with Europe; and the assertion of traditional Victorian family values. See further discussion of Thatcherism in the section on the 1980s.

4 Ron and Reggie Kray were twin brothers who were gangsters in London's East End during the 1950s and 1960s.

5 'The British are coming!' was a comment made by the writer of *Chariots of Fire*, Colin Welland, at the Oscar ceremony in 1982 when the film won the Best Picture award.

6 The Falklands Crisis of 1982 was a period of ten weeks of undeclared war between Britain and Argentina who both claimed sovereignty over the British colony. Britain sent a task force of warships and forced the Argentinian forces to surrender.

7 A Ministry of Defence official, Clive Ponting, was prosecuted when he leaked information during the Falklands Crisis, revealing that the British had torpedoed the *General Belgrano*, killing 368 Argentinian seamen. The 1982 Conservative Party Conference exploited the immediate post-Falklands context to the full. The Party's public-relations advisers were determined to whip up as much nationalist fervour as possible, staging Margaret Thatcher's arrival on the platform to coincide with the singing of a strident British anthem, 'Land of Hope and Glory'.

8 Although an Irish-British-American co-production, *In the Name of the Father* (1993) is an exception as a political film exposing British hypocrisy and the corruption of the criminal justice system in its treatment of the wrongful conviction of 'the Guildford Four' who were accused of bombing a London pub in 1974.

9 There have been one or two horror films since *The Company of Wolves* including *Hellraiser* (Clive Barker, 1987) and *Dream Demon* (Harley Cokliss, 1988), but they do not draw so much on traditions of Gothic horror. Terry Gilliam's *Twelve Monkeys* (1996), a time-travel thriller registered as an American film, has been compared to *Brazil*: see *Sight and Sound*, April 1996: 56.

10 *Sense and Sensibility* is registered as British, but in many respects is an international production with an American executive producer (Sydney Pollack) and an American-Taiwanese director (Ang Lee). Emma Thompson's screen-play (for which she won an Academy Award) is based on Jane Austen's quintessentially English novel and the majority of the cast are British actors.

5   CONTEMPORARY BRITISH CINEMA

1 Although Linda Williams (1983) argues that women recognise a similarity between themselves and the monster in horror, both constituting a threat to conventional male power.
2 See Richard Dyer's entry in Ginette Vincendeau (ed.), *Encyclopaedia of European Cinema*: 204–5.

6   ACTING AND STARS

1 The music-hall was an Edwardian theatre where variety acts, musical entertainment and circus acts were performed.
2 Duncan Petrie argues that, typically, British cinema and television are informed by words not images (Petrie, 1991: 161–64).
3 As Thomas Elsaesser has perceptively commented, the historic relationship between film, television and the theatre is a complex one, and not necessarily negative:

> Stylistically, the weaknesses of the British cinema are intimately connected with its strengths: the close alliance with the theatre – whether one thinks of acting, writing or directing – and now the quite inextricable dependence of both theatre and cinema on television, which of course is mutual and a three-way relationship.

See Thomas Elsaesser, 1984: 267–68.
4 A highly popular form in the nineteenth century. The plays were mostly tales of good vs. evil, heroes and virtuous women vs. fallen women and villains. Acting style was exaggerated, and the staging spectacular.
5 I am grateful to Christine Gledhill for this example from an unpublished paper given to the conference *Moving Performance: The British Experience of Early Cinema*, January 1996, University of Bristol.
6 Barry Salt's *Film Style and Technology* (1983) does not comment on Low's observation.
7 See Stevenson and Cook (1977), and for an interesting critique of their account of the 1930s see Howkins and Saville in *Socialist Register*, 1979. The issue of consensus is also addressed in the chapter on genre.
8 Detailed work on Gracie Fields has not been done in this context, but for a similar approach on how audiences used star images for their own ends, see Stacey (1993).
9 But see Richard Dyer's interesting comments on British restraint in *Brief Encounter*: 'it is common to characterise this way with emotions as inhibited or even emotionless. The English are cold fish with stiff upper lips. Yet this is to mistake restraint for repression and lack of expression for lack of feeling' (Dyer, 1993b: 66).
10 See reports in *Picturegoer* and tables of the most popular feature films at the British box office, 1945–60 in Thumim (1991: 258–59).

11 Landy (1991) is the first book to apply generic analysis to British films. See also Sue Harper's work.
12 For two different approaches to *Victoria the Great* see Harper (1992) and Landy (1991: 68–70).
13 I am indebted to Josie Dolan for allowing me to read a draft of her unpublished thesis for the University of Lancaster, 'National Heroines: Constructing Femininity, Representing the Past in Popular Film and Literature, 1930–55'.
14 See previous reference to the divorcement decrees: Chapter 1, note 7.
15 See, for example, Nina Hibbin (1981: 1122).
16 See Hill (1986) and qualifying remarks by Murphy (1992).
17 See box-office surveys published every December by *Kinematograph Weekly*, which became *Cinema TV Today* in 1971 and thereafter merged into *Screen International*. These reveal a market still dominated by American films, the biggest successes being *The Sound of Music* and other musicals. James Bond films were the most successful British films in the 1960s.
18 Janet Thumim's study of films of the period has shown that

> women in these sixties films, with the important exceptions of Marnie (Tippi Hedren) and Mary Poppins (Julie Andrews) are most notable for their absence. When they do appear on screen, in *Tom Jones*, *Goldfinger* and *Summer Holiday*, for example, it is always and only to partner the primary, male characters or to motivate narrative events which centre on male characters.
>
> (Thumim, 1992: 77)

But also see Robert Murphy's comment that in the social problem films, at least, 'these incandescently intense women have a seriousness, an emotional weight, altogether lacking in the pathetically trivial roles women had to play in most 1950s British films' (Murphy 1992: 33).
19 Connery had done a considerable amount of acting before Bond. He had appeared with Anna Neagle in a stage production of 'Sixty Glorious Years' in Edinburgh. Geoffrey Macnab has commented on this interesting collaboration:

> The fustian matriarch of British cinema, cast by her husband Herbert Wilcox as Edith Cavell or Queen Victoria in a string of tasteful, patriotic middlebrow pot-boilers, made a neat foil for Connery, who, as Bond, would represent an altogether different (but arguably complementary) kind of Englishness. Bond was the renegade kind of adventurer, the man who would be king, on whose shoulders Queen Vic's empire was built.
>
> (1992: 33)

20 Although it must be noted that the film was bound to do well in Britain and it was a relatively cheap film to produce.
21 Mitchell appeared in social problem films in the 1950s, including *Turn the Key Softly* (Jack Lee, 1953), *Yield To the Night* (J. Lee Thompson, 1956), *Woman In a Dressing Gown* (J. Lee Thompson, 1957) and *Sapphire* (Basil Dearden, 1959). In the late 1960s and early 1970s her screen roles were confined to horror films.
22 This diffidence sometimes applied in Hollywood with stars like Grace Kelly who were associated with a regal, high-class image.

8   BORDERLINES II: COUNTER-CINEMA AND INDEPENDENCE

1 French theorist Jacques Lacan contributed to psychoanalytic theory in the late 1960s and 1970s by developing Freudian ideas concerning the early development

of male children and their subjectivity. The 'mirror' phase concerns a child aged 6–18 months and the illusion of unity with his own image in a mirror and also his identification with his mother. This impression of unity is known as the *imaginary order* which is shattered when the child experiences the *Oedipal crisis* which is a major cornerstone of Freudian theory. During this crisis the child becomes aware of his own difference, split-subjectivity, and eventually submits to the *law of the father*, otherwise known as the *symbolic order*, which teaches him that the male is dominant in society and to obtain the power held by his father, he must break with all thoughts of unity with his mother. Because the female does not possess the phallus she is associated with 'lack', reminding men of how they would be disempowered without patriarchy. Once living according to the symbolic order, however, a child remembers the pleasures of the imaginary order and seeks in several forms (including cinema) *ego ideals* which correspond to the memory of the illusion of unity in the pre-Oedipal phase. For further detail on all these concepts see Elizabeth Wright (ed.) (1992) *Feminism and Psychoanalysis: a Critical Dictionary*, Oxford: Blackwell.

2 I am using the terminology suggested by E. Ann Kaplan in *Women and Film: Both Sides of the Camera* (1983) which discusses *Thriller* in Chapter 10.

3 It is useful to remember here that in *Psycho* Marion Crane has stolen money which a rich man intends to put in the bank for safe-keeping until he needs to buy a wedding present for his daughter. Marion's transgression is therefore signalled as being against patriarchy.

4 Patricia Mellencamp argues that in *The Gold Diggers* 'The film is a love story, and the love is lesbian. . . . The actresses are dressed as "femme" and "butch" – Christie as the Princess and Laffont as Prince Charming. The tale can be read as Ruby's coming out, or coming into lesbian consciousness' (Mellencamp, 1990: 162).

5 See Anderson's concept (1983) of 'imagined community' as discussed in the introduction to this book.

6 The Tolpuddle Martyrs were six rural Dorset labourers who were prosecuted for forming a branch of the Labourers' Union. They were transported to Australia in 1834 for seven years because they had been found guilty under an Act of 1797 which forbade the 'administering or taking of unlawful oaths'. Their case was an attempt by the government to curb the growth of trade unions.

7 The NFFC also contributed on the advice of Mamoun Hassan who had moved to the NFFC from the BFI. When he was the BFI's Head of Production, Hassan had persuaded the BFI to fund the first two parts of the Trilogy. His successor, Peter Sainsbury, oversaw the third which was similarly beset with problems.

8 Before the expansion of animation into the art school curriculum it was especially difficult to fund and distribute animated films. Even Rank's animation unit, which was run by an ex-Disney employee, had to close in 1950. For a brief history of British animation see Elaine Burrows (1996).

9 Reich (in Kader and Piontek, 1992: 125) argues that 'genderfuck' has

> the effect of unstable signifying practices in a libidinal economy of multiple sexualities. . . . This process is the destabilisation of gender as an analytical category, though it is not, necessarily, the signal of the end of gender. . . . The play of masculine and feminine on the body . . . subverts the possibility of possessing a unified subject position.

10 Stills from the film can be found in Boffin and Fraser, 1991: 42–50. The film is available on video from Dangerous to Know, 1994.

CONCLUSION

1 Duncan Petrie's *The British Cinematographer* (1996) shows the extent of European influence on British cinematography. Since the publication of the first edition of this book new research has unearthed more about British cinema's close connection with many other European styles and personnel. See Bergfelder, Harris and Street (2007).

2 Muriel Box was a leading screenwriter for Rank and in the 1950s she directed many films, including the successful *Simon and Laura* (1955). Her sister, Betty, headed Islington studios and later worked on the popular *Doctor* . . . series. Jill Craigie made documentaries in the Second World War; Kay Mander worked for the Shell Film Unit, formed a production company with her husband and made a documentary on housing for the Labour Party. Wendy Toye was a dancer who started film directing in the 1950s for Alexander Korda; one of her most notable films was a comedy, *Raising a Riot* (1955), starring Kenneth More. Sally Potter's career and films have been described in Chapter 6.

Bibliography

Adair, Gilbert (1985) 'The British Tradition', in Adair, Gilbert and Roddick, Nick (eds) *A Night at the Pictures: Ten Decades of British Film*, Kent: Columbus Books.

Aitken, Ian (1990) *Film and Reform: John Grierson and the Documentary Film Movement*, London: Routledge.

Aldgate, Anthony and Richards, Jeffrey (1983) *The Best of British: Cinema and Society, 1930–70*, Oxford: Blackwell.

Aldgate, Tony (1983) 'Comedy, Class and Containment: the British Domestic Cinema in the 1930s', in Curran, James and Porter, Vincent (eds) *British Cinema History*, London: Weidenfeld and Nicholson.

—— (1986) *Britain Can Take It: British Cinema in the Second World War*, Oxford: Blackwell.

Ambler, D. (1948), *Close-Up*. [journal]

Anderson, Benedict (1983) *Imagined Communities: Reflections on the Origins and Spread of Nationalism*, London: Verso.

Anstey, Edgar (1947) Review of the Film *Odd Man Out*, *Documentary Newsletter*, April–May.

Anthony, B. (1984) 'Music-Hall and Mirth-makers', in Lloyd, A. (ed.) with Robinson, David (consultant ed.) *Movies of the Silent Years*, London: Orbis.

Ashby, Justine and Higson, Andrew (eds) (2000) *British Cinema, Past and Present*, London: Routledge.

Aspinall, Sue (1983) 'Women, Realism and Reality in British Films, 1943–53', in Curran, James and Porter, Vincent (eds) *British Cinema History*, London: Weidenfeld and Nicholson.

—— and Murphy, Robert (eds) (1983) *Gainsborough Melodrama*, London: British Film Institute Dossier 18.

Balcon, Michael (1969) *Michael Balcon Presents: a Lifetime of Films*, London: Hutchinson.

Barr, Charles (1960) Review of the film *Saturday Night and Sunday Morning*, *Granta*, vol. LXIV, no. 1204.

—— (1977) *Ealing Studios*, London and Devon: Cameron and Tayleur, David and Charles.

—— (1986) 'Amnesia and Schizophrenia', in Barr, Charles (ed.) *All Our Yesterdays: 90 Years of British Cinema*, London: British Film Institute.

—— (1999) *English Hitchcock*, Moffat: Cameron and Hollis.

Bergfelder, Tim (1997) 'Surface and Distraction: Style and Genre in Gainsborough's International Trajectory in the 1920s and 1930s', in Cook, Pam (ed.) *Gainsborough Pictures*, London: Cassell.

Bergfelder, Tim, Harris, Sue and Street, Sarah (2007) *Film Architecture and the Transnational Imagination: Set Design in 1930s European Cinema*, Amsterdam: Amsterdam University Press.

Berry, David and Horrocks, Simon (eds) (1998), *David Lloyd George: the Movie Mystery*, Cardiff: University of Wales Press.

Betts, Ernest (1928) *Close-Up*, July, vol. 3, no. 1.

Bhabha, Homi (1990) 'DissemiNation', in Bhabha, Homi (ed.) *Nation and Narration*, London: Routledge.

—— (1994) *The Location of Culture*, London: Routledge.

Boffin, Tessa and Fraser, Jean (1991) *Stolen Glances*, London: Pandora.

Bordwell, David (1985) *Narration in the Fiction Film*, London: Methuen.

——, Staiger, Janet and Thompson, Kristin (1985) *The Classical Hollywood Cinema: Film Style and Mode of Production to 1960*, London: Routledge & Kegan Paul.

Braun, B. Vivian (1934) 'Film Art Manifesto', *Film Art*, Spring.

British Film Institute Film and Television Handbooks, 1991–2005, London: British Film Institute.

British Screen (1987) *Basic Information for Producers*, London: British Screen.

Brooks, Xan (1999) Review of *Human Traffic*, *Sight and Sound*, vol. 9, no. 6.

—— (2002) Review of *Morvern Callar*, *Sight and Sound*, vol. 12, no. 11.

Brown, Geoff (1986) '"Sister of the Stage": British Film and British Theatre', in Barr, Charles (ed.) *All Our Yesterdays*, London: British Film Institute.

Brunsdon, Charlotte (2007) *London in Cinema: the Cinematic City Since 1945*, London: British Film Institute.

Burch, Noël (1990) 'A Primitive Mode of Representation?', in Elsaesser, Thomas (ed.) *Early Cinema: Space, Frame, Narrative*, London: British Film Institute.

Burrows, Elaine (1986) 'Live Action: a Brief History of British Animation', in Barr, Charles (ed.) *All Our Yesterdays*, London: British Film Institute.

Burrows, Jon (2003) *Legitimate Cinema: Theatre Stars in Silent British Films, 1908–1918*, Exeter: University of Exeter Press.

Caughie, John (1992) 'Halfway to Paradise', *Sight and Sound*, vol. 2, no. 1.

Chanan, Michael (1990) 'Economic Conditions of Early Cinema', in Elsaesser, Thomas (ed.) *Early Cinema: Space, Frame, Narrative*, London: British Film Institute.

Chibnall, Steve (1998) *Making Mischief: the Cult Films of Pete Walker*, Guildford: FAB Press.

—— (2007) *Quota Quickies*, London: British Film Institute.

—— and Murphy, Robert (eds) (1999) *British Crime Cinema*, London: Routledge.

—— and Petley, Julian (eds) (2002) *British Horror Cinema*, London: Routledge.

Christie, Ian (1985) *Arrows of Desire*, London: Waterstone.

—— (1995) *The Last Machine: Early Cinema and the Birth of the Modern World*, London: British Film Institute/BBC.

Ciment, Michel (1985) *Conversations with Losey*, London: Methuen.

Conrich, Ian (2002) 'Horrific Films and 1930s British Cinema' in Chibnall, Steve and Petley, Julian (eds) *British Horror Cinema*, London: Routledge.

Cook, Chris and Stevenson, John (1979) *The Slump: Society and Politics during the Depression*, London: Jonathan Cape.

Cook, Pam (1996) *Fashioning the Nation: Costume and Identity in British Cinema*, London: British Film Institute.

Cox, Alex (2007) 'A Very British Cop-out', *The Guardian*, 15 August.

Dave, Paul (2006) *Visions of England: Class and Culture in Contemporary Cinema*, Oxford: Berg.

Diawawa, Martha (1993) 'Power and Territory: the Emergence of Black British Film Collectives', in Friedman, Lester (ed.) *British Cinema and Thatcherism*, London: University College of London Press.

Dick, Eddie, Noble, Andrew and Petrie, Duncan (eds) (1993) *Bill Douglas: a Magic Lanternist's Account*, London: British Film Institute/Scottish Film Council.

Dickinson, Margaret (ed.) (1999) *Rogue Reels: Oppositional Film in Britain, 1956–90*, London: British Film Institute.

—— and Street, Sarah (1985) *Cinema and State: the Film Industry and the British Government, 1927–84*, London: British Film Institute.

—— and Harvey, Sylvia (2005) 'Film Policy in the United Kingdom: New Labour at the Movies', *Political Quarterly*, vol. 76, no. 3, pp. 420–29.

Dixon, Wheeler Winston (1994) 'The Long Day Closes: an Interview with Terence Davies', in Dixon, Wheeler Winston (ed.) *Re-Viewing British Cinema, 1900–1992*, New York: SUNY.

Docherty, David, Morrison, David and Tracey, Michael (1987) *The Last Picture Show? Britain's Changing Film Audiences*, London: British Film Institute.

Dors, Diana (1950), 'They Made Me a Good Time Girl', *Picturegoer*, 7 October 1950.

Durgnat, Raymond (1970) *A Mirror for England: British Movies From Austerity to Affluence*, London: Faber.

Dusinberre, Deke (1976), 'St George in the Forest: the English Avant-garde', *After-image*, no. 6. Also printed in the Arts Council/British Council (1978), *A Perspective on English Avant-Garde Film* which includes Dusinberre's 'The Ascetic Task'.

—— (1980) 'The Avant-garde Attitude in the Thirties', in Macpherson, Don (ed.) *Traditions of Independence: British Cinema in the Thirties*, London: British Film Institute.

Dyer, Richard (1979) *Stars*, London: British Film Institute.

—— (1987) *Heavenly Bodies: Film Stars and Society*, London: Macmillan.

—— (1993a) '*Victim*: Hegemonic Project', in *The Matter of Images: Essays on Representation*, London: Routledge.

—— (1993b) *Brief Encounter*, London: British Film Institute.

Ebert, Roger (2003) Review of *Morvern Callar*, *Chicago-Sun Times*, 1 January 2003.

—— (2004) Review of *Young Adam*, *Chicago-Sun Times*, 30 April 2004.

Ehrenreich, B., Hess, E. and Jacobs, G. (1992) 'Beatlemania: Girls Just Want to Have Fun', in Lewis, Lisa A. (ed.) *The Adoring Audience: Fan Culture and Popular Media*, London: Routledge.

Ellis, John (1982) *Visible Fictions*, London: Routledge.

Elsaesser, Thomas (1984) 'Images for England', *Monthly Film Bulletin*, September 1984.

—— (1993) 'Images for Sale', in Friedman, Lester (ed.) *British Cinema and Thatcherism*, London: University College of London Press.

Finney, Albert (1994), 'Falling Stars', *Sight and Sound*, May, vol. 4, no. 5.

French, Philip (1995) Review of the film *The Englishman Who Went up a Hill and Came Down a Mountain, Observer Review*, 6 August.

Friedman, Lester (ed.) (1992) *Fires Were Started: British Cinema and Thatcherism*, London: University of London Press.

—— (1993) *British Cinema and Thatcherism*, London: University College of London Press.

—— and Stewart, Scott (1994) 'The Tradition of Independence: an Interview with Lindsay Anderson', in Dixon, Wheeler Winston (ed.) *Re-Viewing British Cinema, 1900–1992*, New York: SUNY.

Fuller, Graham (1996) 'Cautionary Tale', *Sight and Sound*, vol. 6, no. 3.

Geraghty, Christine (1986) 'Diana Dors', in Barr, Charles (ed.) *All Our Yesterdays*, London: British Film Institute.

—— (2000) *British Cinema in the Fifties: Gender, Genre and the New Look*, London: Routledge.

Gifford, Denis (1986) *The British Film Catalogue, 1895–1985*, London: David and Charles.

Glaessner, Veronica (1992) 'Fire and Ice', *Sight and Sound*, vol. 2, no. 4.

Gledhill, Christine (ed.) (1991) *Stardom: Industry of Desire*, London: Routledge.

—— (2003) *Reframing British Cinema 1918–28: Between Realism and Restraint*, London: British Film Institute.

—— and Swanson, Gillian (1984) 'Gender and Sexuality in the Second World War – a Feminist Approach', in Hurd, Geoff (ed.) *National Fictions*, London: British Film Institute.

Gomery, Douglas (1986) *The Hollywood Studio System*, London: British Film Institute.

Gunning, Tom (1990) 'The Cinema of Attractions: Early Film, its Spectator and the Avant-Garde', in Elsaesser, Thomas (ed.) *Early Cinema: Space, Frame, Narrative*, London: British Film Institute.

H. D. (1927) *Close-Up*, July, vol. 1, no. 1.

Hacker, Jonathan and Price, David (1991) *Take 10: Contemporary British Film Directors*, Oxford: Oxford University Press.

Hanson, Stuart (2007) '"Celluloid or Silicon?" Digital Cinema and the Future of Specialised Film Exhibition', *Journal of British Cinema and Television*, vol. 4, no. 2.

Harper, Sue (1987) 'Historical Pleasures: Gainsborough Costume Melodrama', in Gledhill, Christine (ed.) *Home Is Where the Heart Is: Studies in Melodrama and the Women's Film*, London: British Film Institute.

—— (1992) 'Studying Popular Taste: British Historical Films in the 1930s', in Dyer, Richard and Vincendeau, Ginette (eds) *Popular European Cinema*, London: Routledge.

—— (1994) *Picturing the Past: the Rise and Fall of the British Costume Film*, London: British Film Institute.

—— (2000) *Women in British Cinema: Mad, Bad and Dangerous to Know*, London: Continuum.

—— and Porter, Vincent (2003) *British Cinema in the 1950s: the Decline of Deference*, Oxford: Oxford University Press.

Harvey, Sylvia (1986) 'The "Other Cinema" in Britain: Unfinished Business in Oppositional and Independent Film, 1929–84', in Barr, Charles (ed.) *All Our Yesterdays*, London: British Film Institute.

Hebdige, Dick (1979) *Subculture: the Meaning of Style*, London: Methuen.

Hibbin, Nina (1981) 'British New Wave', in *The Movie*, vol. 5, chap. 57, London: Orbis.

Higson, Andrew (1984a) 'Five Films', in Hurd, Geoff (ed.) *National Fictions*, London: British Film Institute.

—— (1984b) 'Space, Place, Spectacle: Landscape and Townscape in the "Kitchen Sink" Film', *Screen*, July–October, vol. 25, nos. 4–5.

—— (1993) 'Re-Presenting the National Past: Nostalgia and Pastiche in the Heritage Film', in Friedman, Lester (ed.) *British Cinema and Thatcherism*, London: University College of London Press.

—— (1995) *Waving the Flag: Constructing a National Cinema in Britain*, Oxford: Oxford University Press.

—— (ed.) (1996) *Dissolving Views: Key Writings on British Cinema*, London: Cassell.

—— (2003) *English Heritage, English Cinema: Costume Drama Since 1980*, Oxford: Oxford University Press.

—— and Maltby, Richard (eds) (1999) *'Film Europe' and 'Film America': Cinema, Commerce and Cultural Exchange, 1920–1939*, Exeter: Exeter University Press.

Hill, John (1986) *Sex, Class and Realism: British Cinema 1956–63*, London: British Film Institute.

—— (1992) 'The Issue of National Cinema and British Film Production', in Petrie, Duncan (ed.) *New Questions of British Cinema*, London: British Film Institute.

—— (1999) *British Cinema in the 1980s*, Oxford: Clarendon, Oxford University Press.

—— (2006) 'British Cinema as National Cinema', in Vitali, Valentina and Willemen, Paul (eds) *Theorising National Cinema*, London: British Film Institute.

Hjort, Mette and Mackenzie, Scott (2000) *Cinema and Nation*, London: Routledge.

Hood, Stuart (1983) 'John Grierson and the Documentary Film Movement', in Curran, John and Porter, Vincent (eds) *British Cinema History*, London: Weidenfeld and Nicholson.

Howkins, Alan and Saville, John (1979) 'The Nineteen Thirties: a Revisionist History', *Socialist Register*.

Hunter, I. Q. (1999) *British Science Fiction Cinema*, London: Routledge.

Hurd, Geoff (ed.) (1984) *National Fictions*, London: British Film Institute.

Hutchings, Peter (1993) *Hammer and Beyond: the British Horror Film*, Manchester: Manchester University Press.

Jarman, Derek (1987) *The Last of England*, London: Constable.

Jarvie, Ian (1990) 'The Postwar Economic Foreign Policy of the American Film Industry: Europe 1945–50', *Film History*, vol. 4.

Johnston, Claire and Dawson, Jan (1969/70), 'Declarations of Independence', *Sight and Sound*, vol. 39, no. 1.

Johnston, Sheila (1985) 'Charioteers and Ploughmen', in Auty, Martyn and Roddick, Nick (eds) *British Cinema Now*, London: British Film Institute.

Jones, Stephen (1987) *The British Labour Movement and Film, 1918–1939*, London: Routledge & Kegan Paul.

Kader, C. and Piontek, T. (guest eds) (1992) 'Essays in Gay and Lesbian Studies', Special Issue of *Discourse*, vol. 15, no. 1.

Kaplan, E. Ann (1983) *Women and Film: Both Sides of the Camera*, London: Routledge.

—— (1992) *Motherhood and Representation: the Mother in Popular Culture and Melodrama*, London: Routledge.

Kolker, Robert Philip (1988) *A Cinema of Loneliness*, second edition, Oxford: Oxford University Press.

Kuhn, Annette (1980) 'British Documentary in the 1930s and "Independence": Recontextualising a Film Movement', in Macpherson, Don (ed.) *Traditions of Independence*, London: British Film Institute.

—— (1995) *Family Secrets: Acts of Memory and Imagination*, London: Verso.

—— (2002) *An Everyday Magic: Cinema and Cultural Memory*, London: I. B. Tauris.

Kulik, Karol (1975) *Alexander Korda, the Man Who Could Work Miracles*, London: Allen & Unwin.

Landy, Marcia (1991) *British Genres: Cinema and Society, 1930–1960*, Princeton, NJ: Princeton University Press.

Langley, Noel (1948) Article on Anna Neagle, *Close-Up*, February.

Lant, Antonia (1991) *Blackout: Reinventing Women for Wartime British Cinema*, Princeton, NJ: Princeton University Press.

Leigh, Jacob (2002) *The Cinema of Ken Loach*, London: Wallflower.

Leigh, Mike (2006) Interview, in *Sight and Sound* vol. 15, no. 1.

LeMahieu, D. L. (1988) *A Culture for Democracy: Mass Communication and the Cultivated Mind in Britain Between the Wars*, Oxford: Oxford University Press.

Lewis, Jane (1984) *Women in England, 1870–1950*, London: Harvester Wheatsheaf.

Light, Alison (1991a) 'Englishness', *Sight and Sound*, July, vol. 1, no. 3, p. 63.

—— (1991b) *Forever England: Femininity, Literature and Conservatism Between the Wars*, London: Routledge.

—— (1993) 'The Importance of Being Ordinary', *Sight and Sound*, vol. 3, no. 9, September.

Lovell, Terry (1990) 'Landscapes and Stories in 1960s British Realism', *Screen*, vol. 31, no. 4, Winter.

Low, Rachael (1949) *History of the British Film, 1906–1914*, London: Allen & Unwin.

—— (1950) *The History of the British Film, 1914–1918*, London: Allen & Unwin.

—— (1971) *The History of the British Film, 1918–1929*, London: Allen & Unwin.

—— and Manvell, Roger (1948) *History of the British Film, 1896–1906*, London: Allen & Unwin.

Lusted, David (1984) '"Builders" and "The Demi-Paradise"', in Hurd, Geoff (ed.) *National Fictions*, London: British Film Institute.

McFarlane, Brian (1986) 'A Literary Cinema: British Films and British Novels', in Barr, Charles (ed.) *All Our Yesterdays*, London: British Film Institute.

McIlroy, Brian (1993) 'The Repression of Communities: Visual Representations of Northern Ireland During the Thatcher Years', in Friedman, Lester (ed.) *British Cinema and Thatcherism*, London: University College of London Press.

Mackenzie, David (2003) Interview, in *Sight and Sound* interview, vol. 13, no. 9.

Macnab, Geoffrey (1992) 'Before Bond', *Sight and Sound*, vol. 2, no. 6.

—— (1993) *J. Arthur Rank and the British Film Industry*, London: Routledge.

—— (2000) 'Tribute to British Screen', *Moving Pictures*, October.

Macpherson, Kenneth (1927a) Editorial, *Close-Up*, July, vol. 1, no. 1.

—— (1927b) *Close-Up*, October, vol. 1, no. 4.

Malik, Sarita (1996) 'Beyond the Cinema of Duty', in Higson, Andrew (ed.) *Dissolving Views: Key Writings on British Cinema*, London: Cassell.

—— (2002) 'Money, Macpherson and Mind-Set', *Journal of Popular British Cinema*, vol. 5.

Marshall, N. (1931) 'Reflections on the English Film', *The Bookman*, October.

Marwick, Arthur (1990) (ed.) *British Society Since 1945*, second edition, London: Penguin.

—— (1996) (ed.) *British Society Since 1945*, third edition, London: Penguin.

Massey, Doreen (1993) 'A Global Sense of Place', in Grey, Ann and McGuigan, J. (eds) *Studying Culture*, London: Arnold.

Mather, N. (2006), *Tears of Laughter: Comedy-Drama in 1990s British Cinema*, Manchester: Manchester University Press.

Mathews, Tom D. (1994) *Censored*, London: Chatto & Windus.

Mayer, J. P. (1948) *British Cinemas and Their Audiences*, London: Dennis Dobson.

Medhurst, Andy (1984) '1950s War Films', in Hurd, Geoff (ed.) *National Fictions: World War Two in British Films and Television*, London: British Film Institute.

—— (1986a) 'Music Hall and British Cinema', in Barr, Charles (ed.) *All Our Yesterdays*, London: British Film Institute.

—— (1986b) 'Dirk Bogarde', in Barr, Charles (ed.) *All Our Yesterdays*, London: British Film Institute.

—— (1993) 'Embarrassment and Beyond', *Sight and Sound*, vol. 3, no. 11.

—— (1995) *The Observer Review*, 30 July.

Mellencamp, Patricia (1990) *Indiscretions: Avant-Garde Film, Video and Feminism*, Bloomington: Indiana University Press.

Miller, Laurence (1994) 'Evidence for a British *Film Noir* Cycle', in Dixon, Wheeler Winston (ed.) *Re-Viewing British Cinema, 1900–1992*, New York: SUNY.

Mitchie, Alastair (1986) 'Scotland: Strategies of Centralisation', in Barr, Charles (ed.) *All Our Yesterdays*, London: British Film Institute.

Monk, Claire (1996) Review of the film *Sense and Sensibility*, *Sight and Sound*, vol. 6, no. 3.

—— (2002a) 'The British Heritage-Film Debate', in Monk, Claire and Sargeant, Amy (eds) *British Historical Cinema*, London: Routledge.

—— (2002b) 'Underbelly UK: the 1990s Underclass Film, Masculinity and the Ideologies of "New" Britain', in Ashby, Justine and Higson, Andrew (eds) *British Cinema, Past and Present*, London: Routledge.

Montagu, Ivor (1975) 'Old Man's Trouble: Reflections on a Semi-Centenary', *Sight and Sound*, vol. 44, no. 4.

Mulvey, Laura (1975) 'Visual Pleasure and Narrative Cinema', *Screen*, vol. 13, no. 3.

Murphy, Robert (1983) 'Rank's Attempt on the American Market, 1944–49', in Curran, James and Porter, Vincent (eds) *British Cinema History*, London: Weidenfeld and Nicolson.

—— (1984) 'The Coming of Sound to the Cinema in Britain', *Historical Journal of Film, Radio and Television*, vol. 4, no. 2.

—— (1986) 'Riff-Raff: British Cinema and the Underworld', in Barr, Charles (ed.) *All Our Yesterdays*, London: British Film Institute.

—— (1989) *Realism and Tinsel: Cinema and Society, 1939–49*, London: Routledge.

—— (1992) *Sixties British Cinema*, London: British Film Institute.

Murray, Jonathan (2005) 'Kids in America? Narratives of Transatlantic Influence in 1990s Scottish Cinema', *Screen*, vol. 46, no. 5.

Neagle, Anna (1974) *There's Always Tomorrow*, London: W. H. Allen.

Neale, Steve (1980) *Genre*, London: British Film Institute.

—— (1986) 'Melodrama and Tears', *Screen*, vol. 27, no. 6.

Noble, Peter (ed.) (1950) *British Film Yearbook, 1949–50*.

Orr, John (1992) *Cinema and Modernity*, Cambridge: Polity Press.

Pearson, George (1957) *Flashback*, London: Allen & Unwin.

Perelli, Patricia (1983) 'A Statistical Survey of the British Film Industry', in Curran, James and Porter, Vincent (eds) *British Cinema History*, London: Weidenfeld and Nicholson.

Petley, Julian (1985) 'Reaching for the Stars', in Auty, Martin and Roddick, Nick (eds) *British Cinema Now*, London: British Film Institute.

—— (1986) 'The Lost Continent', in Barr, Charles (ed.) *All Our Yesterdays*, London: British Film Institute.

Petrie, Duncan (1991) *Creativity and Constraint in the British Film Industry*, London: Macmillan.

—— (ed.) (1993) *New Questions of British Cinema*, London: British Film Institute.

—— (1996) *The British Cinematographer*, London: British Film Institute.

—— (2000) *Screening Scotland*, London: British Film Institute.

Petrie, Graham (1985) *Hollywood Destinies: European Directors in America*, London: Croom Helm.

Pines, Jim and Willemen, Paul (1989) *Questions of Third Cinema*, London: British Film Institute.

Political and Economic Planning (1952), London: PEP.

Potamkin, Harry Alan (1929) Review of the film *Underground*, *Close-Up*, March, vol. 4, no. 3.

Powell, Michael (1986) *A Life in Movies*, London: Heinemann.

Pribram, E. Deidre (ed.) (1988) *Female Spectators: Looking at Film and Television*, London: Verso.

Rattigan, Neil (1994) 'The Last Gasp of the Middle Class: British War Films of the 1950s', in Dixon, Wheeler Winston (ed.) *Re-Viewing British Cinema, 1900–1994*, New York: SUNY.

Redfern, Nick (2007) 'Defining British Cinema: Transnational and Territorial Film Policy in the United Kingdom', *Journal of British Cinema and Television*, vol. 4, no. 1.

Rich, B. Ruby (1992) 'New Queer Cinema', *Sight and Sound*, vol. 2, no. 5.

Richards, Jeffrey (1984) *The Age of the Dream Palace*, London: Routledge & Kegan Paul.

Ritchie, Harry (1988) *Success Stories: Literature and the Media in England, 1950–1959*, London: Faber & Faber.

Roberts, Les (2002) '"Welcome to Dreamland": From Place to Non-Place and Back Again', *New Cinemas: Journal of Contemporary Film*, vol. 1, no. 2.

Robertson, James C. (1985) *The British Board of Film Censors: Film Censorship in Britain, 1896–1950*, London: Croom Helm.

Roddick, Nick (1995) '*Four Weddings* and a Final Reckoning', *Sight and Sound*, vol. 5, no. 1.

—— (2007) 'Almost Rosy: British Cinema Now', *Sight and Sound*, vol. 17, no. 1.

Rowson, Simon (1925) 'The Facts and Figures of the Film Industry', *Kinematograph Weekly*, 2 July.

—— (1936) 'A Statistical Survey of the Cinema Industry in Great Britain in 1934', *Journal of the Royal Statistical Society*, vol. XC1X, pt. 1.

Ryall, Tom (1986) *Alfred Hitchcock and the British Cinema*, London: Croom Helm.

Ryan, Trevor (1983) 'The New Road to Progress: the Use and Production of Films by the Labour Movement, 1929–39', in Curran, James and Porter, Vincent (eds) *British Cinema History*, London: Weidenfeld and Nicholson.

Ryans, Tony (1973/74) 'Reflected Light: Independent Avant-Garde Festival', *Sight and Sound*, vol. 43, no. 1.

Salt, Barry (1983) *Film Style and Technology: History and Analysis*, London: Starword.

Samson, Jen (1986) 'The Film Society, 1925–39', in Barr, Charles (ed.) *All Our Yesterdays*, London: British Film Institute.

Sanjek, David (1994) 'Twilight of the Monsters: the English Horror Film, 1968–75', in Dixon, Wheeler Winston (ed.) *Re-Viewing British Cinema, 1900–1992*, New York: SUNY.

Sargeant, Amy (2005) *British Cinema: a Critical History*, London: British Film Institute.

Seabury, William Marston (1926) *The Public and the Motion Picture Industry*, New York: Macmillan.

Sedgwick, John (1994) 'The Market for Feature Films in Britain, 1934: a Viable National Cinema', *Historical Journal of Film, Radio and Television*, vol. 14, no. 1.

—— (2000) *Popular Filmgoing in 1930s Britain: a Choice of Pleasures*, Exeter: Exeter University Press.

Shail, Robert (2007) *British Film Directors: a Critical Guide*, Edinburgh: Edinburgh University Press.

Sinfield, Alan (1989) *Literature, Politics and Culture in Post-War Britain*, Oxford: Blackwell.

Stacey, Jackie (1993) *Star-Gazing*, London: Routledge.

—— and Street, Sarah (eds) (2007), *Queer Screen: a Screen Reader*, London: Routledge.

Stanbrook, Alan (1984) 'When the Lease Runs Out', *Sight and Sound*, vol. 53, no. 3.

—— (1986) 'The Boys from Tiberias', *Sight and Sound*, vol. 55, no. 4.

Stanton, Gareth (2002) 'New Welsh Cinema as Postcolonial Cinema?', *Journal of Popular British Cinema*, no. 5.

Stevenson, John (1990) *British Society, 1914–45*, London: Penguin.

—— and Cook, Chris (1977) *The Slump: Society and Politics During the Depression*, London, Jonathan Cape.

Street, Sarah (1985) 'The Hays Office and the Defence of the British Market in the 1930s', *Historical Journal of Film, Radio and Television*, vol. 5, no. 1.

—— (1986) 'Alexander Korda, Prudential Assurance and British Film Finance in the 1930s', *Historical Journal of Film, Radio and Television*, vol. 6, no. 2.

—— (2002) *Transatlantic Crossings: British Feature Films in the USA*, New York: Continuum.

—— (2005) *Black Narcissus*, London: I. B. Tauris.

—— (2008) 'Contemporary British Cinema', in *Cambridge Companion to Modern British Culture*, Cambridge: Cambridge University Press.

Stuart, Andrea (1994) 'Blackpool Illumination', *Sight and Sound*, vol. 4, no. 2.

Taylor, B. F. (2006) *The British New Wave*, Manchester: Manchester University Press.

Thompson, Ben (1994) Review of the film *Shopping*, *Sight and Sound*, vol 4, no. 7.

Thompson, Kristin (1985) *Exporting Entertainment: America in the World Film Market, 1907–1934*, London: British Film Institute.

Threadgall, Derek (1994) *Shepperton Studios: an Independent View*, London: British Film Institute.

Thumim, Janet (1991) 'The "Popular", Cash and Culture in the Postwar British Cinema', *Screen*, vol. 32, no. 3.

—— (1992) *Celluloid Sisters: Women and Popular Cinema*, London: Macmillan.

Vaughan, Dai (1983) *Portrait of an Invisible Man: the Working Life of Stewart McAllister, Film Editor*, London: British Film Institute.

Vincendeau, Ginette (ed.) (1995) *Encyclopedia of European Cinema*, London: Cassell/British Film Institute.

Vitali, Valentina and Willemen, Paul (eds) (2006) *Theorising National Cinema*, London: British Film Institute.

Walker, Alexander (1974) *Hollywood, England*, London: Michael Joseph.

—— (1985) *National Heroes: British Cinema in the Seventies and Eighties*, London: Harrap.

Walker, John (1985) *The Once and Future Film*, London: Methuen.

Warren, Patricia (1995) *British Film Studios: an Illustrated History*, London: Batsford.

Weiss, Andrea (1992) *Vampires and Violets: Lesbians in the Cinema*, London: Jonathan Cape.

Wilcox, Herbert (1967) *Twenty-Five Thousand Sunsets*, London: Bodley Head.

Willemen, Paul (1994) *Looks and Frictions: Essays in Cultural Studies and Film Theory*, London: British Film Institute.

Williams, Linda (1983) 'When the Woman Looks', in Doane, Mary Ann, Mellencamp, Patricia and Williams, Linda (eds) *Re-vision: Essays in Feminist Film Criticism*, Los Angeles, CA: American Film Institute Monograph Series, University Publications of America.

—— (2002) 'Escape Artist', *Sight and Sound*, vol. 12, no. 10.

Williams, Michael (2003) *Ivor Novello: Screen Idol*, London: British Film Institute.

Williams, Tony (1994) 'The Repressed Fantastic in *Passport to Pimlico*', in Dixon, Wheeler Winston (ed.) *Re-Viewing British Cinema, 1900–1992*, New York: SUNY.

Winterson, Jeanette (1992) 'Outrageous Proportions', *Sight and Sound*, vol. 2, no. 6.

—— (1994) *Great Moments in Aviation* and *Oranges Are Not the Only Fruit*, London: Vintage Film Scripts.

Wollen, Peter (1972) 'Counter-Cinema: Vent D'Est', *Afterimage*, vol. 4.

—— (1993) 'The Last New Wave: Modernism in the British Films of the Thatcher Era', in Friedman, Lester (ed.) *British Cinema and Thatcherism*, London: University College of London Press.

—— (1994) 'The Western and the Bather', article on artists and cinema in *Sight and Sound* supplement 'Art Into Film', vol. 4, no. 7.

—— (1995) 'Possession: 25 Years On; Peter Wollen Explores Drugs, Decadence and Jagger in *Performance*', *Sight and Sound*, vol. 5, no. 9.

Wood, Linda (ed.) (1983) *British Films, 1971–1981*, London: British Film Institute Library Services.

Wright, Basil (1947) Review of the film *Odd Man Out*, *Documentary Newsletter*, April–May.

Young, Cynthia (1994) 'Revision to Reproduction: Myth and Its Author, in *The Red Shoes*', in Dixon, Wheeler Winston (ed.) *Re-Viewing British Cinema, 1900–1992*, New York: SUNY.

Subject index

Name index

Index of films and television programmes